VEGETARIAN VIỆT NAM

Before eating, monks and nuns pray, shaping the right hand in a symbolic mudra position to aid digestion and metabolism, and to honor the bounty of food and those who prepared the meal.

VEGETARIAN VIỆT NAM

Cameron Stauch

W. W. NORTON & COMPANY
Independent Publishers Since 1923
New York   London

For information about permission to reproduce selections from this book, write to Permissions, W. W. Norton & Company, Inc., 500 Fifth Avenue, New York, NY 10110

For information about special discounts for bulk purchases, please contact W. W. Norton Special Sales at specialsales@wwnorton.com or 800-233-4830

Manufacturing by LSC Kendallville
Book design by Jan Derevjanik
Production manager: Julia Druskin

Library of Congress Cataloging-in-Publication Data

Names: Stauch, Cameron, author.
Title: Vegetarian Viet Nam / Cameron Stauch.
Description: First edition. | New York, N.Y. : W. W. Norton & Company, Inc., [2018] |
    Includes bibliographical references and index.
Identifiers: LCCN 2017048498 | ISBN 9780393249330 (hardcover)
Subjects: LCSH: Cooking, Vietnamese. | Cooking, Southeast Asian. |
    Vegetarian cooking. | LCGFT: Cookbooks. | Cookbooks.
Classification: LCC TX724.5.V5 S73 2018 | DDC 641.59597—dc23
    LC record available at https://lccn.loc.gov/2017048498

W. W. Norton & Company, Inc.
500 Fifth Avenue, New York, N.Y. 10110

www.wwnorton.com

W. W. Norton & Company Ltd.
15 Carlisle Street, London W1D 3BS

1 2 3 4 5 6 7 8 9 0

For Ayesha, Lyla, and Kiran

Two Cao Đài sisters praying with the Divine Eye in the background.

A Buddhist lay believer cooks *bánh khọt*, a mini rice pancake filled with lentils and mushrooms, for a celebratory meal at a temple in southern Việt Nam.

CONTENTS

INTRODUCTION

In late 2012, on a visit to Sài Gòn (also known as Hồ Chí Minh city), I woke up early, threw on some clothes, and headed toward the street food stalls on the outskirts of the city's markets. Hunger—and a desire to investigate the stalls' well-loved breakfast specialties—propelled me.

Zigzagging my way through a residential alley, I came upon a woman stirring a large, stainless-steel pot filled with *phở*, a traditional breakfast soup, its steam pouring forth in billowy clouds. Several diners sat nearby, hunched over large bowls, chopsticks guiding noodles to mouths. Seconds later, I joined them.

Tangles of rice noodles drowned in a clear broth, expertly scented with star anise and cinnamon. I added cilantro, Asian basil, bean sprouts, and slivers of fresh red chile, then hit the phở, with a liberal squeeze of lime. Leaning forward, I breathed deeply and took it all in—the fragrant steam, the communal meal on the street, the entire scene. When I finally loosened the noodles with my chopsticks, discovering oyster-shaped mushrooms, tofu sticks, carrots, and daikon, that's when I realized: the soup was vegetarian, not a shred of chicken or beef in sight.

On the same trip I encountered an elderly woman selling vegetarian sandwiches (called *bánh mì chay*) from her roadside cart. She smeared mushroom pâté on a split baguette, topping it on one side with tofu balls in tomato sauce. On the other side she added cucumber,

pickled vegetables, spring onion, cilantro, chile, and toasted sesame seeds. She sprinkled the tofu with cellophane noodles that had been dusted with toasted rice powder, then squirted soy sauce over it all. Like my vegetarian *phở*, her sandwich rivaled any meat-filled creation I'd ever had then or have had since.

I adore how Vietnamese cooks adjust the flavors of dishes to create a dance of salty, sweet, sour, and spicy. Each diner further personalizes these tastes, deploying squirts of lime juice, slivers of fiery red chile, dustings of toasted ground sesame seed. The more I learn about Việt Nam, the greater my admiration for its people and their culinary ingenuity.

Vegetarian Việt Nam features healthy, modern, simple yet sophisticated recipes I've collected as a chef eating and traveling the length of Việt Nam. These dishes were a revelation to me because they were naturally vegetarian and mostly gluten-free and vegan—something I did not expect to find in my travels through an otherwise meat-loving country. This compendium of recipes, stories, and images celebrates this relatively hidden part of Vietnamese cuisine while also exploring how Vietnamese cooks use local ingredients to create and adapt traditional dishes based on seasonal, cultural, political, and religious influences.

WHY VEGETARIAN?

North American vegetarians and vegans often embrace these alternative diets for environmental, health, or moral reasons. In Việt Nam, religious traditions hold greater sway. Buddhism, specifically the branch of Mahayana Buddhism with its vegetarian traditions, has greatly influenced the distinct character of meat- and seafood-free Vietnamese cuisine.

In Việt Nam, there's no separate vegetarian category of recipes and foods. Rather, the boundary between what's considered vegetarian and what's not is more fluid since vegetarian dishes are generally replicas in look and taste of their meat and seafood relatives. Centuries ago, Chinese monks reportedly did not want to make meat-eating visitors uncomfortable by forcing vegetarian meals on them. Instead, they cleverly replicated meat and seafood dishes through creative use of tofu and wheat gluten (seitan). This culinary approach reached Việt Nam, where it was adopted by those cooking in Buddhist monasteries, royal courts, and eventually in home and restaurant kitchens.

MY BACKGROUND AND MOTIVATIONS

I'm married to a Canadian diplomat. For a chef like me, one whose curiosity is both longstanding and deep-seated, following my wife around the globe and building our lives in some of the world's most vibrant culinary landscapes affords me an extremely rare opportunity: to devote myself fully to researching, exploring, tasting, and understanding local foodways. I don't fly in and fly out after a week or two. While in a new country that I'll call home for several years, I'm immersed. And the knowledge I gain about a country's culture, geography, and history helps me better understand its cuisine. The more information I acquire, the better I appreciate how and why the populations of certain regions eat the foods they do. This process makes me a better cook, a better eater, a better traveler. It also directly informed my approach to writing this book.

I embarked on this project to translate my discoveries into practical, flavor-packed recipes for the home cook. I'm drawing on skills I've long used as a trained chef. In between stints of living overseas when I lived in Canada, for six years I was part of the kitchen team that cooks for the governor general, Her Majesty Queen Elizabeth the Second's representative in Canada. Like those cooking in the White House kitchen, we're required to prepare a variety of food—from daily family meals to creative state dinners—that best represent Canada's culinary landscape while also honoring the flavors of the visiting nation. During these events one of my roles was to prepare meals for guests with dietary restrictions, accommodating those who may be vegetarian or gluten-free or who may suffer from serious food allergies. With each meal or event, I refined my skills in vegetarian global cuisines, drawing upon the dishes and flavors I've encountered while living overseas.

WHY VIỆT NAM?

In early 2000, I followed Ayesha (then my girlfriend, now my wife) to Hong Kong, where she'd started a new job. Just after Christmas that year, we took a trip to Việt Nam's capital, Hà Nội, with her parents. We arrived late in the morning. Ayesha and her parents set out to shop for Vietnamese silk and lacquerware souvenirs while I sought out a famous restaurant I'd read about in a trusted guidebook. I was familiar with *phở*, of course; it's considered Việt Nam's national dish as it is sold throughout the entire country. And I knew about summer rolls (also called salad rolls) and basic pantry ingredients. But until then, I really hadn't experienced Việt Nam's regional specialties.

My first stop that morning was Chả Cá Lã Vọng, a restaurant so well loved an entire street was named after it. I climbed the rickety stairs to the second-floor dining room and took a seat at a table with a small charcoal burner. A young waitress handed me a menu. It said: "Only one dish in our restaurant: Grilled Fish." So that was settled. She then set three small bowls on the table: one with toasted, crushed peanuts; another with a clear sauce with floating red chiles; and a third with a shrimp paste

so pungent I pushed it to the far end of the table. (I'm a curious eater but had my limits in those early days.)

She disappeared, then returned a few minutes later with a skillet of partly-grilled pieces of golden fish and a plastic tray of vermicelli rice noodles, a pile of feathery dill fronds, and thin slices of scallion. Torn lettuce and fragrant herbs lent freshness and color. She mimed that I should finish cooking the fish over the charcoal burner. When she noticed that the fish was almost done, she signaled that I should add the dill and scallions and then briefly sauté the herbs. She even helped me assemble the finished dish, adding some rice noodles to an empty bowl, topping them with greenery, and adding the fish and remaining accompaniments on top. Last, she gestured that I should stir the mixture with my chopsticks before eating. We didn't exchange a single word the entire time.

My first bite of silky rice noodles with all the garnishes stilled me with its complexity and vibrancy. It balanced salty, sour, sweet, and hot flavors, and multiple textural elements, without shortchanging any single component. I've even created a version with tofu so you can experience it for yourself, Turmeric Tofu with Fresh Dill and Rice Noodles (page 75).

I spent the next few days eating my way through Hà Nội's Old Quarter, mesmerized by how skillfully Vietnamese cooks use basic ingredients to produce such bold and nuanced flavors.

That initial trip to Việt Nam piqued my interest, and I couldn't wait to get back to explore its culture, geography, and diversity through its cuisine. I had my chance in 2012, when Ayesha announced our family would be moving to Hà Nội. She'd just been named political counselor at the Canadian Embassy.

MY IMMERSION IN VIETNAMESE VEGETARIAN CUISINE

Since 2012, I've spent years sampling and preparing vegetarian Vietnamese meals. In Huế, the historic imperial capital city, I researched vegetarian street food. Ninety miles (145 km) south in Hội An, a UNESCO World Heritage site with picture-perfect lanterns and Japanese-, Chinese-, and French-influenced architecture, I learned from fellow cooks how to combine seaweed with tofu to create marine flavors. And in Đà Lạt, a city in the Central Highlands, I cooked with monks and nuns in secluded Buddhist pagodas surrounded by forests of pine trees. I even studied Vietnamese cuisine from culinary legend Nguyễn Dzoãn Cẩm Vân, Việt Nam's Julia Child. Ms. Vân, herself a vegetarian, shared family recipes that had been passed from generation to generation, offering me firsthand access to the secrets of home-style Vietnamese cooking.

CHALLENGES AND OPPORTUNITIES

As a professionally trained chef, I've always been mindful about purchasing food locally, seasonally, and from a reliable source. But in Việt Nam, I quickly learned that finding out how and where your meat and produce are grown remains difficult. I was fortunate in Hà Nội to be able to purchase local, seasonal, and (sometimes) organic produce but had no access to a butcher shop or stall that could verify that the meat was antibiotic- or hormone-free. This reality compounded my desire to prepare frequent vegetarian meals for my family. And as our son announced one day he would eat only vegetarian, I increasingly began to treat meat as an accent flavor and

not as the main ingredient, much as is done throughout Asia.

In my quest to become skilled in the vegetarian category of Vietnamese cuisine, I paid particular attention to the ingredients Vietnamese cooks use to replace not only proteins like meat and fish but also the umami flavors from derivatives like fish sauce, a widely used condiment. I knew I'd have to mimic it with an equally flavorful alternative. I also committed to learning the specialized techniques Vietnamese cooks use when transforming nonvegetarian dishes into vegetarian standouts.

It's important to note that I had a particular advantage when developing these recipes: as someone who is not strictly vegetarian, I could easily compare meat-based dishes with their meat-free counterparts to ensure as close an approximation of flavor and texture as possible.

ABOUT THE RECIPES

The recipes in these pages are wide-ranging and versatile. They're also accessible to cooks of all skill levels. If you've ever made a stir-fry, simmered a soup, boiled pasta, made rice, or steamed vegetables, you can cook the dishes in this book. Recipes such as Sautéed Squash with Basil and Peanuts (page 236) and the many recipes for light broths with seasonal vegetables, tofu, and seaweed are easy to prepare and incorporate into weekly meals.

My own family's weekly menu plan, in fact, increasingly includes vegetarian, even vegan, options. Taro Root Mung Bean Spring Rolls (page 107) are one such family favorite. Our six-year-old son always grabs one first while the rest of us are busy wrapping ours in lettuce leaves we've lined with basil and mint. By the time we dip our rolls in the clear sour and sweet chile garlic sauce, he has already pol-ished off two (or even three) rolls. Smart boy.

When we crave comfort food, I fry chunks of tofu and pair them with a quick tomato sauce and sides of garlicky water spinach and steamed rice. The Vietnamese vegetarian table is truly an ideal entry point for anyone who wants to experience the flavors of Southeast Asia. Many of these recipes are quick and weeknight-friendly. Others, like the various noodle soups, do require some advance plan-ning, preparation, and time, but once you've stocked up on pantry basics you can rustle up even a piping-hot bowl of a noodle soup in lit-tle time.

To respect authenticity, I first tasted the vast majority of the dishes in this collection on Vietnamese streets, in market food courts, in monasteries with Buddhists monks or nuns, or in the kitchens of home cooks. (Monks, nuns, and devout lay Buddhists generally avoid members of the allium family such as onion, garlic, leek, shallots, and chiles, believing these ingredients stir passions and make it more difficult for them to maintain ritual purity.) I've tried my best to remain true to the interplay of flavors and ingredients Vietnamese cooks themselves use when preparing these dishes. Some of the recipes are exactly as I experienced them, while others are loosely adapted from one or more sources. I consider them a collaboration.

I've also tossed in a few of my own vegetar-ian interpretations of meat and seafood dishes, such as the Turmeric Tofu with Fresh Dill and Rice Noodles (page 75) and the Green Mango Rice Paper Ribbons (page 117). These special-ties have yet to be converted into vegetarian dishes by Vietnamese cooks, so I've taken the liberty of doing it myself. Consider them a value-add.

HOW TO USE THIS BOOK

Before you begin cooking, please consult the Vegetarian Vietnamese Pantry (page 27) and the Glossary (page 294) to orient yourself and become familiar with key terminology and ingredients. Everyday items—such as rice paper, vermicelli noodles and phở noodles, mushrooms, Asian greens, tofu, lemongrass, ginger, and fresh (Italian) basil, cilantro, dill, and mint—are all readily available at large grocery stores. For the occasional dish you may need to visit an Asian grocer to source pantry items like tofu skin or less common herbs like Thai basil, Vietnamese balm, Vietnamese coriander, or red perilla, also known as *red shiso*. And if you're lucky enough to live near a Latin American grocery store, look for culantro, chayote, jicama, or achiote there, as there's some crossover between the two cuisines when it comes to certain produce. (You'll also find these items in Asian markets, of course.)

In some recipes I've suggested non-Asian vegetables or products that you can use as substitutes for some of the harder-to-find produce items. Vietnamese home cooks them-selves often make such substitutions to use the freshest produce they can get in any given season, so if you do so yourself, you'll be in excellent company.

For most of the recipes, unless speci-fied, use a vegetable oil with a clean, neutral flavor and with a high smoke point. Peanut, sunflower, or organic canola oil is suitable for all kinds of cooking from stir-frying to deep-frying.

In order to economize on space in the ingredients lists of recipes, I've omitted the instruction to peel vegetables such as beets, carrots, chayote, daikon, jicama, and kohlrabi. For the same reason, I've omitted "washed and dried" from greens and herbs. Please peel the vegetables and wash and dry greens and herbs before proceeding with a recipe.

For those of you who are unfamiliar with using Vietnamese herbs, I've provided standardized measurements for accuracy. However, over time I've become accustomed to measuring whole uncut herbs by the handful. If you prefer this laissez-faire approach use the following as a guide: 1/3 cup herbs equals a small handful; 3/4 cup herbs equals a handful; 1 cup herbs equals a generous or large handful.

Last, one request: Please don't leave out any ingredients (or their substitutions) in the recipes. The final flavor of a Vietnamese dish relies on the layering of ingredients. Omit one or two ingredients or components of a layer and the dish will taste flat. Merge them all together and they sing in harmony.

Whether you digest this book in the kitchen, in an armchair, or in preparation for travel to this captivating country, I hope you are as fascinated by Vietnamese vegetarian cuisine as I am. I can't wait to take you on this journey!

The main kitchen at the Zen Buddhist monastery in Long Thành.

A BRIEF HISTORY OF VIETNAMESE CULINARY AND CULTURAL INFLUENCES

As part of its rich history, Việt Nam has been ruled by foreign governments including China and France. Conquerors and missionaries brought religious practices with them, exerting influence and authority over much of Vietnamese society. In the second century, Buddhism arrived in Việt Nam courtesy of Indian Buddhist missionary monks and, later, via a millennium of Chinese domination. The Chinese also introduced Confucianism and Taoism. Vietnamese society adopted and integrated many Confucian, Taoist, and Buddhist culinary, cultural, philosophical, and religious beliefs.

A history of wavering support for Vietnamese Buddhism suggests why certain parts of Việt Nam, such as the Nguyễn imperial city of Huế and the South, have stronger vegetarian traditions than other parts, like Hà Nội or the rest of the North. Following independence from the Chinese in the tenth century, Vietnamese monarchs declared Buddhism the state religion. It flourished for the next four hundred years, before being challenged and usurped in the fifteenth century by the Lê dynasty, which supported Confucianism. During the nineteenth century the Nguyễn dynasty, whose capital was the central city of Huế, returned royal support for Buddhism, but the French occupation of Indochina (including Việt Nam, Cambodia, and Laos) in the late nineteenth century increased Catholicism's influence. In 1954, as part of the process of restoring peace to the Indochina region, following the Indochina War, the so-called Geneva Accords split Việt Nam into two parts: a Communist-governed North and a pro-Catholic South. Strict control of organized religion spread over the entire country following the end of the Vietnam War (or the American War, as it is known in Việt Nam), when the North and South came under Communist rule in 1975. Since 1986, when the Communist government brought about free-market reforms, individuals have been relatively unhindered in their ability to practice officially sanctioned Buddhist traditions.

Mahayana and Theravada Buddhism are the two major schools of Buddhism practiced in Southeast Asia. Buddhists in Việt Nam and northern China primarily follow Mahayana traditions whereas Buddhists in neighboring Cambodia, Laos, and Thailand—and the small southern population of Vietnamese in the

OPPOSITE Monastery kitchens are basic and use firewood as fuel for their cooking. Like this one at a Pure Land Buddhist nunnery outside of Huế

15

Mekong delta of Khmer background—practice Theravada Buddhism. One tenet of Buddhism is not to participate in the killing and suffering of any living thing. In general, Theravada Buddhist monks and nuns believe that it's fine to eat meat or seafood if the meat or seafood was not killed specifically for their consumption. If the food was slaughtered to feed a lay family, for instance, and then offered to a monk or nun for consumption, monks and nuns will eat it. By contrast, Mahayana Buddhists consider animals to be sentient beings. Not eating meat or seafood limits the suffering of animals and is a way to cultivate compassion. Devout Mahayana Buddhists will therefore never eat meat. Lay Mahayana Buddhists may decide to eat vegetarian a couple of times a month or for an entire month, as a form of religious observance. (Interestingly, this custom of eating vegetarian sets Việt Nam apart from its Southeast Asian neighbors.)

Traders seeking new markets and foreign rulers seeking new conquests have also greatly influenced Việt Nam's food. The Khmer Empire, covering much of Cambodia, Laos, Thailand, and southern Việt Nam, introduced coconut milk and spices into Vietnamese cuisine. Dishes such as the thin, crispy dosalike (or crepe-like) *bánh xèo*; a fragrant curried vegetable stew (*cà ri chay*); and a biryani-style rice dish cooked with onions, garlic, ginger, spices, lemongrass, and coconut milk (*cơm nị*) were likely brought to Việt Nam from India through the trading routes of the Cham people. The French colonial period left a legacy of fresh baked baguettes, used for *bánh mì* sandwiches, and a thirst for coffee and condensed milk, creating a café culture that transformed how members of Vietnamese society socialized and passed the time. The French also added vegetables such as carrots, potatoes, onions, asparagus, artichokes, and lettuce. Support and regular interactions between Communist Việt Nam and Russia may have brought beetroot to the Vietnamese table.

Both cooks and eaters celebrate Vietnamese food for its subtle, invigorating flavors, layered textures, and vibrant colors incorporated through the use of fresh seasonal vegetables. The Vietnamese also adhere to the Chinese philosophy of yin and yang and the principles of the five elements theory (wood, fire, earth, water, and metal) in their cuisine. Dishes and ingredients are selected based on seasonal and climatic conditions and an effort to achieve harmony among colors, flavors, textures, and also for one's health. If someone in the family is unwell, for whatever the reason, the cook, typically one of the older women of the household, will choose ingredients and dishes to prepare to help rebalance the health of the ailing family member. An interesting lasting legacy of Chinese influence in Việt Nam is the extensive use of chopsticks at most meals. In other Southeast Asian countries they're used primarily for noodle dishes.

PRACTICING VEGETARIANS
IN TODAY'S VIỆT NAM

Buddhist monks and nuns fully abstain from eating meat and seafood, but some do consume dairy products such as milk and yogurt; they don't believe animals suffer during the production of these ingredients. Lay Buddhists adopt "temporary" vegetarianism on preassigned dates as a rite of abstinence or purification. They eat vegetarian as a reminder to avoid doing or saying bad things and to increase good luck for themselves, their families, and their ancestors for the new month. Typically the period of abstinence falls on the first and fifteenth day of each lunar month, although for some observers it can be up to ten times or even a month-long abstinence period, depending on individual devoutness. Vegetarian meals may also be served on the first day of the Lunar New Year (*Tết*) to bring luck, happiness, and health for the coming year.

Followers of a unique homegrown religion called Cao Đài—an amalgamation of Buddhism, Taoism, and Confucianism—practice vegetarianism on certain sacred days. They start with six days each lunar month, increasing to ten days with the hope that they will practice vegetarianism full time.

Both Mahayana Buddhists and Cao Đài followers practice vegetarianism for similar reasons: to cultivate compassion, to live a life of higher consciousness, and because they believe that one living creature should not be killed for the survival of another.

Throughout my travels I spoke with young and old and found that an increasing number of Vietnamese follow a vegetarian diet. Many seniors have recently begun to reduce the frequency of their meat consumption as they feel it improves their health. The majority of diners eating in vegetarian restaurants, though, are part of the younger generation—largely university students and recent graduates. Since vegetarian meals tend to be cheaper, some students eat this way regularly to save money. Others, as lay Buddhists, continue to eat vegetarian, maintaining the practice introduced by their parents and grandparents. Still others have adopted a vegetarian lifestyle for ecological and moral reasons, similar to many vegetarians in the West.

There's also been a recent increase in the number of followers of Vietnamese Zen Buddhism (Trúc Lâm/ Thiền), which focuses on the practice of meditation and of being present in the moment. This uptick may be due to the popularity and writings of monks such as Thích Nhất Hạnh, who resides in Plum Village in the South of France, and Thích Thanh Từ, who is based in Đà Lạt. Both monks enjoy international followings.

HOW TO FIND VEGETARIAN OFFERINGS IN VIỆT NAM

You may assume that eating vegetarian in Việt Nam would be challenging, but it doesn't have to be. In fact many restaurants, private homes, and temple kitchens throughout the country regularly offer meat-free options (for more detailed information, see Finding Vegetarian and Vegan Restaurants in Việt Nam, page 288). Periodically, Buddhist monks and nuns, with the assistance of followers, prepare vegetarian meals for the public at the pagoda for celebrations such as Buddha's birthday, a senior monk or nun's birthday, to mark funerals or death anniversaries, or to feed needy citizens.

Greater numbers of vegetarian restaurants are found in the center or South of the country, where there is a higher concentration of devout followers of vegetarian Buddhist practices. On days of the new and full moon street food vendors in central and southern Việt Nam switch to vegetarian versions of their meat- or seafood-based dishes.

At food markets in Việt Nam, vegetarian ingredients and vendors are organized near each other to facilitate shopping. This is echoed, with vegetarian ingredients stocked together, at Vietnamese and Chinese grocers in North America.

Monks and nuns eat two meals a day: a simple breakfast following their early morning (4:30 a.m.) meditations and the day's main meal, which they take in the late morning. Operating in large, often dimly lit kitchens on a rotating work schedule, designated monks and nuns prepare simple, nourishing dishes using seasonal produce harvested from their own gardens (or from donations from lay followers) and using basic kitchen equipment like vegetable peelers, knives, graters, and mortars and pestles. In small monasteries with fewer than 20 monks, dishes are cooked in standard-size woks, pots, and pans. In larger monasteries, much larger cookware and industrial-size steamers allow them to cook at scale.

Using wood, branches, and leaves they collect from the surrounding forests, monastery cooks do most of their cooking over wood-fueled burners. Cooking over wood saves money, of course, but they also believe the wood adds an elusive flavor that makes food and rice taste better. Meals are taken family style.

Meals are simple and austere. The main meal in smaller monasteries may include a fresh or pickled vegetable dish, a tofu or gluten dish, and a simple soup consisting of one or two vegetables and steamed rice. In larger monasteries with more resources, meals remain basic yet ingredients are higher quality thanks to donations of money or provisions. Large groups may eat meals "hot pot" style (see page 190), with up to ten diners per table eating from a shared communal pot. Dessert consists of a piece of seasonal fruit or a sweet treat donated by lay followers. When there's a celebration—for the abbot's birthday, for example—meals tend to be more extravagant.

EATING AND MINDFULNESS

For monks and nuns eating is an act of mindfulness. Before a meal, the entire monastic community, called a *sangha*, and any lay believers who happen to be dining with them scoop some rice into their own eating bowl in preparation for the ritual of prayer. Out of respect for Buddha, they symbolically hold the bowl at eye level as a headmaster leads the sangha through a recitation of chants honoring nature's bounty and the farmers and cooks responsible for producing the food. They offer appreciation and gratitude for being worthy of receiving a nourishing offering that strengthens and medicates their bodies. Diners eat in complete silence, freeing the mind of all distractions. To immerse themselves fully in the experience of eating, they chew each small mouthful of food slowly, savoring it. They believe that eating in this manner will improve digestion and help them be less greedy.

When I dined with a small group of nuns in

The female elders of the Cao Đài Holy See in Tây Ninh enjoy lunch.

their pagoda on the outskirts of Huế, following these rituals was a challenge. Our simple lunch consisted of stir-fried leafy greens, sautéed matchsticks of preserved daikon, a clear soup, and rice. Following prayers I added some greens and daikon to my rice, then popped three pieces of daikon into my mouth, perhaps more greedily than I'd intended. I closed my eyes to focus on the flavors. When I started to chew the daikon, I made loud successive crunches, like those you make automatically when biting into a cool, crisp pickle. Nervous, I opened my eyes, hoping I wasn't as loud as I'd feared. The entire table of nuns stared at me, quietly giggling at my maiden but enthusiastic attempt at mindful eating.

Because monks and nuns eat their main meal of the day around 10:30 or 11:00 a.m., if you ever find yourself at a pagoda around this time, you may receive an invitation to dine with them and other lay Buddhists. Do yourself a favor and accept.

A simple lunch of stir-fried leafy greens, sautéed preserved daikon, soup, and rice at a nunnery outside of Huế. The mindfulness bell on the table is used for prayer.

MENU GUIDANCE

It's easy to incorporate Vietnamese dishes into your weekly meals. Prepare a dish or two to complement other Asian dishes. Or try your hand at cooking an entire multidish rice meal.

In general, look to the Rolls, Bánh Mì, and Street Snacks chapter (page 89) for light lunch ideas or fun finger foods to serve to your family and friends.

Select a dish from Bowls of Noodles (page 171) or one of the rice porridges in the Grains of Rice chapter (page 197) when you crave a comforting one-bowl meal. In Việt Nam, one-bowl noodle soups are typically eaten for breakfast or at lunch, but you can eat them for any meal. With prior planning you can easily and quickly assemble one of these delicious dishes. It's worth getting a large deep soup bowl, one for each member of the family, to accommodate the noodles, garnishes, and broth. I learned to eat them with a pair of chopsticks in one hand and a soupspoon in the other, first spooning up some broth to establish its taste and then slurping up the noodles using my chopsticks. You can personalize your soup by adding some chile slices, a squirt of lime, herbs, and beansprouts. For any of the one-bowl meals you really don't need to serve anything else as they're unexpectedly filling, though I don't know many who can resist a hot, crispy spring roll.

Throughout Việt Nam multidish rice-based meals are normally served in the evening with family and friends. When you plan to prepare a multidish vegetarian rice meal, try to include one or two vegetable dishes, a tofu or wheat gluten dish, a salad, and perhaps a light soup served with steamed, long-grained white or brown, rice. You can replace rice with a stir-fried noodle dish, if you wish.

Provide each person with their own bowl, chopsticks, and Chinese or Western soup-spoon. Consider including a small side plate and individualized dipping bowls if you're going to serve fresh or fried spring rolls.

Try to organize yourself in the kitchen so all of the dishes come to the table at the same time. Serve the food family style on small platters or in serving bowls. Pass the dishes around the table or spoon portions onto others' plates. Serving the meal in this manner adds intimacy, plus it means that seconds, and thirds, are always an option.

When planning a multidish rice meal, refer to dishes in the following chapters for inspiration: Tofu and Seitan (page 57); Vibrant Salads (page 127); Light Soups (page 153); From the Market and Garden (page 223). Follow Vietnamese cooks and consider what's in season and think about balancing flavors. Serve lighter dishes, like salads or stir-fried vegetables alongside richer or spicier dishes. To help get you started here are some suggested seasonal or family friendly multidish rice meal menus to feed four to six people.

Menu 1

Tofu with Fresh Tomato Sauce

Vermicelli Noodles with Fresh Turmeric, Tofu, and Chinese Chives

Stir-Fried Water Spinach

Kohlrabi and Carrot Salad

Squash and Sweet Potato Coconut Milk Soup

Menu 2

Lemongrass Chile "Chicken" Strips Stir-Fry

Tender Boiled Vegetables with Fermented Tofu, Lemongrass, and Chile Sauce

Stir-Fried Romaine Lettuce with Tomatoes and Peanuts

Banana Blossom (or Green Cabbage) Salad

Magenta Beet Tofu Soup

Menu 3

Tomatoes stuffed with Meatless Ground and Tofu

Bamboo Shoots and Wild Mushrooms with Peanuts and Sesame Seeds

Soy Ginger Glazed Eggplant

Palate-Cleansing Pomelo Salad

Clear Broth Soup with Tofu and Leafy Greens

Menu 4

Tofu with Tangy Tamarind Sauce

Sautéed Squash with Basil and Peanuts

Stewed Jackfruit with Vietnamese Coriander

Cucumber and Shredded Tofu Skin Salad

Plate of boiled green vegetables or Clear Broth Soup with Tofu and Leafy Greens

Monk's lunch at Long Vân pagoda outside Biên Hòa: (1) stir-fried rice noodles with vegetables, (2) rice, (3) fresh mangoes, (4) braised tofu skin sausage (page 44), (5) lightly pickled bean sprouts and carrot, (6) salad greens, (7) soy dipping sauce, (8) banana coconut tapioca pudding (page 277).

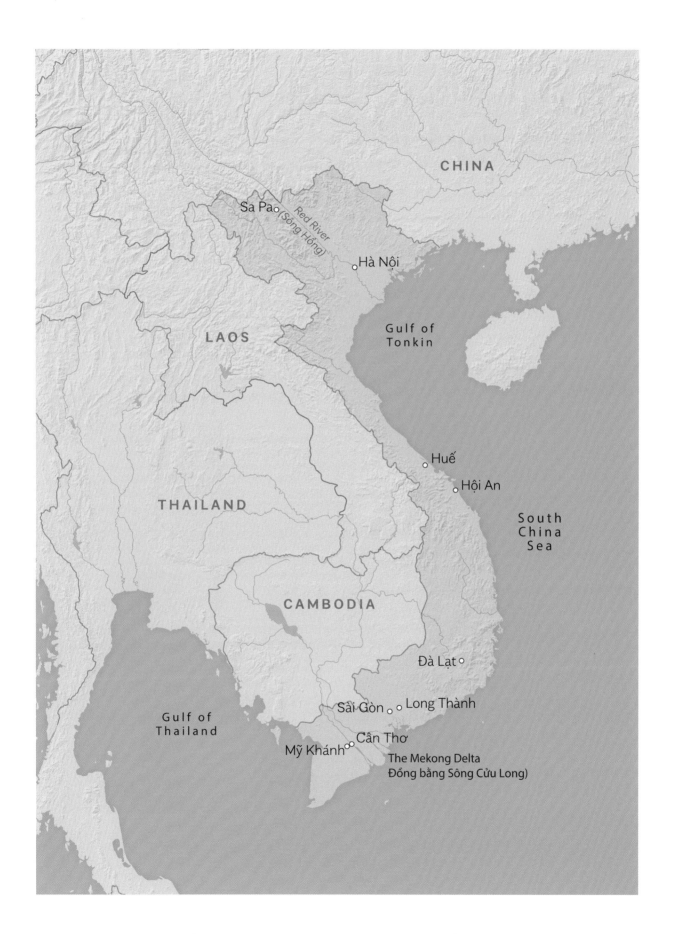

CHINA

Sa Pa
Red River (Sông Hồng)

Hà Nội

Gulf of
Tonkin

LAOS

Huế

Hội An

THAILAND

South
China
Sea

CAMBODIA

Đà Lạt

Sài Gòn   Long Thành

Gulf of
Thailand

Cần Thơ

Mỹ Khánh

The Mekong Delta
Đồng bằng Sông Cửu Long)

TRANSFORMATIVE VEGETARIAN STAPLES

The foods below will increase the umami or "meatiness" of a dish in the absence of meat, seafood, and fish sauce.

SOY SAUCE is used as seasoning, in dipping sauces and in braised vegetables or tofu dishes. To obtain the saltiness of fish sauce without having an overwhelming soy sauce flavor, use a combination of tamari or soy sauce and salt.

FERMENTED SOYBEANS are made when whole roasted soybeans are mixed with salt, water, at times glutinous rice, and naturally fermented into a dark brown salty paste or whole soybeans rich in umami. Mash them into a paste for dipping sauces or add to stir-fries or soups.

FERMENTED TOFU OR BEAN CURD. At Asian grocers, look for small glass jars with white cubes of fermented tofu surrounded in its fermentation liquid. It's often called *stinky tofu* or *bean curd cheese* because of its strong odor, which mellows when heated. For added complex flavors, spoon it in small amounts—start with ½ teaspoon—into noodle soups, rice porridge, or plain rice or make a flavorful sauce to serve with boiled vegetables.

TOFU SKIN, also called *dried bean curd* or *yuba*, its Japanese name, is the thin delicate skin that forms on the surface when fresh warm soy milk is heated in large shallow pans. It's carefully lifted off and hung on rods to cool briefly and kept fresh or dried. Dried bean curd sticks are another form of tofu skin. Fried or braised tofu skin adds a chewy texture and savory flavor to dishes.

SEITAN, also known as *wheat gluten* or *mock meat*, because of its chewy meatlike texture, is a protein-rich substitute eaten by vegetarians, lay Mahayana Buddhists and Mahayana Buddhist monks or nuns.

DRIED SHIITAKE MUSHROOMS are the most important mushroom to the vegetarian kitchen. These fragrant, earthy mushrooms, rich in umami components and meaty when reconstituted, add a depth of savoryness to dishes. The intense, slightly smoky flavor of dried shiitake is more pronounced than in fresh ones, which are not perfect substitutes.

SEA VEGETABLES (OR ALGAE) provide another layer of umami richness to dishes. Powdered, chopped, or whole pieces of **hijiki**, **wakame**, or **nori** are sometimes used to imitate a marine flavor in a recipe.

A makeshift street-side store sells basic pantry items in Hà Nội.

BLACK PEPPER. Devout Mahayana Buddhists add a generous pinch of fresh, medium-coarse black pepper right before serving, in place of "internal-heat-producing" chiles. Vietnamese black peppercorns, especially those from Phú Quốc island, are known for their intense fruity, citrusy aroma, and mild flavor.

MISO. Cooks in vegetarian restaurants in Việt Nam have recently started to use miso, the protein-rich soybean paste, made by salting and fermenting soybeans and a grain (rice or barley) with a mold, as a background flavor enhancer in noodle soups. Use red-brown miso (aka miso).

THE VEGETARIAN VIETNAMESE PANTRY

OPPOSITE *Clockwise from top*: seitan; fresh tofu skin (small light colored square); dried tofu skin (manila envelope color, larger piece); dried tofu skin sticks; shiitake mushrooms; wakame; nori; fermented soybean paste; red miso; black peppercorns; soy sauce; fermented tofu

The recipes in this chapter are essential building blocks that give dishes their unique Vietnamese identity. If you've ever cooked Chinese, Southeast Asian, or South Asian recipes, you're probably already familiar with at least some of them. Others may be new. Embrace them.

Pantry staples are the best way to give all your home-cooked Vietnamese meals added oomph. In every Vietnamese neighborhood you'll find vendors who prepare and sell pantry staples. I can't tell you how convenient this is. After I purchased my vegetables and tofu, I'd drive my red Vespa up to one of these pantry vendors and, still seated on my scooter, buy some dried tofu sticks or roasted crushed peanuts or sesame seeds. It was quick and efficient.

Of course, not everyone lives just a scooter stop away from a Vietnamese pantry vendor. Now that I no longer have such immediate access, instead of wallowing in self-pity I do the next best thing: I make essential pantry items from scratch.

Staples such as vegetable stock (pages 30 and 31) or Annatto Seed Oil (page 35) added at the beginning of a recipe build foundational flavor. Garnishes like Toasted Sesame Seeds (page 33) and roughly chopped fresh herbs come in at the end, adding texture and sparkle. Umami-laden vegetarian ingredients—such as Mushroom Powder (page 36), fermented soybeans, and fermented tofu—will deepen the flavor profile or mimic the salinity and savory quality of fish sauce.

Keep a small jar of Lemongrass Chile Satay (page 54), Soy Chile Dipping Sauce (page 51) or Everyday Table Sauce (page 49) on the table so diners can customize their bowl of noodles or plate of rice to their liking. These condiments give finished dishes their punch, yes, but they also ensure that the vegetarian version of a traditionally meat- or seafood-containing dish will still remain recognizably Vietnamese, even without the meat, fish, or seafood.

True, you can buy ready-made bottles and jars of many of these items, but your from-scratch versions will taste much fresher. Plus, you'll control the quality of all the ingredients.

In the time it takes me to make a homemade vegetable stock, I can assemble many of the pantry items in this chapter. I toast sesame seeds and rice, infuse oils, grind shiitake mushrooms, and crisp shallots while my stock simmers away. The best part? Once they're stored airtight in the fridge, freezer, or even on the kitchen counter, they'll serve you well for a good long while.

VEGETABLE STOCKS

Once a month or so, when I have a free morning to relax at home, I make a double batch of stock in my large stockpot. This quantity satisfies my family's weekly soup cravings for several weeks. I extend the cooking time to 1½ hours to draw out more flavor from the larger volume of ingredients. Once the strained stock has cooled I freeze it in 1-quart (1-liter) and 2-cup (500 ml) containers or zip-top freezer bags.

It's best to use vegetables that have clean, mild flavors and don't break down during cooking to achieve a clear, well-balanced, and flavorful stock.

Here are some helpful tips to maximize the flavor and yield of your stocks:

- Cut vegetables into ½-inch (1½ cm) thin slices or ½-inch (1 cm) cubes. Sometimes I grate vegetables like zucchini, eggplant, and kohlrabi. This exposes a greater surface area and enables flavors to emerge more quickly and fully.

- Strain the stock immediately after it has finished cooking. Vegetables tend to absorb moisture if cooked for a long time, and some may overpower the stock or turn it bitter if left to steep for too long.

- While straining the stock, press the vegetable solids, using the back of a ladle or spoon, against the sieve. Doing so will help you maximize the amount of liquid you have to work with.

LIGHT VEGETABLE STOCK

This clear, delicate broth illustrates how Vietnamese cooks prepare vegetable stock. Each cook I've met has a personal preference for which produce to use when making stock. Some add chayote, green papaya, or even a little pineapple, apple, or sugarcane to bring forth sweet, fruity notes. Others stick with vegetables, as I have here, changing them according to the season and their availability. This stock is particularly well suited for Tomato and Creamy Tofu Noodle Soup (page 181), Savoy Cabbage and Tofu Parcels in Broth (page 159), and any of the light vegetable soups (*canh*) in Chapter Five.

Makes about 3½ quarts (3½ liters)

2 tablespoons vegetable oil

1 pound (454 g) carrots, thinly sliced (3 cups)

½ pound (227 g) green cabbage, roughly chopped into 1-inch (2.5 cm) pieces (3 cups)

¾ pound (340 g) jicama, thinly sliced (3 cups)

¾ pound (340 g) daikon, thinly sliced (2½ cups)

½ pound (227 g) leeks, green and white parts, thinly sliced (2 cups)

1½ teaspoons salt

4 quarts (4 liters) water

Heat the oil in a 6-quart (6-liter) pot over high heat. Toss in the vegetables and salt and cook, stirring occasionally, for 10 minutes. Don't worry if they brown lightly as they wilt. It adds flavor to the stock. Pour in the water and bring to a boil over high heat. Cover, reduce the heat to low, and simmer gently for 1 hour.

Carefully strain through a fine-mesh sieve positioned over another large pot or bowl in batches. Using the back of a spoon or ladle, gently press the vegetables in the sieve to extract any extra liquid. Discard and repeat with the remaining stock and vegetables.

Use immediately to make broths in other recipes or refrigerate in a covered container for up to 1 week. If you plan to freeze the stock, let it cool to room temperature, pour into containers with tight lids or zippered freezer bags, and freeze for up to 3 months.

VEGETABLE SUBSTITUTES

For green cabbage: Napa cabbage, bok choy

For jicama: celery, celeriac, zucchini, Chinese celery, chayote

For daikon: kohlrabi, rutabaga, turnip

For leeks: onions or shallots, without skin; scallions

RICH VEGETABLE STOCK

This vegetable stock has great depth of flavor, and it's versatile enough to suit many cuisines beyond Vietnamese. Adding garlic and umami-boosting ingredients like tomatoes or dried shiitakes creates a richly flavored base for the Star Anise Cinnamon Scented Pho Noodle Soup (page 175), Fragrant Lemongrass Hué-Style Noodle Soup (page 179), and Wild Mushroom and Leafy Greens Noodle Soup (page 186). **Makes about 3½ quarts (3½ liters)**

2 tablespoons vegetable oil

1 pound (about 2 medium) onions, thinly sliced

1 pound (454 g) carrots, thinly sliced (3 cups)

½ pound (227 g; 3 or 4 stalks) celery, thinly sliced

4 garlic cloves, smashed

1½ teaspoons salt

¼ pound (112 g; 1 whole) plum tomato, roughly chopped

¾ cup (1 ounce; 30 g) dried shiitake mushrooms, rinsed

¼ pound (120 g) fresh mushrooms or ½ pound (227 g) eggplant, chopped (2 cups)

4 quarts (4 liters) water

Heat the oil in a 6-quart (6-liter) pot over high heat. Toss in the onions, carrots, celery, garlic, and salt and cook, stirring occasionally, for 10 minutes. Don't worry if they brown as they wilt. It adds flavor and color to the stock. Add the tomato, shiitake mushrooms, and fresh mushrooms and cook for a few minutes. Pour in the water and bring to a boil over high heat. Cover, reduce the heat to low, and simmer gently for 1 hour.

Carefully strain through a fine-mesh sieve positioned over another large pot or bowl in batches. Using the back of a spoon or ladle, gently press the vegetables in the sieve to extract any extra liquid. Discard and repeat with the remaining stock and vegetables.

Even though you washed and rinsed the shiitake mushrooms, some dirt and grit may be released when the mushrooms are cooking. Allow the stock to sit for 15 minutes for any small grit particles to settle on the bottom of the pot. Check to see if there is any sediment on the bottom. If there is, when transferring the stock to a clean pot or storage containers, try to disturb the bottom of the stock as little as possible. Discard the last remaining ½ cup or so of gritty stock.

Use immediately to make broths in other recipes or refrigerate in a covered container for up to 1 week. If you plan to freeze the stock, let it cool to room temperature. Pour into containers with tight lids or zippered plastic bags and freeze for up to 3 months.

continues

VEGETABLE SUBSTITUTES

For onions: leeks or shallots, with skin; scallions

For celery: celeriac, zucchini, eggplant with skin on, kohlrabi, daikon, Chinese celery, chayote

For mushrooms: Any fresh mushroom will do. If using portobello mushrooms, remove the gills from the underside of the mushroom cap and discard—they will darken the stock too much. You can use other dried mushrooms, but it's best to rinse them quickly in some water to remove any dust and debris.

Note:

I have yet to find a store-bought vegetable stock that meets my standards. But if you plan on using boxed vegetable stock, select one that is low-sodium and relatively clear (not an orangey-red cloudy color).

To add some umami goodness to a boxed vegetable stock, pour 2 quarts (2 liters) into a pot and add ¾ cup (1 ounce; 30 g) dried shiitake mushrooms. Bring to a boil, cover, and reduce the heat to low. Simmer gently for 20 minutes. Drain. It's now ready for use.

TOASTED SESAME SEEDS

NƯỚNG MÈ or VỪNG

The simple act of sprinkling toasted sesame seeds over a salad or grinding and adding them to a dipping sauce (like the Coconut Soy Dipping Sauce on page 100), can dramatically transform a dish. In monasteries, monks and nuns spoon toasted sesame seeds over rice or vegetables. In fact, the seeds make such a frequent appearance—sometimes whole, sometimes coarsely ground—that they sit in a tiny jar on the dinner table (much as you'd find ketchup in an American diner). The seeds' deep nuttiness enlivens even the simplest rice-based meal. **Makes ½ cup**

½ cup (2½ ounces; 80 g) white sesame seeds

Place the sesame seeds in a 10-inch (25 cm) frying pan over medium heat. Leave undisturbed for several minutes. At this point some of the seeds, particularly around the edges of the pan, will take on a faint golden color. Shake the pan to mix and distribute the seeds.

For the next 5 minutes, allow the seeds to toast evenly for about 45 seconds and then give the pan another shake. When you notice that about one-third of the seeds are golden brown, regularly swirl or stir the seeds around the pan. A fragrantly nutty aroma will gradually fill the kitchen as oil from the seeds is released. When most of the seeds are a deep golden brown, remove the pan from the heat and transfer the seeds to a bowl to cool. If at any time during this process you feel the seeds are getting too dark too quickly, reduce the heat.

Store in a glass jar at room temperature for up to a week or refrigerate or freeze in a tightly sealed container or zippered plastic bag for up to a month.

TOASTING BLACK SESAME SEEDS
Follow the same process but listen carefully as they toast. Black sesame seeds are toasted when they begin to pop, after 3 to 5 minutes.

GROUND SESAME SEED SALT

MUỐI MÈ or VỪNG

Adding a touch of salt deepens the flavor of toasted ground sesame seeds.

Makes scant ½ cup

½ cup (2½ ounces; 80 g) cooled Toasted
  Sesame Seeds (page 33)

¼ teaspoon salt

Crush the seeds and salt in a mortar and pestle or pulse in an electric coffee grinder until most are broken and roughly ground. Depending on the size of your mortar and pestle or the efficiency of your electric coffee grinder, you may need to do this in two batches.

Store in a glass jar at room temperature for up to a week or refrigerate or freeze in a tightly sealed container or zippered plastic bag for up to a month.

ANNATTO SEED OIL

DẦU HẠT ĐIỀU

Annatto seed oil gives soups and stews a lovely orange-reddish hue. When used in Tomato and Creamy Tofu Noodle Soup (page 181) and Fragrant Lemongrass Huế-Style Noodle Soup (page 179), its sweet nuttiness makes a statement without being overwhelming. Make sure not to overheat the oil or the seeds will burn and turn bitter.   **Makes 1 cup (250 ml)**

1 tablespoon annatto seeds
1 cup (250 ml) vegetable oil

Place the annatto seeds and oil in a small saucepan over low heat. After 5 minutes, tiny bubbles will slowly rise to the surface. As the oil becomes warmer it will start to take on a noticeable sweet aroma and turn light red in color, and bubbles will appear at a faster rate and increase slightly in size. When this occurs and the oil's color is a deeper orange-red, after 12 to 15 minutes, remove from the heat and set aside for at least 30 minutes to allow the annatto seeds to infuse more color and the oil to cool.

Strain through a fine-mesh strainer into a bowl and transfer to a covered glass jar. Store at room temperature for a month or in the fridge for up to 2 months.

MUSHROOM POWDER

Mushroom powder is magical. It's meaty, smoky, and filled with intense umami flavor. I prefer the natural glutamates found in dried mushrooms, although Vietnamese vegetarian cooks often turn to a manufactured vegan mushroom seasoning called *hạt nêm nấm* to impart added savoriness. I add it habitually in small amounts, like salt and pepper, to soups, stir-fries, and braises.

Due to their intensity, shiitakes are the ideal mushrooms for this powder. You could substitute sliced Italian porcini although their flavor is more pronounced, and they're more expensive, as is the shiitake or porcini powder you'll find in some specialty grocery stores. **Makes a scant ½ cup**

1 ounce (30 g) dried shiitake mushrooms

Break the mushrooms into smaller pieces with your hands, scissors, or a knife. (Break off the hard stems of large shiitakes and store in the freezer to use when making vegetable stock.) Put into a spice or coffee grinder (or a blender with a narrow bowl) and grind for a couple of minutes. Stop occasionally to use a spoon or spatula to loosen any large pieces that may get stuck under the blades. (Note: When stopping the grinder, leave the top on for a minute or two to allow the mushroom dust to settle.)

Tip the powder into a small bowl. Gently tap the grinder cover over the bowl or use a spatula or a clean, dry brush to collect any powder that has stuck to it.

Transfer to a clean, dry jar and store indefinitely in a cool, dry place.

Dried shiitake mushrooms

CRISPY FRIED SHALLOTS

HÀNH PHI

If you find these crisp sweet mini "onion" rings as addictive as I do, double the shallots in the recipe. They're an indispensable garnish for salads and some noodle dishes. Evenly cut slices will cook most uniformly, so here's a great place to practice good knife skills. For optimal crispness and texture, make these the same day you plan to eat them. (Humid weather will blunt their crispness, but their fabulous flavor will remain.)

Ready-made fried shallots are available at Asian grocery stores in the West, but they lack the characteristic richness of those you make from scratch. When you've finished frying, reserve the fragrant oil to use in other dishes. **Makes 1 cup**

½ pound (225 g) shallots
1 cup (250 ml) vegetable oil

Peel the shallots, leaving the root ends intact. Thinly slice crosswise, resulting in small shallot rings. Discard the root end bits or use in vegetable stocks. On a cutting board or in a bowl, loosely break the layers of rings apart to ensure that they cook evenly.

Line a plate or baking sheet with paper towel. Pour the oil into a wok or large skillet over medium heat. After 2 or 3 minutes, drop a few pieces into the oil. If they sizzle lightly, add the remaining shallots. If they do not and sink to the bottom of the pan, the oil is not hot enough. Wait for them to rise and then add the remaining shallots.

The shallots will soften and begin to give off their moisture, resulting in many tiny bubbles. Every minute or so, stir using a spider or slotted spoon. After 5 or 6 minutes some of the shallots around the edge of the oil will take on some color. For the next 5 minutes or so, stir regularly to move them around. When about three-quarters are uniformly light golden brown, move the pan off the heat. (The shallots will continue to cook out of the oil, so take them out when they are a light golden brown instead of a darker color, when they may taste bitter).

To remove, briefly tilt the spider or spoon against the side of the pan to let any excess oil drip back into the pan. Transfer to a paper-towel-lined plate and spread them out to cool and crisp up. Transfer to an airtight jar or container and store for up to 1 week at room temperature (or freeze during humid weather).

continues

IF DOUBLING THE RECIPE

Use a total of 1¼ cups (310 ml) of oil. Cook as directed, but the shallots will take on some color after 12 to 15 minutes and turn golden brown during the following 5 minutes.

FRAGRANT SHALLOT OIL

Let the oil cool and pass it through a fine-mesh strainer into a clean jar. Cover and store in a cool, dry place for up to a month. Use it for stir-fries or when specifically suggested in a recipe.

Shallots and garlic

TOASTED RICE POWDER

THÍNH

If you've ever eaten Aromatic Cellophane Noodle Roll-Ups (page 101), you've likely encountered toasted rice powder (although you may not have realized it). With its delicate texture and earthy flavor, this garnish adds complexity to fresh rice paper rolls, salads, and dumplings. Make sure to toast through the entire rice grain evenly, which can take a good 15 to 20 minutes. Try not to rush it. You're looking for the rice to change color from sandy to bronze to a burnished copper brown.   **Makes a scant ½ cup**

½ cup (3½ ounces; 100 g) white or brown jasmine rice or sticky rice

Place the rice in a heavy 10-inch skillet over medium-low to medium heat. Leave undisturbed for 3 to 4 minutes, then shake to mix and distribute the rice. Every 45 seconds to 1½ minutes, for the next 8 to 10 minutes, shake the pan or stir the rice to prevent the grains from darkening too much. Depending on the type of rice you're using, some grains may pop and you may notice a light smoky haze coming from the skillet. Pay attention to the edges of the skillet as grains tend to brown more quickly there. Gradually the rice will turn from a light brown to a deeper golden brown. (If at any time you feel the rice is browning too quickly, reduce the heat.) Reduce heat to low and continue to toast, stirring regularly, for another 3 to 5 minutes. Remove the pan from the heat and transfer the toasted rice to a plate to cool.

When cool, transfer to a blender and grind on high for 30 seconds. Stop, uncover, and stir the rice powder. Re-cover and grind on high for another 30 seconds. If need be, gently shake the blender as it grinds to disturb the rice powder. When done, the powder should resemble fine sand. (Alternatively, grind toasted rice in several batches in an electric coffee grinder designated for grinding spices.) Store in an airtight glass jar for several months.

Note:
If your blender does not grind the rice well or you see any coarse grains, sift it through a fine-mesh strainer to get rid of any large pieces.

TAMARIND LIQUID

NƯỚC ME

The liquid made from sour tamarind pulp infuses some central and southern Vietnamese dishes with a smoky-sweet tang. Because the pulp is semidried, you must first soften it with hot water, then mash and strain it. Since I also use it in Indian, Thai, and Mexican dishes, I double the recipe and freeze it in ice cube trays. Once hardened, I pop out the frozen cubes and store them in a zip-top freezer bag. **Makes about 2 cups (500 ml) or a tray of 16 ice cubes**

7 to 8 ounces (200 to 225 g; ½ block)
    tamarind pulp
2½ cups (600 ml) boiling water plus ½ cup
    (125 ml) warm water

Break the block of tamarind pulp into 2-inch (5 cm) chunks and place in a large bowl. Pour the boiling water over them and let sit for a couple of minutes. Mash with a potato masher or the back of a large fork to dissolve and loosen the pulp from the fibers and seeds.

When the mashed pulp is cool enough to handle but still warm, transfer it to a large fine-mesh sieve placed over a deep bowl or pot. Use one hand, a spatula, or the back of a large spoon to push and gently scrape the pulp through the sieve. Periodically lift the sieve and scrape the thick puree from the underside into the bowl.

Transfer the seeds and fibers to a small bowl and pour ½ cup (125 ml) warm water over them. Squeeze or mash the pulp to release any remaining puree. Pass through the sieve and discard the fibers and seeds. The tamarind liquid is now ready to use. Refrigerate for several days to a week (it will turn moldy after that) or freeze in an ice cube tray and store in a zip-top plastic bag for future use.

OPPOSITE *Clockwise from top right*: black sesame seeds; lemongrass chile satay; pickled carrots and daikon; toasted rice powder (*center*); ground sesame seed salt; crispy fried shallots; annatto seed oil (*top left*); toasted sesame seeds; tamarind liquid

TOFU SKIN CHIPS

ĐẬU HŨ KY CHIÊN

Bowls of noodles and rice porridge are perfect comfort foods, and it's hard to improve on perfection. But scattering in fried tofu skin chips does just that. Frying fresh or rehydrated dried tofu skin (also called *bean curd skin*) transforms its texture from chewy to shatteringly crisp. Work in batches and resist the urge to crowd the pot. If they stick to each other while frying, don't fret: you can ease them apart once they're cool. **Serves 4 as a garnish**

1 ounce (30 g) dried or 2 ounces (60g) fresh tofu skin

1½ to 2 cups (375 to 500ml) vegetable oil

Heat the oil in a wok or large skillet over medium-high heat.

If using dried tofu skin: Fill a large bowl with lukewarm water. Break or cut with scissors tofu skin sheets into large pieces that will fit in the bowl. Slide the dried tofu skin into the water and soak for about 5 minutes. (Slightly thicker or older tofu skin may require a longer soak. Check every 5 minutes and, if need be, separate the folds of any sheets and turn and push the tofu skin under the water.) When it's soft, flexible, and has turned to the shade of cream, it is ready. Drain into a colander set in the sink. Gently shake the colander over the sink. One at a time, lift each piece, pausing briefly to allow any excess water to fall back into the sink, and transfer to a cutting board.

As the oil heats up, separate the fresh or rehydrated dried tofu skin layers from each other and cut them with scissors or a sharp knife into triangles shaped like tortilla chips, about 3 inches (8 cm) on a side. If using dried tofu skin, lay the rehydrated triangles briefly on a clean kitchen towel to blot dry.

Lay a couple of layers of paper towel on a large plate and set beside the stove.

The oil is ready when it reaches 325°F (163°C) or when you touch the bottom of the wok or pot with a wooden chopstick and small oil bubbles immediately form on the surface around the chopstick. One at a time, carefully slip several tofu skin triangles into oil. Within seconds they will make a crackling sound and partially blister. Quickly use a spider or a pair of tongs to push them under the surface for a couple of seconds (after 30 seconds, try to turn the pieces over, gently agitating and pushing them under the surface).

When they've turned a light golden brown color and the small bubbles have mostly stopped (45 seconds to a minute), lift them from the oil, pausing briefly to let some oil drip back into the wok, and transfer to a fine-mesh sieve. Gently shake the sieve and carefully transfer them to the paper-towel-lined plate.

If the chips darken too quickly, your oil is too hot. To cool the oil, reduce the heat slightly and pour in a ¼ to ½ cup (62.5 to 125 ml) of room-temperature oil.

Repeat until the rest of the tofu skin is fried.

The chips stay crispy for a couple of days, but in humid weather it's best to make them shortly before serving.

VARIATIONS

CRISPY TOFU SKIN STRIPS

Cut rehydrated or fresh tofu skin into strips ¼ inch wide by 2 inches long(06. by 5 cm) and fry until golden brown, about 45 seconds.

CRISPY TOFU SKIN STICKS

If you are using crumpled tofu sticks (see page 301), rehydrate them (see long or short soak methods below) before frying to ensure the entire stick will fully cook. Squeeze and dry them on a clean kitchen or paper towel to remove as much water as possible to prevent oil from sputtering from the wok. Fry as you would for regular tofu skin chips, but increase the cooking time to 2 to 2½ minutes.

TO REHYDRATE THE TOFU SKIN STICKS

LONG SOAK METHOD

Eight hours before you plan to fry the tofu sticks, place them in a casserole dish (snap them, trying to keep them in long lengths if they're too long for the dish). Fill the casserole dish with hot tap water. Since the tofu skin sticks will float, use a small-mesh rack (you can lay a large stainless-steel spoon, or something that won't float, across them) to keep them immersed. The tofu skin sticks will rehydrate overnight (or put them in the water before leaving for work).

QUICK SOAK METHOD

If you've forgotten to soak them and need to speed up the process, turn your oven to 200°F (95°C) and add the casserole dish (filled with hot water). The constant gentle heat quickens the process of the water penetrating the sticks' center. They should be ready after 1 to 1½ hours. A quick boil, like boiling pasta, won't work, because the sticks will lose their shape and become slimy instead of fully hydrated.

The tofu skin sticks are fully hydrated when they have turned a lighter color and when you cut through them there are no dried parts at the core of the stick.

Cut the sticks into 2-inch (5 cm) lengths. Discard any parts that are tough (this tends to be the thin curved part that touched the stick or rack when drying). Place the tofu sticks in a bowl or on a plate, cover with a damp towel, and wrap with plastic wrap so that they don't dry out.

TOFU SKIN SAUSAGE

CHẢ (GIÓ) LỤA CHAY

When you hear the word *charcuterie*, you think of cured meat, right? Not so fast. Charcuterie plays an unexpected role in the Vietnamese vegetarian kitchen, where cooks cunningly shape tofu skin into "sausages" for use as a meat substitute in Bánh Mì Sandwiches (page 113), Star Anise Cinnamon Scented Pho Noodle Soup (page 175), and Fragrant Lemongrass Huế-Style Noodle Soup (page 179), among other dishes. Tofu skin is chewier and more toothsome than block tofu, so don't substitute the latter for the former. I consistently have great success using thin dried tofu sheets, but you can also find fresh tofu skin at Vietnamese markets or Hodo Soy brand at some well-stocked grocers. (Fresh tofu skin is stickier, and therefore binds more easily, which is a plus. And its texture is fantastic.)

This recipe will teach you how to roll the tofu into a secure, tight cylinder, and your first bite will make you wonder how you ever lived without homemade tofu skin sausage in your pantry.   **Makes two ½-pound (225 g) sausages**

FROM THE PANTRY/MAKE AHEAD

½ teaspoon Mushroom Powder (page 36)

————

½ pound (225 g) dried or 1 pound (454 g) fresh tofu skin

1 tablespoon finely chopped scallion, white part only

2 teaspoons coarsely ground black pepper

1 teaspoon soy sauce

1 teaspoon vegetarian mushroom-flavored stir-fry sauce or vegetarian hoisin sauce

1 teaspoon salt

¼ teaspoon sugar

Prepare the Mushroom Powder.

If using dried tofu skin: Fill a large bowl with lukewarm water. Cut the tofu skin sheets into large pieces that will fit in the bowl. Place the dried tofu skin in the water and soak for 5 minutes. (Slightly thicker or older tofu skin may require up to 25 minutes of soaking. Check every 5 minutes and, if need be, separate the folds of any sheets and turn and push the tofu skin under the water.) When it's soft, flexible, and has turned to the shade of cream, it is ready. Drain into a colander. Lift it above the colander and gently shake off any excess water. Grab a third of it and squeeze out as much water as you can. Transfer to a large bowl. Repeat two more times with the remaining tofu skin. You should have 3 to 3⅓ packed cups (600 g) of rehydrated tofu skin.

If using fresh tofu skin: Separate the sheets, not worrying if some stick together.

Trim and discard any hard edges from the fresh or rehydrated tofu skin. Cut it into rough 1½-inch (4 cm) squares and place in a large bowl. Sprinkle all of the seasonings over the top. Use your hands to mix the seasonings evenly all over the surface of the tofu skin.

Clean a 2-foot (61 cm) area on your countertop, then moisten it with a damp, clean dish towel. Tear off a piece of plastic wrap about 2 feet (61 cm) long and lay it flat horizontally on the moistened countertop. Make an 8-inch (20 cm) mound with half of the seasoned tofu skin (9 to 10½ ounces; 255 to 300 g) centered and over the bottom half of the length of the plastic wrap, about 1½ inches (4 cm) from the edge closest to you. In one quick motion, roll up the bottom edge of the plastic over the tofu skin, trying to hold it in place, as tightly as possible. Gently press the ends of the shaped tofu toward the center of the cylinder. Tighten the cylinder by twisting one end of the plastic wrap several times against the tofu skin. Repeat on the other side, twisting in the opposite direction. Bring both ends of the plastic toward the center and press together. You should have a cylinder 6 or 7 inches (15 to 18 cm) in length.

Moisten the countertop again and tear off another piece of plastic the same length, laying it in the same manner as before. Before placing the cylinder on the plastic wrap, use a toothpick to prick the cylinder about 5 times where you can see some air bubbles that developed as you rolled the tofu. Center the cylinder horizontally along the bottom edge of the plastic.

Roll up the cylinder tightly to gently press out any air bubbles. Don't worry if you press a little liquid out. Once the ends are twisted and tightened, bring the extra wrap from the ends together and tie in a knot just tight enough to rest against the cylinder. Lightly prick the cylinder four more times where you can see any air bubbles that developed during the second rolling. About ¾ inch (2 cm) from one end, tightly tie a piece of string, about 10 inches (26 cm) long, around the cylinder. Repeat with four or five more strings, about ¾ inch (1 cm) apart. Set the cylinder aside and repeat with the remaining half of the seasoned tofu skin.

Fill a wok or steamer pot with an inch or two of water. Place both cylinders in the steamer basket, cover, and set the steamer basket into the wok. Bring the water to a boil and steam for 40 minutes for fresh tofu skin and about 1 hour for dried. Every 20 minutes, remove the lid, allowing the steam to dissipate to avoid being burned, and use tongs to turn each cylinder halfway. Also check the water level, adding more hot water if necessary. Re-cover and steam until done.

Remove the cylinders and transfer to a plate to cool to room temperature. Refrigerate for several hours or overnight to firm up before slicing.

Store for up to 1 week in the refrigerator or up to a month in the freezer. (Once the roll is completely cooled, I cut away the strings, gently unwrap it, and rewrap it in plastic. I find this keeps it fresher for longer.)

TO USE IN A RECIPE

Cut the tofu skin sausage, through the plastic wrap, into ⅓-inch (1 cm) slices. Peel away the plastic wrap and use as needed.

NUTTY MUSHROOM PÂTÉ

Use mushroom pâté for greater umami in Bánh Mì Sandwiches (page 113) and Grilled Rice Paper with Mushroom Pâté, Egg, and Sriracha (page 120). Stick with a single mushroom type or opt for a variety (think cremini, oyster, portobello, or fresh shiitakes) for added complexity. Just make sure to brown the mushrooms well to bring forth their deepest, smokiest flavors.   **Makes about 1½ cups**

FROM THE PANTRY/MAKE AHEAD

½ teaspoon Mushroom Powder (page 36)

———

1 pound (454 g) fresh mushrooms

2 tablespoons vegetable oil

1 small shallot, minced (1 tablespoon)

1 tablespoon minced garlic

½ teaspoon salt

½ teaspoon freshly ground black pepper

2 tablespoons roasted unsalted peanuts, or Toasted Sesame Seeds (page 33), ground

1 tablespoon soy sauce

Prepare the Mushroom Powder.

Clean the mushrooms of any dirt or debris with a soft brush or a damp paper towel.

Finely chop the mushrooms by hand, or in a food processor or grate them on the large holes of a grater. (If using a food processor, halve or quarter them to facilitate mincing before placing in the processor.)

Heat the oil in a medium skillet over medium heat. Add the shallot and cook, stirring frequently, for about 2 minutes, or until soft and translucent. Add the garlic and cook until the garlic releases its fragrance, about 30 seconds. Toss in the mushrooms, salt, and pepper and increase the heat to medium-high. Stir occasionally to spread the mushrooms around the bottom of the pan to help evaporate any liquid that is released. After 5 minutes, as they begin to dry out, stir less until lightly browned. Scrape any caramelized nutty bits from the bottom of the pan.

Stir in the ground peanuts or sesame seeds, soy sauce, and mushroom powder. Cook for another minute or two, until everything is well blended.

Remove from the heat and transfer to a clean container to store. Refrigerate for up to 5 days.

VARIATION

NUTTY MUSHROOM AND TOFU PÂTÉ

Replace half of the mushrooms with ½ pound (225 g) of firm or extra-firm tofu. Mash the tofu with a fork or your hands. Add it with the peanuts and cook for 2 or 3 minutes, until some of the water evaporates from the tofu.

PICKLED CARROTS AND DAIKON

ĐỒ CHUA (South); DƯA GÓP (North)

Carrot and daikon pickles add a bright sweet-and-sour crunch to a huge variety of dishes. Cut the vegetables into thick matchsticks for a Bánh Mì Sandwich (page 113) or thinner ones for salads, Rainbow Rice Paper Rolls (page 95), and Tasty Rice Noodle Bowl (page 188). Sprinkling a bit of salt on the vegetables before pickling draws out excess moisture, creating crisper pickles.

When you're ready to branch out, replace the daikon with kohlrabi or even green papaya. Pro tip: A wide-mouth canning jar makes it easier to fish the pickles out of the brine. **Makes 3 cups (750 ml)**

½ **pound (225 g) carrots (1 large) cut into matchsticks**

½ **pound (225 g) daikon peeled and cut into thick matchsticks**

2 teaspoons salt

½ **to** ¾ **cup (100 to 150 g) sugar**

1 cup (250 ml) rice vinegar

1 cup (250 ml) water

Place the carrots and daikon in a large colander in the sink or over a large bowl. Sprinkle salt over them and massage for about a minute. Allow the vegetables to stand for at least 15 minutes.

Add the ½ cup sugar, the vinegar, and the water to a small pot and warm gently over low heat. Stir until the sugar is completely dissolved. Remove from the heat and taste. If you prefer the brine to be sweeter, add the remaining ¼ cup sugar and stir until completely dissolved. Cool until lukewarm.

Rinse the vegetables under cold running water for a minute. Drain and squeeze out any extra water. Place in the container you plan to store them in.

Pour the lukewarm pickling liquid into the container, making sure the liquid fully covers the vegetables. Marinate the vegetables for at least 1 hour before using. Store refrigerated in an airtight container for up to 1 month.

Note:
Daikon or other types of radish or turnips often release a funky odor when stored in a container for a while. Leave the top off for 10 minutes or so to let the odor dissipate. It should not affect the overall taste of the vegetables, but sample a bit before including in a dish.

continues

QUICK PICKLED CARROTS

Here is a small-quantity pickle recipe you can make in 15 minutes if you don't have time to make a larger batch but still want some of the sour and sweetness. It's best to make it before preparing the rest of the recipe you plan to use the carrots in.

3 tablespoons rice vinegar

3 tablespoons sugar

¼ teaspoon salt

1 medium carrot (3 ounces; 85 g), cut into matchsticks

Place the vinegar, sugar, and salt in a medium bowl and stir until the sugar is fully dissolved. Add the carrot and massage gently with the liquid. Marinate for 15 minutes before using.

Pickled carrots and shallots stored in a jar on a street food cart.

EVERYDAY TABLE SAUCE

NƯỚC CHẤM CHAY

Traditionally made with fish sauce, *nước chấm* is a fixture on restaurant tables throughout Việt Nam. Clear, light, and endlessly versatile, this dipping sauce has the magical ability to bring together many distinct flavors into a cohesive whole.

My version is, of course, vegetarian, and it works wonders as a dipping sauce for fresh and fried spring rolls and Crispy Rice and Mung Bean Crepes (page 217). I also drizzle it over a Tasty Rice Noodle Bowl (page 188). I tasted many vegetarian versions at street food stalls, in homes, and in monasteries, and after some tinkering I've managed to achieve the ideal balance of sweet, sour, salty, and spicy.   **Makes just over ½ cup (125 ml)**

3 tablespoons sugar

¼ cup (62.5 ml) water

2 tablespoons rice vinegar

1 teaspoon soy sauce

1 tablespoon plus 1 teaspoon fresh lime juice

½ teaspoon salt

1 fresh red Thai bird chile, finely chopped or thinly sliced

1 garlic clove, finely chopped

Put the sugar, water, rice vinegar, soy sauce, lime juice, and salt into a bowl. Stir until the sugar is fully dissolved. Add and mix in the chile and garlic. Taste and adjust the seasoning if needed. Let the sauce sit for 10 minutes before serving to allow the flavors to intermingle.

Serve in one medium bowl with a spoon so guests can drizzle some extra sauce into their spring rolls following their initial bite. Or double the recipe and serve in small individual bowls.

VARIATIONS

- For a sweeter sauce, add 2 teaspoons to 1 tablespoon more sugar.

- Whisk in 1 teaspoon fermented tofu or a tablespoon of the fermented tofu brine.

- Stir in ¼ to ½ teaspoon wakame or hijiki powder.

- Use fresh coconut water (not milk) instead of tap water.

- Add 1½ teaspoons finely chopped lemongrass.

Note:

You can mix the sugar, water, vinegar, soy sauce, lime juice, and salt together up to a day in advance. Stir in the chile and garlic 10 to 15 minutes before serving.

Using, Storing, and Preparing Chiles

Mahayana Buddhist monks, nuns, and very devout followers who eat a vegetarian diet rarely use chile in their cooking. However, lay Buddhists who eat vegetarian twice a month continue to consume chiles. For the majority of the recipes I've decided to follow their lead. You can omit the chiles if you cook for a very devout practitioner.

Besides one recipe that uses dried chile flakes (ớt khô) two types of fresh chiles you'll find in Việt Nam and in Asian and well-stocked grocery stores are used in this book. Fresh red Thai bird chiles (ớt hiểm), 1½ inches (4 cm) in length, are fiery, while fresh long red chiles, 3 to 4 inches (7.5 to 10 cm) long, are only mildly spicy. If need be, substitute serrano chiles for the Thai bird chiles and Fresno or jalapeño chiles for the long red chiles.

Store chiles in a loosely covered container or paper bag for up to a week and a half in the refrigerator. Or, if you're forced to buy a large quantity, freeze them in a zip-top plastic bag for at least several months.

When I've felt it necessary to decrease the amount of heat level in a recipe, I've suggested you seed the chile (scrape out and discard the seeds). Otherwise, if this is not indicated, chop or slice the chile seeds and all.

Fresh red Thai bird chiles (*foreground*); fresh long medium-hot red chiles (*center*)

SOY CHILE DIPPING SAUCE

NƯỚC TƯƠNG or NƯỚC SIÊU

Sometimes you need a no-frills, all-purpose dipping sauce. Here it is. Slightly sweetened soy sauce, a touch of vinegar for tang, and hot chile slices for heat are all you need to create this high-impact, low-effort sauce. Drizzle it over Tasty Rice Noodle Bowl (page 188), use it to flavor and moisten baguettes for Bánh Mì Sandwich (page 113), or tap it to accompany Crispy Half-Moon Pillows (page 110) or Translucent Mung Bean Dumplings (page 123). You can even add some minced garlic to change things up.   **Makes about ¾ cup (187.5 ml)**

½ cup (125 ml) soy sauce

2 tablespoons water

2 tablespoons rice vinegar

2 tablespoons sugar

1 fresh red Thai bird chile, thinly sliced (optional)

1 garlic clove, minced (optional)

Pour the soy sauce, water, rice vinegar, and sugar into a small bowl. Stir until the sugar is fully dissolved. Add the chile and garlic and serve. Store refrigerated in a glass jar for up to 1 week.

Note:
The chile and garlic flavors get stronger as they sit, so I often mix everything else together and store in the fridge. Right before serving I add the chile and/or garlic for a more balanced flavor.

VARIATION

BÁNH MÌ SANDWICH SUPER SAUCE

If making Bánh Mì (page 113), make half of the recipe, without the garlic. Add 2 thinly sliced scallions, a diced ¼ plum tomato, and 1 teaspoon Toasted Sesame Seeds (page 33). Mix well and drizzle into the bánh mì sandwich.

NUTTY FERMENTED SOYBEAN DIPPING SAUCE

NƯỚC LÈO CHAY

I learned how to make this divine central Vietnamese sauce from Bội Trân, a well-known Huế artist and cook (see page 241). Its rich, salty flavor comes from fermented soybeans (*tương*). Pureeing half of the toasted peanuts and sesame seeds thickens the sauce and adds body. The rest are finely chopped and added to the sauce at the end. For an extra kick I often add finely chopped garlic and chile.

Pair this sauce with Fresh Swiss Chard Rolls (page 103), small bundles of wrapped Crispy Rice and Mung Bean Crepes (page 217), or Tasty Rice Noodle Bowl (page 188). Or follow Bội Trân's lead and serve it alongside raw and Tender Boiled Vegetables (page 227) as part of a simple rice meal.

Makes 1 cup (250 ml)

1 teaspoon vegetable oil

1 tablespoon finely chopped scallion, white and light green parts only

2 tablespoons fermented soybeans or soybean paste

2 tablespoons roasted unsalted peanuts

2 tablespoons Toasted Sesame Seeds (page 33)

1 teaspoon sugar

¾ cup plus 1 tablespoon water (202.5 ml)

1¼ teaspoons cornstarch

Heat the oil in a small saucepan over medium heat. Add the scallion and cook for about 1 minute, until softened. Add the fermented soybeans, 1 tablespoon each of the peanuts and sesame seeds, the sugar, and ¾ cup of the water. Give it a good stir. Immediately remove the pot from the heat and transfer all of the contents to a blender.

Puree briefly on the blender's lowest setting and then increase to medium or high speed for a minute. Pour the sauce back into the saucepan. Mix the cornstarch and 1 tablespoon cold water in a small bowl, then stir it into the sauce. Bring the sauce to a boil over medium heat. Reduce the heat slightly and simmer for a couple of minutes, or until it is slightly thickened and lightly coats the back of a spoon. Transfer to a serving bowl to cool.

Finely chop the remaining peanuts. Stir them and the remaining sesame seeds into the sauce. Serve at room temperature. The sauce can be made in advance and kept refrigerated for several days. If made more than a day in advance, it may separate a touch. Give it a quick stir before serving.

VARIATIONS

· Replace the scallion with 2 garlic cloves and 1 stemmed fresh red Thai bird chile, both finely chopped, and cook for about 30 seconds before adding the other ingredients. Squeeze the juice of ½ lime into the cooled sauce.

· Substitute coconut milk for the ¾ cup water and reduce the cornstarch to 1 teaspoon.

A young nun peels peanuts as part of her daily active meditation.

LEMONGRASS CHILE SATAY

ỚT XẢ TẾ or SẢ TẾ

With a red hue from annatto seed oil and fiery heat thanks to chiles, this sauce calls for frying an entire stalk of lemongrass. (Most recipes use the bottom two-thirds only.) It's one of my favorite pantry condiments, perfect for stirring into noodle soups, adding to dipping sauces, or even mixing with mayonnaise for a Bánh Mì Sandwich (page 113). **Makes about 1¼ cups**

FROM THE PANTRY/MAKE AHEAD
¼ cup Annatto Seed Oil (page 35)

---

4 lemongrass stalks (140 g), rinsed
½ cup (125 ml) vegetable oil
3 fresh red Thai bird chiles, minced
3 tablespoons (23 g) dried chile flakes
1 tablespoon sugar
1 teaspoon salt

Prepare the Annatto Seed Oil.

Remove two or three outer layers from the lemongrass. Trim off the root end and thinly slice. You should have about ¾ cup. Place in a food processor (a smaller insert bowl or mini food processor works nicely) or blender and mix until finely chopped. You may need to occasionally stop and push any lemongrass that has crept up on the edges of the bowl down with a spatula.

Heat the oil in a medium saucepan or skillet over medium-low heat. Add the lemongrass and cook, stirring frequently, repeatedly spreading it evenly over the bottom of the pan. Give particular attention to the edges of the pan as they color first. After 10 to 12 minutes, or when the lemongrass is fragrant and a nutty golden brown color, add the annatto seed oil, fresh and dried chiles, sugar, and salt and cook, stirring constantly, for 3 to 5 minutes more. Remove from the heat to cool. While still a little warm, transfer to a glass jar, pressing down on it so that some oil rises to the top if necessary. Cool completely before covering and storing at room temperature or in the fridge.

VARIATION
Add a couple tablespoons each of minced garlic and shallots if you like. Stir in along with 3 more tablespoons of oil about 5 minutes after you start cooking the lemongrass.

TOASTED SESAME RICE CRACKERS

BÁNH TRÁNG ĐA MÈ TRẮNG or MÈ ĐEN NƯỚNG

Think of these crackers as the Vietnamese (rice-based) equivalent of the Mexican (corn-based) tortilla chip. They make a grabbable snack on their own or can be deployed to scoop up dips or to spoon up salads.

Traditionally, the crackers are toasted over a clay pot oven or barbecue. Toasting them in a hot oven is quicker and more practical.

8½-inch (22 cm) untoasted rice crackers, with white or black sesame seeds

Put a rack in the middle of the oven and heat to 400°F (200°C) (or set a toaster oven to broil). Place a cracker directly on the rack. After 30 seconds to 1½ minutes, it will puff up with tiny bubbles on the surface, curl a touch, and turn white starting from the edges and moving toward the center. When that occurs, use tongs to turn it over. Toast for another 1½ to 2 minutes (for a total of 3 to 4 minutes), occasionally rotating or flipping if an edge or curled part is becoming too dark or your oven has hot spots. The cracker is done when fully crisp and lightly golden brown around the edges and/or center.

Make the toasted crackers in advance. They'll stay crisp for several days stored in a zip-top plastic bag.

2

———

TOFU AND SEITAN

OPPOSITE Fresh and fried tofu, tofu skin, and seitan at a market stall in Sài Gòn.

For more than a millennium, cooks have creatively manipulated tofu and seitan, both rich sources of nonanimal protein. Over time, Mahayana Buddhist monastics, in particular, became increasingly skilled at transforming tofu, tofu skin, and seitan (also called *wheat gluten*) into imitation meats. This culinary art filtered into Việt Nam by way of China, and its influence on Vietnamese culture persists to this day.

Today in Việt Nam, the gastronomic illusion of imitation meat remains popular, as market vendors sell ingredients and cooks prepare dishes that try to closely resemble meat and seafood dishes in color, taste, texture, and flavor. (See page 9 for a further discussion on this topic.)

At markets throughout the country, there's always a stall or two selling small blocks of freshly made tofu. In central or southern Vietnamese communities with a high concentration of vegetarians, such as the Cao Đài in Tây Ninh or those with a strong Chinese tradition, you'll often find an even greater concentration of tofu and seitan stalls. The sheer scope and variety are impressive: you'll find firm fresh tofu blocks; batons, cubes, triangles, or small blocks of fried tofu; fresh tofu skin sold in wrinkled packages; tofu rolled and steamed into thick tofu skin sausages (See my recipe on page 44); tofu wrapped into drumsticks around small lengths of lemongrass; and tofu curved into small mock shrimp. And that's just for starters.

Steamed or fried seitan is sold variously as small ovals (whole or cut into thin slices or torn into shreds), as rolled coils, or as small bite-sized balls.

In North America, you'll find tofu, seitan, and meat analog products, from raw to cooked, grouped together in the refrigerated, and sometimes frozen, sections of well-stocked grocers and Vietnamese and Chinese markets. In areas with large Vietnamese and Chinese populations you may find outstanding small artisanal tofu makers at community grocery stores.

Tofu and seitan absorb seasonings easily, particularly when first frozen, and flavorful sauces cling to their surfaces. For the recipes in this and other chapters (excluding those in the sweets chapter), opt for firm or extra-firm tofu. The best way to enhance the flavor and texture of tofu is to follow the lead of Vietnamese cooks, who generally shallow-fry or deep-fry it to create a golden crust while maintaining a creamy yet toothsome interior. Or freeze tofu in advance to transform it into chewy meat- or fish-mimicking chunks.

Incorporating seitan into your diet is a great way to get extra protein. It's not hard to make it at home, so I've included a basic recipe here as well. You may also purchase packaged, lightly seasoned seitan for use in the recipes. Several small, regional companies in the United States make and sell packaged seitan.

Finally, over the last few years, there's been considerable advancement in the development of meat analogs—those foods made from textured soy and/or vegetable proteins—that closely mimic the texture and flavor of chicken and beef. Although such products are not sold in Việt Nam, I believe if Vietnamese vegetarian cooks had access to them they would quickly adopt them in their cooking. I've highlighted a couple of recipes using these products, including Lemongrass Chile "Chicken" Strips Stir-Fry (page 71) and Tomatoes Stuffed with Meatless Ground and Tofu (page 79).

TIPS FOR PREPARING TOFU

Prior to using tofu, I generally recommend shallow-frying or deep-frying it. Doing so not only creates that alluring crust but, more important, the oil that clings to the tofu adds a rich fattiness and mouthfeel, which can especially benefit vegetarian dishes such as these. You can also panfry or bake tofu, but the results will be less full-bodied.

While deep-frying tofu produces a crispy exterior, the interior remains warm and custardy. You can even fry it ahead of time: cubes or slabs of deep-fried tofu will keep for up to a week in the refrigerator. They freeze well, too, although the texture becomes a bit chewier (which isn't at all bad). If you're organized, you can prepare other deep-fried garnishes, like tofu skin chips, at the same time.

All that being said, even I'm not the best weekly meal planner, so I often shallow-fry tofu immediately before adding it to recipes. To shallow-fry tofu, use just enough oil so it comes about halfway up the sides of the slabs. If shallow-frying cubes, turn them frequently to ensure even cooking.

PRESSING TOFU FOR DEEP-FRYING, SHALLOW-FRYING, OR PANFRYING

Before cooking or cutting tofu, you first must drain, blot dry and press the blocks to rid them of excess moisture. Tofu sold at Vietnamese markets is so fresh and spends such a short time in water that it doesn't require much, or any, pressing before being fried, but this isn't true of most of the packaged tofu sold in the West. Tofu that's too wet will aggressively spurt oil, and you'll run the risk of both burning yourself and ruining the dish.

Here's what to do: Drain off the liquid from the package and cut the tofu into the thickness or shape indicated in a recipe. When cutting tofu into cubes, try to keep it close together, in a rectangular shape, as I find it easier to blot dry and press out the water that way. Line a large plate with a double thickness of paper towels or a clean kitchen towel. Arrange the tofu (cubes or slabs) on top. Cover the tofu with a second, folded, clean kitchen towel or another double layer of paper towels. If you'll be shallow-frying, leave the tofu to drain for at least 10 minutes as you prepare the rest of your ingredients. For deep-frying, you'll need to press out more water. Set a plate or tray atop the second towel layer and weight it down with something heavy, like a few 28-ounce (783 g) cans of tomatoes. Leave it for about 30 minutes. Blot off any residual outside moisture before frying.

DEEP-FRYING TOFU

When you're ready to fry, set a plate or tray lined with paper towel next to the stove. Heat 3 to 4 cups of cooking oil with a high smoke point (peanut, sunflower, or canola) in a Dutch oven over medium to medium-high heat to 350°F (177°C) on a deep-fry thermometer. Alternatively, you may use a wok filled with 2½ to 3 cups of oil.

Remove the tofu from the plate and blot any lingering moisture. Place several pieces of tofu onto the mesh of a spider (or a slotted metal spoon or tongs) and lower the tofu carefully into the hot oil. Repeat with several more pieces of tofu, but don't crowd the pot. (Tofu has a tendency to stick together, so after about 2 minutes without touching it, nudge any clingy pieces apart with your spider, spoon, or even a chopstick.) Then gently turn the tofu. After 3 to 4 minutes, it should puff up and become crispy and light golden in color. Start lifting it from the oil at this point, pausing to allow any oil to drip back into the pot. Transfer to the paper-towel-lined plate and set it aside until ready to use in a recipe. Repeat as needed.

To reuse the oil, let it cool. Strain it (a fine-mesh strainer lined with a coffee filter works well) into a tighty sealed container and store in a cool, dark place. You can reuse the oil several times. Discard it when the oil darkens or begins to smell off.

SHALLOW-FRYING TOFU

Set a paper-towel-lined plate or tray next to the stove. In a wok or large skillet, heat ¼ cup plus 2 tablespoons to ½ cup cooking oil over medium-high heat. When the oil is hot, carefully add the tofu. Use caution as the oil may sputter as the tofu releases moisture. Cook tofu slabs for 4 to 5 minutes per side, or until lightly golden, then flip. Cook tofu cubes for about 3 minutes for the first side, then 2 to 2½ minutes for each of the other sides, ensuring that each side of the cube colors and crisps.

Tofu is ready when it's puffy, crispy, and golden. Transfer it to the lined plate and set aside until ready to use.

PANFRYING TOFU

Heat 3 tablespoons of oil in a large nonstick skillet over medium-high heat. Transfer the pressed tofu to the skillet and panfry for 4 to 5 minutes per side (2 to 3 minutes per side for cubes) until golden. Use as directed in the recipe.

BAKING TOFU

Preheat the oven to 400°F (200°C). Place cut, pressed tofu onto a parchment-lined baking sheet and drizzle with 1 tablespoon oil. Turn to coat evenly. Bake in the center of the oven for about 40 minutes, turning the tofu every 15 minutes, until it's slightly puffed and golden. Use as directed in a recipe.

FREEZING TOFU

Freezing tofu is a simple and convenient way to easily change the texture of tofu and use up excess portions of tofu. Freezing changes the structure of tofu, making it denser and chewier, and increases its capacity to absorb flavorings or liquids. You freeze, defrost, then squeeze out the water from the tofu before using it in a recipe. I like to add frozen silken tofu to simple soups and prefer to panfry cubes or rectangles of frozen medium or firm tofu before adding them to sauces or noodle soups.

Remove one 14-ounce (420 g) block silken, medium, or firm tofu from its water and briefly drain on paper towels. (You can also place the packaged tofu straight into the freezer, if you like.) Cut the block into four even pieces or into bite-sized cubes (leftover chunks or slabs of tofu are good too) and place, not touching, on a parchment-lined plate or tray and put it in the freezer. (Cutting it into smaller portions allows it to unfreeze quicker and you can use some of it rather than using the entire block of tofu.)

Freeze overnight or until hard. If you're not planning to use the tofu right away, wrap it in plastic or store in a zip-top bag (freeze silken tofu up to 2 weeks and medium or firm tofu for up to 2 months).

Thaw the frozen tofu in a shallow bowl at room temperature for several hours or in the fridge for about a day, occasionally pouring off any expelled water.

Over the bowl or a sink, gently press the thawed tofu between your palms to expel as much water as possible. Cut the tofu into the desired size. Store the thawed tofu covered in the fridge for up to a day (do not refreeze).

You can add it directly to soups or sauces and briefly simmer it before serving. If you want to fry it before adding to a recipe, first blot it dry on paper towels.

OPPOSITE *Clockwise from top right:* crispy tofu skin strips (page 43); fried tofu cubes; fried tofu rect-angles; tofu skin chips (page 42); crispy tofu skin sticks (page 43)

HOMEMADE SEITAN

MÌ CĂN

There are several ways to make seitan (wheat gluten) from scratch. The traditional, lengthier method involves first making a stiff wheat flour dough, kneading it to develop the gluten, letting it rest for several hours, then rinsing and squeezing away the starch until you're left with strands you can squeeze together into a ball or log.

    A second, much easier and quicker method (and my preferred method, detailed in this recipe) involves making a dough from vital wheat gluten flour (the gluten protein from wheat in powdered form available at natural food pantries or well-stocked grocers) and vegetable stock or water. As you stir the liquid into the vital wheat gluten, a dough forms almost instantly. Knead the dough for a few minutes, simmer it to tenderize, then use as directed in recipes. For added flavor, panfry slices or shreds until lightly brown and crisp before stir-frying (with lemongrass and chile, page 54) or tossing in a sauce. If using in soup, shallow-fry the slices until golden first. (Otherwise they'll soak up too much broth.) **Makes about 10 ounces (275 g) dough**

FROM THE PANTRY/MAKE AHEAD

1½ teaspoon Mushroom Powder (page 36)

FOR THE DOUGH

½ cup plus 2 tablespoons (155 ml) Light or Rich Vegetable Stock (page 30 or 31) or water

1 teaspoon soy sauce

1 cup (130 g) vital wheat gluten, or more if needed

½ teaspoon salt

FOR THE SIMMERING BROTH

4 to 5 cups (1 to 1.25 liters) Light or Rich Vegetable Stock or water

1 tablespoon soy sauce

1 teaspoon salt

Prepare the Mushroom Powder.

For the dough: Mix together the vegetable stock and soy sauce in a small bowl. Place the vital wheat gluten, mushroom powder, and salt in a large bowl. Stir the dry ingredients together with a fork and, as you continue to stir, pour in almost all of the vegetable stock (hold back a tablespoon or two) in a steady stream. Quickly stir together until it clumps into a shaggy mass.

Drizzle the remaining tablespoon of liquid over any stray dry vital wheat gluten and briefly knead to pick up and incorporate all of the vital wheat gluten. Transfer the dough to a clean counter and knead for a minute or two. (Resist mixing it in a food processor or using a dough hook as overmixing it makes the end product tough and too chewy.) It will still look rough and should feel a touch moist but not wet (if it feels too wet, knead in a couple of teaspoons to a tablespoon more of vital wheat gluten). Shape into a rough baguette-shaped loaf 7 to 8 inches (18 to 20 cm) in length. Cut in half crosswise and reshape each half into a small rough baguette, about 3½ inches (9 cm) long.

Place the dough halves in a medium pot and pour over 4 cups (1 liter) of the vegetable stock or water, the soy sauce, and the salt. The liquid should almost cover the dough (if it doesn't, top it up with some more stock or water). Bring the liquid to a boil over high heat. Reduce the heat to low or medium-low, enough for a gentle simmer, and partially cover with a lid. As the dough simmers it will puff up and some of it will float above the broth's surface. Simmer, rotating it every 15 minutes to ensure even cooking, for about 45 minutes. Remove from the liquid if you plan on using it right away. Otherwise, turn off the heat and cool in the broth. Store the seitan in the broth in the refrigerator for a couple of days or wrap it well in plastic and freeze for up to a month. (If you've used vegetable stock for the simmering, you can save it to make a noodle soup.)

Note:
If you like to cook with seitan often, I recommend preparing a double recipe. Use a larger pot and increase the total amount of broth or liquid for simmering to 6 to 8 cups (1.5 to 2 liters).

TO PANFRY SEITAN

Remove the seitan from the liquid and squeeze out any excess liquid. Cut the loaf lengthwise if you want smaller pieces (I like two-bite-sized pieces). Slice into thin (⅛-inch; 3 mm) slices. Pat dry with paper towels. Heat a couple of tablespoons of vegetable oil in a large skillet over medium-high heat. Add the slices and panfry on each side for 2 to 3 minutes, until browned.

TO SHALLOW-FRY SEITAN

Follow the directions above for slicing the seitan. Add ¼ cup of vegetable oil to a wok or medium skillet and heat over medium-high heat. Working in batches, shallow-fry slices for a minute or two, occasionally turning over, or until lightly golden brown. Remove to a paper-towel-lined plate. Add the slices to noodle soups like Star Anise Cinnamon Scented Pho Noodle Soup (page 175) and Fragrant Lemongrass Huế-Style Noodle Soup (page 179) about 5 to 10 minutes before planning to serve.

TO MAKE SEITAN CRUMBLES

Cut the seitan into smaller chunks. Add chunks to a food processor and pulse until coarse and crumbly. Overprocessing will make it too pasty. Use the seitan crumbles as a part of the filling in stuffed tomatoes (page 79) or tofu pockets (page 77).

TOFU WITH FRESH TOMATO SAUCE

ĐẬU PHỤ SỐT CÀ CHUA

Tofu with fresh tomato sauce is common in homes and casual restaurants throughout Việt Nam. Think of it as the country's spaghetti marinara. With tofu cubes that are crispy on the outside and meltingly tender within, paired with a deeply flavorful tomato sauce, this comfort food creates a simple yet satisfying meal, especially when plated alongside some vegetables. (See Chapter Eight for options.)   **Serves 4 as a multidish meal**

FROM THE PANTRY/MAKE AHEAD

¼ teaspoon Mushroom Powder (page 36)

───

1 pound (450 g) firm tofu, cut into 1½ inch (4 cm) cubes

1 tablespoon vegetable oil

1 tablespoon finely chopped garlic

¾ pound (340 g) ripe plum tomatoes, finely chopped (1¾ cups)

1 tablespoon soy sauce

½ teaspoon sugar

¼ teaspoon salt

⅓ cup (80 ml) water, mushroom-soaking liquid, or Light or Rich Vegetable Stock (page 30 or 31)

¼ cup scallions, thinly sliced

¼ teaspoon freshly ground black pepper

1 tablespoon roughly chopped cilantro

Prepare the Mushroom Powder.

Shallow-fry or deep-fry the tofu cubes (see page 60)

Heat the oil in a wok or skillet over medium heat. Add the garlic and stir-fry until fragrant, about 20 seconds. Toss in the tomatoes, soy sauce, sugar, salt, and mushroom powder. Simmer for about 5 minutes, stirring occasionally, until the tomato breaks down. Add the water and simmer gently for about 10 minutes, until the sauce thickens. Stir in the tofu, scallions, and black pepper and cook for another minute to coat the tofu lightly with the sauce. Transfer to a serving dish and sprinkle the cilantro over the top.

Note:

When ripe tomatoes are not in season, substitute a small (14.5-ounce; 410 g) can of plum tomatoes with their juices, roughly chopped, and reduce the cook time by a few minutes.

OPPOSITE Vermicelli Noodles with Fresh Turmeric, Tofu, and Chinese Chives (page 191); Tofu with Fresh Tomato Sauce (page 67); Stir-Fried Water Spinach (page 231)

TOFU WITH TANGY TAMARIND SAUCE

ĐẬU PHỤ SỐT ME

This sauce, a perfect foil for tofu, gets its fruity, sweet, salty, and sour flavors from a combination of tamarind liquid, soy sauce, salt, and sugar. Portioning cubes of tamarind liquid and storing them in your freezer (see page 41) makes this tangy dish quick and easy to assemble. Brighten it further with finely chopped lemongrass and ginger. **Serves 4 as part of a multidish meal**

FROM THE PANTRY/MAKE AHEAD

½ cup Tamarind Liquid (page 41)

———

1 pound (454 g) firm tofu, cut into 1-inch (2.5 cm) cubes, 2 by 1 by ½-inch (5 by 2.5 by 1.5 cm) rectangles, or ¾-inch (3 cm) slices of Nori-Wrapped Tofu Roll (page 85)

½ cup (125 ml) water

2 tablespoon plus 2 teaspoons sugar

1 tablespoon soy sauce

½ teaspoon salt

1 tablespoon vegetable oil

1 shallot, finely chopped

1 garlic clove, minced

½ fresh medium-hot long red chile (optional), seeded and minced

Juice of ¼ lime

½ teaspoon freshly ground black pepper

1 tablespoon roughly chopped cilantro

Prepare the Tamarind Liquid.

Shallow-fry or deep-fry tofu (see page 60) or panfry slices of the tofu rolls and set aside.

In a small bowl, stir the tamarind liquid, water, sugar, soy sauce, and salt together until the sugar is fully dissolved. Adjust the flavors,

balancing sour and sweet with sugar, remembering that the liquid will reduce slightly.

Heat the oil in a wok or medium skillet over medium heat. Stir-fry the shallot, garlic, and chile, if using, until fragrant, about 30 seconds. Add the tofu, pour in the tamarind sauce, and simmer, occasionally turning the tofu over in the sauce or spooning the sauce over slices of nori-wrapped tofu. As the water evaporates and the sauce thickens, the bubbles will become slightly larger and the sauce will become a touch louder. Squeeze in the lime juice and sprinkle black pepper over the tofu. If you find the sauce a touch thick, thin it with a tablespoon of warm water. Transfer to a serving dish and garnish with cilantro.

VARIATION

TOFU WITH TANGY LEMONGRASS GINGER TAMARIND SAUCE

Stir in 1 tablespoon finely chopped lemongrass and 2 teaspoons minced ginger with the shallot and garlic. Stir-fry for about a minute before adding the tofu and tamarind sauce. Continue cooking as directed.

FIVE-SPICE-GLAZED TOFU

ĐẬU PHỤ RIM NGŨ VỊ

I adore this versatile tofu dish so much that I regularly make a double batch to add to meals throughout the week. The plain tofu acts as a true blank canvas, soaking up and absorbing the notes of star anise, cinnamon, and clove in the five-spice marinade. I often catch carnivorous friends reaching for seconds (actually, thirds). Sublime as it is this way, you can also prepare it with thick and meaty portobello mushrooms, or even seitan, in place of the tofu. Serve hot or cold in Bánh Mì Sandwiches (page 113) thinly sliced in rice paper rolls, or cut into bite-sized chunks for Tasty Rice Noodle Bowl (page 188).

Serves 4 as part of a multidish meal

FROM THE PANTRY/MAKE AHEAD

1 tablespoon Annatto Seed Oil (page 35)

---

1 pound (450 g) firm tofu

3 tablespoons soy sauce

3 tablespoons vegetarian hoisin sauce or vegetarian mushroom-flavored stir-fry sauce

1 tablespoon sugar

2 teaspoons five-spice powder

½ cup (125 ml) Light or Rich Vegetable Stock (page 30 or 31), water, or mushroom-soaking liquid

1 scallion, thinly sliced

1 tablespoon roughly chopped cilantro

Prepare the Annatto Seed Oil.

STOVETOP METHOD

Cut the tofu into ½ inch-thick (1 cm) slices and then into 1½-by-4-inch rectangles (4 cm by 10 cm).

In a small bowl, mix together the annatto seed oil, soy sauce, vegetarian hoisin sauce, sugar, and five-spice powder. Place the tofu in a large skillet and pour the soy sauce mixture over the top. Turn the tofu in soy mixture to coat evenly and marinate for at least 15 minutes.

Pour the stock over the marinated tofu, shaking the pan to dilute and disperse the marinade. Use a spatula to scrape any marinade that is sticking to the sides of the pan to the bottom. Set the pan over medium heat and bring to a simmer. Reduce the heat to medium-low and simmer for about 15 minutes, carefully flipping the tofu every 5 minutes. As the water evaporates the bubbles from

continues

the simmering sauce will become larger and the soy marinade will begin to glaze the tofu lightly. If necessary, reduce the heat a little to prevent the marinade from burning. When a couple of tablespoons of sauce remain in the pan remove it from the heat and transfer the glazed tofu and any sauce to a serving dish. Garnish with the scallions and cilantro.

OVEN-ROASTED METHOD

Place the tofu in a 9-by-13-inch (23 by 33 cm) ovenproof baking dish, pour the soy sauce marinade over the tofu, and marinate for at least 15 minutes before baking. Pour the stock over the marinated tofu, shaking the pan to dilute and disperse the marinade. Use a spatula to scrape any marinade that is sticking to the sides of the baking dish to the bottom.

Heat the oven to 350°F (175°C). Bake the tofu, uncovered, carefully turning the tofu over every 15 minutes. Bake for a total of 45 minutes, or until most of the marinade is absorbed and glazes the tofu (a couple of tablespoons will remain). Remove from the heat, transfer to a serving dish, and garnish with the scallions and cilantro.

VARIATIONS

FIVE-SPICE-GLAZED PORTOBELLO MUSHROOMS

Heat the oven to 400°F (200°C). Arrange ¾ pound (340 g; about 6 medium-large) portobello mushrooms stem side up, in a casserole dish and drizzle a teaspoon of vegetable oil over each one before placing the dish in the oven. Roast for 10 to 12 minutes, until the mushrooms release some of their juices. (While the mushrooms roast, prepare a half recipe of the marinade). Spoon or brush the marinade over both sides of the mushrooms. Roast for 15 more minutes spooning some sauce over each cap halfway through, or until about 2 tablespoons of sauce is left in bottom of the casserole dish. Transfer the mushrooms to a shallow dish and pour on any remaining sauce. The mushrooms can be made to this point up to 3 days in advance. Cut the mushrooms into 1-inch-thick (2.5 cm) slices and garnish with the scallion and cilantro if serving as part of a meal. Or stuff 4 or 5 slices into baguette to make a Bánh Mì Sandwich (page 113) (don't forget to drizzle some of the lovely spiced sauce over the crumb of the bread).

FIVE-SPICE-GLAZED SEITAN

In a small bowl, mix together the marinade ingredients and pour over Homemade Seitan (page 64; if using store-bought seitan, cut it into two or three chunks, about the thickness of a cucumber). Marinate for at least 15 minutes. Follow the directions for the stovetop method, occasionally turning and spooning the sauce over the seitan. When cool enough to handle, thinly slice and use in your chosen recipe.

LEMONGRASS CHILE "CHICKEN" STRIPS STIR-FRY

GÀ CHAY XÀO XẢ ỚT

This uncomplicated dish, with its big hit of aromatic lemongrass, is best made just before serving so friends or family can enjoy the aroma as it fills the kitchen. Cubes of fried tofu would be fine (and in fact traditional) here, but I prefer using strips of moist and tender plant-based chicken alternatives. The recipe is also marvelous with fleshy mushrooms or even seitan. It's great as part of a rice meal but also stellar in a Bánh Mì Sandwich (page 113), as a topping for a Tasty Rice Noodle Bowl (page 188), or even used as part of a filling in rice paper rolls (page 92). **Serves 4 as part of a multidish meal or for bánh mì**

FROM THE PANTRY/MAKE AHEAD

½ teaspoon Mushroom Powder (page 36)

---

1 tablespoon plus 1½ teaspoons soy sauce

½ teaspoon sugar

¼ cup water or mushroom-soaking liquid or Light or Rich Vegetable Stock (page 30 or 31)

1 tablespoon plus 1½ teaspoons vegetable oil

2 lemongrass stalks, bottom 5 inches (13 cm), peeled and finely minced (¼ cup) 2 tbsp

1 tablespoon finely minced garlic

1 fresh red Thai bird chile, finely chopped

¾ pound (340 g) vegetarian chicken strips (plain or lightly seasoned)

4 scallions, thinly sliced (¼ cup)

1 lime quarter

2 tablespoons roughly chopped cilantro

Prepare the Mushroom Powder.

Stir the soy sauce, sugar, mushroom powder, and water together in a small bowl until the sugar is fully dissolved.

Heat the oil in a wok or large skillet over medium-high heat. Add the lemongrass and garlic and stir-fry for 1½ minutes, until fragrant and the raw garlic flavor mellows. Add the chile and stir-fry for 30 seconds. Add the vegetarian chicken strips and scallions and stir-fry for another 30 seconds. Pour in the soy sauce mixture and stir-fry for another 3 minutes, or until most of the liquid is reduced and the lemongrass, garlic, and chile moistly coat the vegetarian chicken strips. Squeeze in the lime juice, sprinkle in the cilantro, and transfer to a serving dish

continues

VARIATIONS

STIR-FRIED MUSHROOMS WITH LEMONGRASS AND CHILE
(NẤM XÀO XẢ ỚT)

Cut or tear 1 pound of oyster mushrooms into bite-sized pieces—or use quartered button mushrooms or portobello mushroom cups, halved and then cut into ½-inch-thick (15 cm) slices. Add the mushrooms and scallions following the chile and stir-fry for 3 minutes (the mushrooms may give off some liquid). Pour in the soy sauce mixture (reduce the water to 2 tablespoons) and stir-fry for another couple of minutes. Garnish with cilantro before serving.

STIR-FRIED TOFU WITH LEMONGRASS AND CHILE
(ĐẬU HỦ XÀO XẢ ỚT)

Cut a ¾-pound (340 g) block of tofu into 2-inch (5 cm) strips, each ⅜ inch (1 cm) thick, and stir-fry in the same manner as the vegetarian chicken strips. (Alternatively, shallow-fry or panfry the tofu strips until golden brown before adding to the wok.

STIR-FRIED SEITAN WITH LEMONGRASS AND CHILE
(MÌ CĂN XÀO XẢ ỚT)

Slice ½ pound (225 g) seitan into thin slices. Heat 1 tablespoon of vegetable oil over medium heat in a wok or large skillet and panfry the slices for about 4 minutes on each side, until colored or golden brown. Add the panfried seitan to the pan at the same time as you would the vegetarian chicken strips.

OPPOSITE Lemongrass Chile "Chicken" Strips Stir-Fry

TURMERIC TOFU WITH FRESH DILL AND RICE NOODLES

ĐẬU HŨ 'CHẢ CÁ HÀ NỘI' CHAY

Before my initial visit to Hà Nội over a decade ago, I had read about this dish and was intrigued by the abundant use of fragrant herbs. When I arrived in the city, I walked along the thirty-six streets that make up Hà Nội's Old Quarter, quickly realizing that each street is named for those goods or foods in which the shopkeepers on that street specialize. Chả Cá Street, for example, is named for this fish dish, made popular by the family that has run Chả Cá La Vong Restaurant for generations. It's heavy with both scallion and dill.

Walking into the restaurant that day, I was greeted first by those aromas: first onions, then herbs. It's so good that I've adapted the recipe to use tofu and a vegan version of nước chấm, the traditional clear dipping sauce, in place of the fish and fish sauce in the original dish. **Serves 4 as a light one-dish meal**

FROM THE PANTRY/MAKE AHEAD

Everyday Table Sauce (page 49) seasoned
    with fermented tofu

---

1 small head Bibb lettuce, torn into bite-sized
    pieces

¾ cup Thai basil leaves

¾ cup cilantro leaves

½ pound (225 g) dried rice vermicelli noodles

1 to 1½ pounds (450 to 680 g) firm tofu

½ cup rice flour

1 teaspoon ground turmeric

¼ teaspoon salt

¼ cup vegetable oil

3 cups scallions (2 bunches) 1-inch (2.5 cm)
    lengths

2 cups (large bunch) roughly chopped
    stemmed fresh dill

½ cup roasted, unsalted peanuts, roughly
    chopped

Soy sauce (optional)

Prepare the Everyday Table Sauce and put in a small bowl or two. Mix the lettuce, basil and cilantro together in a serving bowl or on a large plate.

Bring a large pot of water to a boil. Drop in the noodles and use chopsticks or tongs to untangle and loosen. Boil until tender, 3 to 5 minutes, then drain and immediately flush with cold water. Gently squeeze four to five times to get rid of any excess water. Set aside on two medium plates, loosely covered with a clean kitchen towel.

OPPOSITE Turmeric Tofu with Fresh Dill
and Rice Noodles

continues

Cut the block of tofu into ½-inch-thick (1.5 cm) rectangles. Then cut each block into smaller rectangles about 1½ inches by 2 inches (3.8 by 5 cm). Mix the rice flour, turmeric, and salt in a large bowl. Add the tofu, toss to coat lightly, and transfer to a plate.

Heat the oil in a wok or 10-inch skillet over medium-high heat. Carefully place some tofu in the oil and fry until each side is crispy and golden, 3 to 4 minutes per side. You may need to cook the tofu in two batches. Transfer briefly to a paper-towel-lined plate and arrange on a serving platter. Carefully pour out most of the oil, leaving 1 tablespoon. Reheat the oil over medium-high heat. Stir-fry the scallions for about 1 minute before tossing in the dill. Stir-fry for another 30 seconds and arrange nicely over the tofu. Sprinkle the peanuts on top.

To eat, each diner puts some noodles in a bowl and some dilled tofu on top. They can add some of the lettuce and herbs and then a good drizzle of the table sauce. Toss together before eating. Add a splash of soy sauce for extra seasoning, if desired.

MUSHROOM-STUFFED TOFU POCKETS IN TOMATO SAUCE

ĐẬU PHỤ NHỒI NẤM SỐT CÀ CHUA

Stuffing tofu pouches with a filling of mushrooms, kohlrabi, carrots, and tofu skin sausage yields unusually impressive results. This is an adaptation of a recipe Bội Trân (see page 241) taught me, in which she shallow-fries tofu slices until crispy and golden brown. As they cook and then cool, they shrink considerably, but don't worry: they're not difficult to stuff.

Frying actually strengthens the tofu's exterior, making it easy to slit and form a sturdy pocket for the filling. You can vary the filling, if you like, using meatless ground (see page 301), finely chopped sautéed greens with garlic (page 231), or other cooked, finely chopped vegetables. (Just make sure to blot the filling dry before stuffing it into the tofu pockets.)

Serves 4 to 6 as part of a multidish meal

FROM THE PANTRY/MAKE AHEAD

½ teaspoon Mushroom Powder (page 36)

One 14-ounce (400 g) block firm tofu

¼ cup plus 3 tablespoons (100 ml) vegetable oil

1 cup packed (3 to 4 ounces; 90 g) finely chopped fresh button or portobello mushrooms or ½ cup packed finely chopped rehydrated shiitake or wood ear mushrooms or a combination

¼ cup finely chopped carrot

¼ cup finely chopped kohlrabi, chayote, or jicama

½ teaspoon salt

¼ teaspoon freshly ground black pepper

½ small bundle (½ ounce; 12 g) cellophane noodles, soaked in hot water for 20 minutes, drained, squeezed dry, and finely chopped (¼ cup packed)

¼ cup finely chopped Tofu Skin Sausage (page 44) or ¼ cup rehydrated, finely chopped shiitake or wood ear mushrooms

2 scallions, finely chopped

1 recipe tomato sauce from Tofu with Fresh Tomato Sauce (page 67)

Prepare the Mushroom Powder.

Cut the block of tofu widthwise into eight even slices, about ½-inch thick (1.5 cm). Press the tofu rectangles to dry (see page 60) and leave to drain naturally for at least 10 minutes, as you prepare the filling.

Heat 1 tablespoon of the oil in a large skillet over medium-high heat. Add the mushrooms, carrot, kohlrabi, salt, mushroom powder, and black pepper and cook, stirring regularly, for

continues

2 minutes, until the vegetables soften and release their liquid. Toss in the cellophane noodles, chopped tofu skin sausage, and scallions and cook for another minute. Transfer the filling to a bowl. At this point the filling can be refrigerated for up to 2 days. Wash and dry the skillet.

Set a plate lined with paper towel next to the stove. Heat the remaining oil in the skillet over medium-high heat. As the oil heats up, lift the tofu rectangles and, before adding to the hot oil, blot the outside dry. Be careful as oil may sputter from the skillet as the tofu releases moisture. Shallow-fry the tofu for 4 to 5 minutes, or until lightly golden, before turning over. (To avoid splashing hot oil in your direction, use tongs or chopsticks or a spatula and turn the tofu away from you.) If you notice your pan does not heat evenly, gently slide the tofu around to brown evenly. When the tofu is slightly puffy and crispy and golden in color, transfer it to the paper-towel-lined plate to cool. At this point you can refrigerate the tofu, wrapped, for up to 1 day. Bring it back to room temperature before you cut and stuff it.

When the tofu is cool enough to handle, lay a slice down on a cutting board. You want to create a tofu pocket, much like an envelope, where three sides are sealed to hold the filling in and one side is open. With one of the long sides of the rectangular tofu slice facing you, gently press two or three fingertips from the other hand on the top of the tofu to hold it in place. Cut into that long side horizontally, with

your knife parallel to the cutting board, to make a deep slit (not so deep as to pierce the other side), starting ¼ to ½ inch from one end and cutting across to just short of the other side. You should end up with a whole tofu piece where one long side is slit open and the other three sides remain sealed.

Hold the tofu slice in one hand, open the slit, and use your opposite index finger to gently push into the corners to stretch it slightly more open. Spoon a tablespoon of filling into the open pocket and press it with your index finger and middle fingers to fill the outer corners. Spoon approximately another tablespoon of filling into the pocket and press it to make it compact and flush with the cut edge. Set aside on the plate. Repeat until the rest of the fried tofu slices are stuffed.

Prepare the tomato sauce and add the stuffed tofu to the skillet when you add the liquid. Every couple of minutes, carefully turn the stuffed tofu over to heat through. When the tofu and filling are hot and the sauce is slightly thickened, transfer to a serving dish.

VARIATION

MEATLESS GROUND
STUFFED TOFU POCKETS IN
TOMATO SAUCE

Replace the mushrooms with ½ cup packed (100 to 120 g, depending on the brand) of meatless ground and cook as directed for the filling.

TOMATOES STUFFED WITH MEATLESS GROUND AND TOFU
CÀ CHUA NHỒI THỊT CHAY VÀ ĐẬU PHỤ

Tomates farcies, French for "stuffed tomatoes," is a comforting classic in both France and Việt Nam. The Vietnamese version, adopted during the period of French occupation, is extremely popular in homes and on the lunch buffets of Vietnamese diners (*cơm bình dân*) because it's filling, easy to make, and affordable. I use a combination of beefy meatless ground and tofu for the filling, but you can also stuff them with just tofu or even sautéed greens with garlic (page 231). If you purchase plump, vine-ripened tomatoes instead of meaty plum tomatoes, cut the top quarter off each one, then finely chop them and use them in the sauce.   **Serves 4 as part of a multidish meal**

FROM THE PANTRY/MAKE AHEAD

½ teaspoon Mushroom Powder (page 36)

_____

¾ cup packed (6 ounces; 170 g) firm or extra-firm tofu

1 cup (6 ounces; 170 g) meatless ground

1 small bundle (1 ounce; 25 g) cellophane noodles, soaked in hot water for 20 minutes, drained, squeezed dry, and finely chopped (scant ½ cup)

2 to 3 medium dried shiitake mushrooms, soaked in hot water for 15 minutes, drained, squeezed dry, stemmed and finely chopped (2 tablespoons)

1 dried wood ear mushroom, soaked in hot water for 15 minutes, drained, squeezed dry, stemmed and finely chopped (2 tablespoons)

¼ cup finely chopped scallion

½ teaspoon salt

½ teaspoon freshly ground black pepper

1 to 2 tablespoons tapioca flour (depending on how moist the filling is)

4 plum tomatoes

1 tablespoon vegetable oil

1½ teaspoons soy sauce

¼ teaspoon salt

¼ teaspoon sugar

A few cilantro sprigs for garnish (optional)

Prepare the Mushroom Powder.

Roughly chop the tofu, place it in a medium bowl, and mash thoroughly with a fork or your hands. Crumble the meatless ground and add it to the bowl. Toss in the cellophane noodles, mushrooms, scallion, salt, pepper, ¼ teaspoon of the mushroom powder, and 1 tablespoon tapioca powder and mix together (if the meatless ground you're using is moist or you find the filling too moist, add another tablespoon of tapioca flour).

continues

Slice a sliver from the nonstem end of each tomato so that it will sit flat in the pan. Cut each tomato in half crosswise. Use a teaspoon to scoop out the meaty, juicy pulp from each half into a separate bowl to form a hollow tomato. Pick out any large pulpy pieces from the bowl, finely chop, and return to the bowl.

Spoon and press a generous tablespoon or more of filling into each tomato half so that the filling is slightly rounded and set on a plate.

Heat the oil in a medium skillet over medium-high heat. Place the tomato halves, filling side down, in the skillet and cook for

2 minutes, or until filling is golden brown. Carefully turn the tomatoes over with a spatula and transfer to the plate.

Reduce the heat to medium and add the tomato pulp, soy sauce, salt, a pinch of sugar, and the remaining 1/4 teaspoon mushroom powder. Cook for 30 seconds, then return the tomatoes, flesh side down, to the skillet. Simmer the tomatoes in the tomato sauce for 4 to 5 minutes, or until the skin begins to wrinkle and the flesh softens. Transfer to a serving dish, filling side up, and garnish with cilantro, if using.

OPPOSITE *Clockwise from top right*: Clear Broth Soup with Tofu and Leafy Greens (page 155); fresh mangoes; boiled Chinese broccoli and green beans (page 227); Tomatoes Stuffed with Meatless Ground and Tofu (page 79); Cooling Bitter Melon Apple Salad (page 147)

TURMERIC TOFU WRAPPED IN WILD BETEL LEAVES

ĐẬU PHỤ CUỐN LÁ LỐT

This recipe, for sunny-hued, turmeric-spiced tofu and mushrooms wrapped in fresh betel leaves, also called wild pepper leaves, was shared with me by a cook who works in a rustic yet stylish beer hall (*bia hơi*) in Hà Nội's West Lake neighborhood. Cooking the wild betel leaves releases their warm, herbal fragrance. (The leaves themselves are both bittersweet and spicy.)

Look for wild betel leaves in Asian stores or even large grocers that serve a Vietnamese or Thai clientele. If you can't locate them, simply shape the filling into small patties. Serve the rolls or patties as an hors d'oeuvre with Everyday Table Sauce (page 49), Soy Chile Dipping Sauce (page 51), or as part of a Tasty Rice Noodle Bowl (page 188). **Makes 12 small rolls or patties**

½ pound (225 g) firm tofu

8 medium dried shiitake mushrooms, soaked in hot water for 15 minutes, drained, squeezed dry, stemmed, and finely chopped (scant ½ cup)

4 dried wood ear mushroom, soaked in hot water for 15 minutes, drained, squeezed dry, stemmed, and and finely chopped (½ cup packed)

¼ cup chopped cilantro

1 tablespoon vegetarian mushroom-flavored stir-fry sauce or vegetarian hoisin sauce

1½ teaspoons ground turmeric

1 teaspoon freshly ground black pepper

½ teaspoon salt

1 cup (60 g) bean sprouts, roughly chopped

¼ cup tapioca flour

12 wild betel leaves, wiped clean with a damp cloth

2 scallions, thinly sliced

1 tablespoon roasted unsalted peanuts, roughly chopped

In a large bowl, mash the tofu with a fork or your hands until it no longer has any clumps. Add the mushrooms, cilantro, stir-fry sauce, turmeric, and black pepper and mix together. Sprinkle the bean sprouts and tapioca starch over the top and mix well to fully incorporate the tapioca flour. The starch in the tapioca helps to bind the mixture together. Set aside.

Trim the stems of the wild betel leaves slightly so that at least ½ inch (1.5 cm) of stem remains, if necessary. Place a leaf on a clean work surface, with the shiny smooth side down and the pointy end closest to you. Spoon 2

OPPOSITE Turmeric Tofu Wrapped in Wild Betel Leaves

continues

tablespoons of the filling slightly above the pointy end of the leaf, roughly shaping it into a 3-inch (7.5 cm) log. Roll the pointy end snuggly over the filling to form a roll. When you reach the stem end, use the remaining part of the stem to fasten the leaf together (if there is no stem, use a small toothpick to fasten it). Place the roll stem side down on a plate and repeat with the remaining leaves. At this point the rolls can be refrigerated for several hours before cooking.

You can either panfry the wrapped wild betel leaves on the stovetop or cook them under the broiler in the oven.

STOVETOP METHOD

Place a paper-towel-lined plate next to the stove.

Brush each wrapped leaf lightly with oil. Heat 1 teaspoon of oil in a large skillet over medium-high heat. Arrange the rolls seam side down in the pan. As the rolls cook, the moisture from the leaves may create the occasional sharp popping sound. Panfry for 3 to 4 minutes before rotating by a third with tongs. Cook for another 1½ to 2 minutes before rotating one more time and cook for another 1½ to 2 minutes. When done, the leaves will have shrunken around the filling and be toasted and lightly browned. Transfer briefly to the paper-towel-lined plate and then to a serving dish. Garnish with the sliced scallions and chopped peanuts.

BROILER METHOD

Alternatively, set an oven rack to the top third of your oven and preheat the broiler to high. Lightly brush some oil over each side of each roll and place on foil-lined baking sheet. Slide the baking sheet into the top third of the oven and bake for 2 to 3 minutes. Turn the rolls over and cook for another 2 to 3 minutes. Repeat one more time. When done, the leaves will have shrunken around the filling and will be toasted and lightly charred. Transfer to a serving dish and garnish with the sliced scallions and chopped peanuts.

VARIATION

SHAPED PATTIES

Take 2 tablespoons of filling and squeeze it in your hands to shape it into a ball. Flatten the ball to form a ⅜-inch thick (1 cm) patty. Set aside on a plate. Repeat with the remaining filling. Heat 1 tablespoon of oil in a large skillet over medium-high heat. Add the patties and cook for 4 minutes, or until golden brown, before turning them over. Cook for another 4 minutes, or until they're nicely golden brown. (Reduce the heat to medium if you feel they're browning too quickly.) Transfer briefly to a paper-towel-lined plate and then to a serving dish.

NORI-WRAPPED TOFU ROLL

CÁ CHIÊN CHAY

Nori gives this unusual dish, which I first encountered at a small vegetarian restaurant in Sài Gòn, its briny flavor and playful look: when wrapped around the tofu and tapered, the resulting "package" mimics a crosswise slice of fish. A home cook named Loan taught me how to shape the tofu using tofu skin and nori and how to bind the squeezed, mashed tofu back together.

Do make sure to grind the dried seaweed (hijiki or wakame) to a powder. Any large seaweed pieces will rehydrate and expand during cooking and prevent the tofu from sticking together properly. Also, if you have a bamboo sushi-rolling mat, use it here. It will help keep the tofu roll nice and compact.   **Makes two 8-inch-long (20 cm) rolls**

FROM THE PANTRY/MAKE AHEAD

½ teaspoon Mushroom Powder (page 36)

---

1 pound (454 g) firm or extra-firm tofu, drained

1 tablespoon dried seaweed powder (hijiki or wakame)

½ teaspoon soy sauce

⅛ teaspoon salt

⅛ teaspoon sugar

1 or 2 sheets dried or fresh tofu skin

2 sheets nori

Prepare the Mushroom Powder.

Roughly cut the tofu into large cubes and place half of it in the center of a clean dish towel. Gather the cloth up and, over the sink or a bowl, gradually twist it around the tofu to make a rough ball. As you do this some water will drip from the cloth. Squeeze the tofu a few times to expel more water. Unwrap the cloth and check that the tofu is a little moist but not wet. Transfer the tofu to a medium bowl. Repeat with rest of the tofu. You should have about 1½ cups packed (11 to 12 ounces: 310 to 340 g) of squeezed tofu.

Use a mortar and pestle or a clean electric coffee grinder used for spices to grind the dried seaweed to a rough powder. You should have about 1½ teaspoons. Sprinkle the seaweed powder, mushroom powder, soy sauce, salt, and sugar over the tofu. Use your hands to mix in the seasonings and mash the tofu until it's very crumbly.

Unwrap and lay a sheet of fresh or dried tofu skin on a cutting board and place a sheet of nori on top of it. Use the nori sheet as a template to cut the tofu skin into two identical pieces and set aside one piece of tofu skin and one nori while you work with the other.

continues

Dampen a clean dish towel or a small folded square of paper towel. Lay a piece of tofu skin flat on the cutting board. (If using dried tofu skin, use the damp cloth or paper towel to wipe each side to moisten and soften it.) Shape half of the seasoned mashed tofu (about ¾ cup packed; 6.5 ounces; 180 g) into an even log and mound over the entire length of the tofu skin, about 1 inch (2.5 cm) from the edge closest to you. In one quick motion, roll up the bottom edge of tofu skin over the tofu, trying to hold it in place with your index and middle fingers, as tightly as possible. Push in any tofu that comes out of the sides.

Arrange a bamboo sushi mat on the cutting board and lay the piece of nori shiny side down on it. Gently and quickly wipe the nori with the damp towel to lightly moisten it to help the roll stick together. Place the roll along the bottom edge of the nori so the edges are aligned. Lift the edge of the bamboo mat closest to you over the roll and roll away from you, pressing gently yet firmly, to pack the tofu together. Push in any tofu that comes out of the sides. Place seam side down on the counter while you shape the second roll.

Moisten the countertop with the damp dish or paper towel. Tear off a piece of plastic wrap about 1½ feet long (46 cm) long and lay it flat horizontally on the moistened countertop. Center one cylinder horizontally along the bottom edge of the plastic. Roll up the bottom edge of the plastic over the seaweed tofu roll snuggly and tightly. Use a toothpick to prick the cylinder about 5 times along its length to help reduce any air bubbles that developed as you rolled it. Gently press the ends of the shaped roll toward the center of the cylinder. Secure the roll by twisting one end of the plastic wrap several times against the end of the

roll. Repeat on the other side, twisting in the opposite direction. On each end, tie the extra plastic wrap into a knot as close to the end of the roll as possible. Trim the extra plastic length if necessary. Set aside and repeat for the other roll.

Fill a wok or a steamer pot with an inch or two of water. Place both the rolls in the steamer basket, cover, and set into the wok. Bring the water to a boil and steam for 15 minutes. Halfway through the steaming, remove the lid and wait for a moment to allow the steam to dissipate (to avoid being burned), then use tongs to turn each roll halfway. Also carefully check the water level, adding more hot water if necessary. Cover again and steam until done: (Poke the middle of the roll using the thin metal stem of a cooking thermometer (or cake tester) or the tip of a paring knife, leave it there for 5 seconds, then touch it just below your lower lip. If it feels hot, it's done. Remove the cylinders from the steamer and transfer to a plate to cool (see Note) for at least 1 hour before slicing, or place in the fridge for a couple of hours or overnight to firm up the tofu some more.

Store the rolls for up to 1 week in the refrigerator or up to a month in the freezer. (Freezing the roll transforms the tofu into a chewy, fishlike texture.)

Note:
You can slightly flatten the rolls into an oblong shape. Once you've transferred the rolls from the steamer to a plate, place a small cutting board or another plate on top of the rolls and weigh them down with several 28-ounce (800 g) cans of tomatoes or a small stack of plates. Leave the weight on the rolls as they cool for at least 30 minutes for them to stay in that shape.

BLACK PEPPER SOY GLAZED NORI TOFU ROLL

3 tablespoons soy sauce

1 tablespoon vegetarian mushroom-flavored stir-fry sauce or vegetarian hoisin sauce

⅓ cup (80 ml) coconut water or water

1 teaspoon sugar

¼ teaspoon freshly ground black pepper

In a small bowl, stir together the soy sauce, stir-fry sauce, coconut water and sugar and set aside.

Slice the roll on a 45-degree angle into ½ to 1-inch-thick (1.3 to 2.5 cm) slices. Heat a tablespoon or two of oil in a skillet over medium heat. When the oil is hot, carefully add the tofu slices to the skillet. Cook for about 3 minutes, or until the tofu is golden brown, before turning it over. Panfry on the other side until golden brown. (If serving with a different sauce, like Tangy Tamarind Sauce, page 68, briefly transfer to a paper-towel-lined plate, prepare the sauce, and add slices to the prepared sauce.)

Pour the soy sauce mixture over the top. Simmer for several minutes, occasionally spooning the sauce over the slices, until they're glazed and 1 to 2 tablespoons of liquid remain in the skillet. Transfer to a serving dish and garnish with freshly ground black pepper.

3

ROLLS, BÁNH MÌ, AND STREET SNACKS

OPPOSITE A woman makes rice paper in Trảng Bàng, northwest of Sài Gòn.

Every Vietnamese region—every city, almost—has its own spring roll. Fresh and fried, wrapped in rice paper or vegetable leaves, the variations alone could fill an entire book. Common to many are fillings of shredded, raw, pickled, or cooked vegetables; mashed or slivered tofu; fresh herbs; and perhaps rice noodles or boiled mung beans. Dipping sauces bring all these elements together.

Choose deep-fried spring rolls when feeling decadent or healthy rice paper rolls (also called *summer rolls* or *salad rolls*) when feeling virtuous. Either way, rolls make an irresistible snack or appetizer and are guaranteed crowd-pleasers. And though their elements are many, rolling and filling them isn't difficult. In fact, when my daughter turned eleven, she and I would assemble the filling together the night before school at least twice a month. She'll roll them herself and tuck them in her lunchbox, making extras for her friends.

If throwing a party, prepare the filling in advance. When guests arrive, enlist them to help with the rolling. With many hands, the assembly goes faster than you might expect.

The French-inspired bánh mì sandwich is perhaps Việt Nam's most famous grab-and-go meal. With a couple of pantry items on hand, it's easy to assemble a homemade version that satisfies from early morning to late at night. I've been known to both start and finish my day munching on a bánh mì.

Snacking is a hugely popular part of Việt Nam's food culture. So in addition to rolls and sandwiches, I've shared recipes for snacks inspired by vegetarian street food, like Crispy Half-Moon Pillows (page 110) and Translucent Mung Bean Dumplings (page 123). I've also created vegetarian versions of nonvegetarian street food. They're so good, I want you to experience them.

Green, unripe mangoes (see recipe on page 117) and scale

TIPS FOR PREPARING AND ROLLING RICE PAPER ROLLS

Here's a list of helpful tips for preparing and rolling rice paper rolls. While some are specific to fresh summer rolls, you can apply many of the tips when you make deep-fried spring rolls. Don't worry if the first few times you make the rolls your cuts aren't the exact width or your rolls don't look perfect. They'll still taste fabulous. Once you've made either type of roll a few times you'll easily get the hang of the process and can customize the fillings.

Cut ingredients, like tofu and vegetables, into thin strips of varying thicknesses and lengths. It facilitates rolling the rice paper and makes them easier to eat. Cut root vegetables like carrots and daikon radish into thin ⅛-inch thick (3 mm) matchsticks. I like to cut panfried tofu, raw jicama, and cucumber into strips ¼ inch (6 mm) thick, like shoestring French fries. For large (8½-inch; 22 cm) rice paper, cut ingredients into strips 3 to 4 inches (8 to 10 cm) long. For small (6-inch; 16 cm) rice paper, cut them into 2½-inch (6 cm) lengths. A Japanese mandoline or julienne vegetable peeler helps to quickly cut vegetables into matchsticks or slices of even thickness (see page 130).

Prepare all of the filling ingredients before you begin rolling. Wash and dry lettuce and herbs with a salad spinner. Cut ingredients into desired widths and lengths. Panfry or stir-fry any ingredients that need to be cooked.

Select soft, buttery large leaves from heads of lettuce such as Boston, Bibb, or butter leaf and tear them into palm-sized (3-to4-inch; 8 to 10 cm) pieces. The leaves from stiffer lettuces like romaine can be used, but trim them from the firm ribs (save the ribs for a stir-fry or as a salad plate garnish) as they may pierce the delicate rice paper. The tiny shoots of chard, beet tops, or other lettuce leaves that make up the convenient grocery store mesclun mixes are fine to use, but trim off any tough stems.

Pick off the upper delicate stems of cilantro and other herb leaves from tough stems. Tear large Thai basil, mint, or Vietnamese balm leaves in half. Flavorful sprouts of broccoli, cress, mustard, or radish are tasty inclusions.

Resist the urge to mix all of the ingredients together before placing them on the rice paper. It quickens the assembly but doesn't guarantee each bite is as flavorful as it can be with a little bit of everything in it. Sometimes I'll mix together a couple of ingredients like matchsticks of carrots and daikon.

Divide some of the ingredients cut into strips—from matchsticks to ½-inch-thick (1.5 cm) strips—into small bundles. Then you can eyeball the portion of filling for each roll. It also helps prevent you from running out of some of the filling ingredients too early.

continues

Organize all of your ingredients on a large plate or tray beside one another in the order that you'll lay them down on the rice paper. I like to set up my tray in this order: lettuce, rice noodles, tofu, vegetable matchsticks or bean sprouts, broken rice crackers, and herbs.

Soften rice paper in warm to hot tap water for about 5 seconds. (It should be warm but cool enough to comfortably stick your fingers in it.) When the water cools, you have two options: heat the water on a burner until warm or discard the cold water and refill the frying pan or shallow container with warm tap water. Dip the entire rice paper in the hot water for 3 to 5 seconds. Any longer and it will become too soft and easily tear. The rice paper should remain slightly firm when removed from the water. As it rests on the cutting board, it continues to absorb moisture.

Layer and evenly spread out the ingredients. Lay the soft lettuce leaves and rice noodles down first, to act as a protective barrier, and to prevent any harder ingredients from piercing the rice paper. Evenly spread the ingredients the length you want the roll to be. Leave sides of the rice paper uncovered to facilitate the rice paper sticking to itself and to make the rolling easier.

Roll the rice paper roll snugly. Use your index and middle fingers to guide and hold the filling in place. Rolled too loose, the filling will fall out. Rolled too tight and the rice paper may break.

An extra pair of hands is helpful when rolling a large number of rolls. Or better yet, prepare the filling ingredients in advance and have a party where you teach guests how to assemble and roll their own.

Serve with a well-balanced flavorful dipping sauce. In most of the fillings there is little or no salt or seasoning. The sauce seasons the roll and brings all of the elements together in one bite. Serve the sauce in individualized condiment bowls or in a single bowl with a small spoon so that diners can drizzle some sauce into their rice paper roll.

Store the rolls in a single layer on a plate or tray, covered with a lightly dampened clean dish towel and wrapped in plastic, in the fridge for up to several hours before serving.

Cut large rolls in half or into thirds or use smaller rice paper for hors d'oeuvres.

RAINBOW RICE PAPER ROLLS

GỎI CUỐN CHAY

Light and flavorful, these beautiful rolls make perfect hot-weather food. They're easy to assemble too. Just wrap soft, translucent rice paper around vermicelli rice noodles, tender lettuce, crunchy vegetables, and herbs—then dip it in a lively sauce.

When I'm at the farmers' market, I seek out multicolored carrots and watermelon radish for their bold visual impact, and, availability permitting, I encourage you to follow suit. That way, when you take a bite, you expose the rolls' vibrant, almost kaleidoscopic interior. Native to Sài Gòn, these rolls are a southern Vietnamese specialty.

Makes 16 rolls with 8½-inch (22 cm) round rice papers

4 ounces (113 g) dried vermicelli rice noodles

1 medium carrot, cut into matchsticks (1 cup) (see Note)

¼ pound (113 g) watermelon radish or daikon, cut into matchsticks (1 cup) (see Note)

¼ pound (113 g) jicama, cut into 32 strips 3 to 4 inches (7.5 to 10 cm) long and ¼ inch (6 mm) wide (1 cup)

1 head green or red Bibb or Boston lettuce, torn into palm-sized pieces

1 cup packed cilantro leaves

¾ cup packed mint or Thai basil leaves or a combination

16 rice paper rounds, 8½ inches (22 cm) in diameter

Everyday Table Sauce (page 49)

Bring a large pot of water to a boil. Drop in the noodles and use chopsticks or tongs to untangle and loosen. Boil until tender, 3 to 5 minutes, then drain and immediately flush with cold water.

Squeeze gently four or five times to get rid of any excess water. Set aside on a plate, loosely covered with a clean kitchen towel. (You should have about 2 cups of noodles).

Mix the carrot and radish together and divide into four piles on a large plate. Place, along with the jicama, lettuce, cilantro, mint, and rice paper, next to a clean cutting board, preferably next to the stove.

Place a large shallow skillet or a 9- or 10-inch (23 to 25 cm) pie plate filled with warm to hot tap water on an unlit burner closest to the cutting board. Dip one rice paper into the water for a few seconds to soften and lay it flat on

continues

the cutting board. Place a lettuce leaf on the bottom third of the rice paper, leaving a border of 1½ inches (4 cm) on either side. Place 1½ to 2 tablespoons of noodles on the lettuce and spread into a 4-½-inch (11 cm) line. Line three leaves of cilantro and a leaf or two each of mint and basil over the top. Grab a portion of the carrot/radish mixture (a quarter of each pile is one portion) and two jicama strips and spread over the length of the noodles, overlapping if necessary.

Carefully lift the bottom edge of rice paper over the filling and roll over once into a tight cylinder. Fold in the sides and continue to roll into a cylinder 4 to 5 inches (10 to 12. 5 cm) in length. Place on a clean plate or serving platter loosely covered with a damp clean dish towel. Repeat with the remaining rice paper and filling. (When the water is no longer warm, gently reheat it or discard the cold water from the pie plate and refill with warm to hot water.)

Store the rolls in a single layer on a plate or tray covered with a damp clean dish towel and wrapped with plastic in the fridge for up to several hours before serving.

Make the Everyday Table Sauce. Serve the rolls on a platter or individual plates and dip into the sauce before eating.

Note:
If you have some pickled carrots and daikon (page 47) in the fridge, substitute 2 drained cups of it for the carrot and radish.

SUBSTITUTION
Replace the Everyday Table Sauce with the Nutty Fermented Soybean Dipping Sauce (page 52).

OPPOSITE Rainbow Rice Paper Rolls

CUCUMBER PINEAPPLE ROLLS
WITH COCONUT SOY SAUCE
GỢI CUỐN DƯA CHUỘT VÀ DỨA CHẤM VỚI NƯỚC TƯỚNG

Parched after a long bike ride through the quiet streets of Hội An, an ancient port town, I wandered into a small vegetarian restaurant seeking nourishment and shade. Although the restaurant was closed, the cook and server invited me in to join their staff for lunch. The cook showed me how to assemble these herb-filled rolls, a study in contrasting textures and flavors. Cool cucumbers, fruity pineapple, crunchy rice crackers, and bright herbs join together, creating the best restaurant meal I've never had to order.

Makes 16 rolls with 8½-inch (22 cm) round rice papers

FROM THE PANTRY/MAKE AHEAD

One 10-inch (25 cm) Toasted Sesame Rice Cracker (page 55) broken into ½-inch pieces

——

¼ cup vegetable oil

½ pound (225 g) firm tofu, cut into ½-inch (1 cm) slabs and patted dry on paper towel or a clean dish towel

3 small cucumbers (Kirby or Persian) or ½ English cucumber, unpeeled (for the English cucumber, seeds removed) and cut into 4-by-¼-inch (10 cm by 0.6 cm) sticks

4-by-¼-inches (10 cm by 0.6 cm) fresh peeled pineapple, sixteen sticks

1 head Boston lettuce, leaves torn into palm-sized pieces

¾ cup packed mint leaves, larger leaves torn in half

¾ cup packed Thai basil or Italian basil, larger leaves torn in half

¾ cup packed Vietnamese balm or lemon basil (see Note)

1 cup packed cilantro sprigs

1 cup bean sprouts (50g)

¾ cup thinly sliced banana blossom or green or red cabbage

16 rice paper rounds, 8½ inches (22 cm) in diameter

Coconut Soy Dipping Sauce (recipe follows)

Prepare the Toasted Sesame Rice Cracker.

Heat the oil in a large skillet over medium-high heat. Add the tofu and cook for 4 minutes, until golden brown. Carefully turn the tofu over using chopsticks, tongs, or a spatula and cook for another 3 to 4 minutes, until golden brown. Transfer to a large plate lined with paper towel. When cool, thinly slice into sixteen ¼-inch-thick (6 mm) sticks and set aside on a large plate or tray.

continues

OPPOSITE Cucumber Pineapple Rolls with Coconut Soy Sauce

Organize the cucumbers, pineapple, and rice cracker pieces in separate bunches on the same plate as the tofu. On another large plate, arrange separate piles of lettuce, herbs, bean sprouts, and banana blossom. Place the plates next to a clean cutting board, preferably next to the stove.

Place large shallow skillet or a 9- or 10-inch (23 to 25 cm) pie plate filled with warm to hot tap water on an unlit burner closest to the cutting board. Dip one rice paper into the water for a few seconds to soften and lay it flat on cutting board. Place a leaf of lettuce on the bottom third of the rice paper, leaving a border of 1½ inches (4 cm) on either side.

Line two or three leaves each of mint, basil, Vietnamese balm, and a couple sprigs of cilantro on top. Spread a pinch of bean sprouts and banana blossom over the herbs. Put a piece of tofu, cucumber, pineapple, and a couple pieces of rice cracker on top. Carefully lift the bottom edge of the rice paper over the filling and roll over once into a tight cylinder. Fold in the sides and continue to roll into a cylinder 4 to 5 inches (10 to 12.5 cm) in length. Place on a clean plate or serving platter loosely covered with a damp clean kitchen towel. Repeat with the remaining rice paper and filling. (When the water is no longer warm, gently reheat it (or discard the cold water from the pie plate and refill with warm to hot water.)

Serve immediately on a platter or individual plates and dip into the coconut soy dipping sauce before eating.

Notes:
- If Vietnamese balm or lemon basil is not available, increase each of the other herbs by ¼ cup or replace with one of the suggested substitutions.
- Prepare these rolls just before serving. If made too far in advance, the rice cracker pieces lose their crunchiness.

SUBSTITUTIONS
- Replace some of the herbs with roughly chopped greens like Chinese celery, sorrel, chard, or arugula.
- Replace the banana blossom with matchsticks of green papaya, green mango, jicama, or even a tart apple.

COCONUT SOY DIPPING SAUCE

The addition of toasted and then ground sesame seeds or tahini brings a luxurious rich nuttiness to this unique dipping sauce. **Makes about 1 cup**

1 garlic clove

½ fresh red Thai bird chile, cut in half lengthwise and seeds removed

1½ tablespoons Toasted Sesame Seeds (page 33), ground or 1 tablespoon tahini

¼ cup (60 ml) soy sauce

¼ cup plus 2 tablespoon (90 ml) coconut milk

1 tablespoon fresh lime juice

½ teaspoon Chinese five-spice powder

Roughly chop the garlic and chile and add to a blender along with the ground sesame seeds, soy sauce, coconut milk, lime juice, and five-spice powder. Puree for a minute, or until the garlic and chile are finely chopped and well blended. Refrigerate for up to 3 or 4 days.

AROMATIC CELLOPHANE NOODLE ROLL-UPS

BÌ CUỐN CHAY

Finely minced wild lime leaves impart an elusive, tropical flavor to these fragrant rolls. Buttery lettuce and lively herbs add a double dose of freshness. For a light, summery lunch, serve these rolls with nothing more than a tangy dipping sauce and a cool drink.

Makes 16 rolls using 8½-inch (22 cm) round rice papers

FROM THE PANTRY/MAKE AHEAD

(3 to 4 tablespoons) Toasted Rice Powder (page 39)

———

A medium bundle (1.8 ounces; 50 g) cellophane noodles

3 wild lime leaves, center stem of leaf cut out and discarded and leaf very finely chopped

¼ cup plus 1 tablespoon vegetable oil

½ pound (225 g) medium-firm or firm tofu, drained, cut into ½-inch (1 cm) slabs, and patted dry on a paper towel or a clean dish towel

½ pound (225 g) jicama, cut into ¼-inch-thick (6 mm) slices

½ pound (225 g) taro root, cut into thin matchsticks

½ pound (225 g) Asian sweet potato, cut into thin matchsticks

1 head green or red Bibb or Boston lettuce, washed, dried, and torn into palm-sized pieces

A large handful Vietnamese balm leaves (¾ cup packed)

A handful cilantro or mint leaves (1 cup packed)

16 rice paper rounds, 8½ inches (22 cm) in diameter

Everyday Table Sauce (page 49)

Make the Toasted Rice Powder.

Place the cellophane noodles in a large bowl and cover with boiling water. Untangle using chopsticks or tongs. Let sit for about 10 minutes, until they're clear, flexible, and softened. Drain, shaking the colander several times, then squeeze gently four or five times to get rid of any excess water. Leave in the colander for 10 minutes to air-dry. Transfer to a large bowl and toss with 3 tablespoons of the toasted rice powder and the chopped wild lime leaves until the noodles are completely coated. If you feel they are not completely coated, sprinkle with another tablespoon of toasted rice powder. Set aside, loosely covered with a clean dish towel.

Heat ¼ cup of the vegetable oil in a large skillet over medium-high heat. Add the tofu and cook for 4 minutes, until golden brown. Carefully turn over using chopsticks, tongs, or a spatula and cook for another 3 to 4 minutes, until golden brown. Transfer to a large plate lined with paper towel.

Carefully add the jicama slices to the skillet. Cook undisturbed for about 3 minutes, until the side against the skillet is lightly golden.

continues

Turn over and cook for another 2 to 3 minutes, until lightly golden. Transfer to a large plate lined with paper towel. When cool, thinly slice the tofu and jicama into ¼-inch-thick (6 mm) sticks and set aside on a large plate.

Add the remaining tablespoon of oil to the skillet. Carefully sprinkle the taro root matchsticks over the entire surface. Some of the matchsticks will stick to each other, so use a pair of chopsticks or tongs to stir to try to separate them. Cook undisturbed for a couple of minutes. Give a good stir and cook undisturbed for a couple more minutes. Repeat this three more times, for a total of about 10 minutes, or until the matchsticks are crispy and mostly golden in color. Transfer to the paper-towel-lined plate.

Add the sweet potato matchsticks to the skillet and cook in the same manner as for the taro root for about 12 minutes, or until they're completely tender (some parts of them will be browned and others not). Transfer to the paper-towel-lined-plate and cool to room temperature. In a medium bowl, mix together the taro root and sweet potato matchsticks.

Organize the lettuce and herbs on a plate next to the tofu and jicama. Arrange all of the ingredients next to a clean cutting board. Place a large shallow skillet or a 9- or 10-inch (23 to 25 cm) pie plate filled with warm to hot water on an unlit burner closest to the cutting board. Dip one rice paper round into the hot water for a few seconds to soften and lay it flat on the cutting board. Place a leaf of lettuce on the bottom third of the rice paper, leaving a border of 1½ inches (4 cm) on either side of the rice paper. Place about 1 tablespoon of noodles on the lettuce and spread them out into a 4½-inch (11 cm) line. Line a leaf or two of Vietnamese balm, mint, or three sprigs of cilantro on top of the length of the noodles. Lay a piece of tofu, a couple sticks of jicama, and a good pinch of the taro/sweet potato mixture on the lettuce next to the noodles.

Carefully lift the bottom edge of the rice paper over the filling and roll over once into a tight cylinder. Fold in the sides and continue to roll into a cylinder 4 to 5 inches (10 to 12.5 cm) in length. Place on a clean plate or serving platter loosely covered with a damp clean dish towel. Repeat with the remaining rice paper and filling. (If at any point the water is no longer warm, turn the burner on low to gently reheat it or discard the cold water from the pie plate and refill with warm to hot water.)

Store the rolls in a single layer on a plate or tray covered with a damp clean dish towel and wrapped with plastic in the fridge for up to several hours before serving.

Make the Everyday Table Sauce.

Serve on a platter or individual plates and dip into the dipping sauce before eating.

SUBSTITUTIONS
- For the tofu, substitute rehydrated shredded tofu skin.
- For the jicama, substitute kohlrabi or yellow-fleshed potato.
- For the taro root, substitute parsnip or celery root.
- For the Asian sweet potato, substitute orange-fleshed sweet potato.

FRESH SWISS CHARD ROLLS

CUỐN DIẾP CHAY

I consistently order this exceptionally beautiful fresh roll at vegetarian restaurants in Sài Gòn. I adore how a bit of the filling, vermicelli noodles with sautéed cabbage, carrots, and fresh herbs, peeks out the sides, begging for a dip in a creamy peanut sauce. They're easy to assemble and fabulous to serve as part of a light summer meal or as an hors d'oeuvres.

I've substituted Swiss chard, which serves as the wrapper, for the traditional mustard leaves, as they're available year round in grocery stores. Try to select bunches with young tender leaves, 4 to 5 inches (10 to 13 cm) wide, that lie flat. In the summer months it's worth looking for peppery Asian mustard leaves at Asian grocers, as ruffled, large-leaved American mustard leaves are too sharp for this recipe. Other leafy greens (lacinato kale, collard greens, or even kohlrabi leaves) make fine substitutes. When using larger leaves or other greens (unless they're tender and lie flat), blanch them first in boiling water, refresh them in cold water, pat them dry, and trim away the thick central ribs before using.   **Makes 16 rolls**

2 dried wood ear mushrooms

20 scallions (plus a few extra in case a couple break when tying), or a bunch of long chives

4 ounces (113 g) dried vermicelli rice noodles

1 tablespoon vegetable oil

1 cup (¼ pound; 113 g) shredded green cabbage

½ cup packed grated carrot (½ medium)

¼ teaspoon salt

⅛ teaspoon freshly ground black pepper

16 or more young tender Swiss chard leaves or whole Asian mustard leaves, each one 7 to 8 inches (18 to 20 cm) long and 4 inches (10 cm) wide

32 Thai basil leaves, torn or cut in half lengthwise if large

32 cilantro sprigs with 2 or 3 leaves each

Nutty Fermented Soybean Dipping Sauce (page 52)

Soak the wood ear mushrooms in warm water for 20 minutes. Drain and squeeze out any excess water. Cut off any hard, chewy centers and thinly slice into 1-inch (2.5 cm) lengths.

Bring a large pot of water to a boil over high heat. Set a bowl of ice water next to the stove. (If using another type of green as wrapper, blanch it before the scallions.) Trim

continues

the scallions at a point about 2 inches (5 cm) from the root end, just below the part where they turn from light green to dark green (reserve scallion whites for another use). Blanch the scallion greens (or chives) for 10 seconds and transfer to the ice water to stop them from cooking and to preserve their bright green color. After a few minutes, drain well. This process helps strengthen scallion greens for tying the Swiss chard or mustard leaves. Gently squeeze out the water and carefully spread out on a clean dish towel to dry.

Drop the noodles into boiling water and use chopsticks or tongs to untangle and loosen them. Boil until tender, 3 to 5 minutes, then drain and immediately flush with cold water. Gently squeeze four or five times to get rid of any excess water. Set aside on a large plate, loosely covered with a clean dish towel, as you prepare the remaining ingredients. (You should have about 2 cups of noodles.)

Heat the oil in a medium saucepan over medium heat. Add the cabbage, carrot, mushrooms, salt, and pepper. Cook, stirring occasionally, for about 4 minutes, or until soft but still a little crunchy. Transfer to a large plate to cool for a few minutes.

Lay a Swiss chard leaf or mustard leaf, with the darker green side facing down and the bottom stem pointing toward you, on a cutting board. Trim the stem off at the point where the leaf ends. To remove the thicker, less flexible part of the stem, cut out a 1½-inch (4 cm) narrow V shape along either side of the bottom part of the stem. (If the leaves you have are less than 7

inches/18 cm long, place a second one on top of the bottom leaf, slightly overlapping in the middle, to make a "leaf" 8 inches/20 cm long.)

Lay a blanched scallion green beside and perpendicular to the Swiss chard or mustard leaf on the board.

Place approximately 2 tablespoons of noodles over the bottom third of the leaf, trying to cover the middle 3 inches (8 cm). Spread a tablespoon of vegetables over the noodles. Place 2 basil leaves and 2 cilantro sprigs on top.

Gently yet tightly, pull the bottom of the leaf over the filling and continue to roll until all of it is rolled up. Lift the leaf package and place on the middle of the scallion, if possible trying to line it up with the midrib of the leaf. Tie the scallion using two quick knots, to secure the roll. Use a knife or scissors to trim any long ends of the scallion if need be. Set aside on a serving platter and repeat until all of the remaining ingredients are used up.

Make the Nutty Fermented Soybean Dipping Sauce.

Refrigerate the rolls, covered with plastic wrap, for up to a couple of hours or serve immediately with the dipping sauce.

VARIATION

ROLLS USING LARGER SWISS CHARD LEAVES, LACINATO KALE, OR COLLARD GREENS

Select cheerful bunches of greens with no holes in the leaves. For all of the leaves, trim the stem off at the point where the leaf stops

OPPOSITE Fresh leaf rolls made with red Swiss chard

continues

to keep leaves intact and to prevent them from tearing when blanched and being handled. When you get some smaller leaves, particularly lacinato kale, which may not be as wide as mustard greens, simply adjust the amount of filling accordingly. You may notice when some of the blanched leaves, such as Swiss chard, are rolled they seal themselves and may not need to be tied with a blanched scallion or chive.

1 bunch red or white chard (large leaves), lacinato kale (leaves at least 7 inches/18 cm long) or collard greens (6 to 7 large leaves)

Bring a large pot of water to a boil over high heat and set a large bowl of ice water next to the stove.

Boil chard for 15 seconds, lacinato kale for 1 to 1½ minutes, and collard green for 2 to 2½ minutes.

Immediately plunge the leaves into ice water until cold. Lift out of the ice water and transfer to a colander set in the sink. Spread a clean dish towel or two on a clean countertop or baking sheet. Carefully open a leaf and place it on the towel. Repeat for all of the leaves. Use another clean dish towel to dab the top side of each leaf dry. Transfer to a plate (or if they are on a baking sheet) and set it aside next to a cutting board.

TRIMMING THE LEAVES

Lay a whole chard or collard green leaf, with smooth side facing up and bottom stem pointing toward you, on a cutting board. Starting from the top, completely trim away the tough stem/midrib that runs down the middle of the leaf. Try to stay as close as possible on either side of the stem. Trim each end of a chard leaf to make the leaf about 7 inches (18 cm) long; if using collard greens, trim each half into a 4-by-7-inch (10 by 18 cm) rectangle (depending on the size of the leaves, you may be lucky and get four rectangles from one leaf. Assemble and roll as directed.

If using lacinato kale, cut the same way as described for the mustard greens. Since its midrib is a touch tougher than mustard greens, cut an inch (2.5 cm) or more of it away. Make sure that at least the top 4 inches (10 cm) of the leaf are not cut. Just before laying the ingredients on the kale leaf, slightly overlap the cut part of the leaves. Assemble and roll as directed.

TARO ROOT MUNG BEAN SPRING ROLLS

CHẢ GIÒ CHAY (South); NEM RÁN CHAY (North)

Fried spring rolls served in the center and South of Việt Nam are commonly filled with boiled mung beans mashed with crispy taro root shreds. Taro root tends to be starchy and prone to sticking, so when browning the taro root shreds, be sure to move them around the pan. Serve smaller rolls as hors d'oeuvres or as part of a multidish meal, or cut them into bite-sized pieces to add to a Tasty Rice Noodle Bowl (page 188).

Makes about 16 large or 32 small spring rolls

FROM THE PANTRY/MAKE AHEAD

½ teaspoon Mushroom Powder (page 36)

———

½ pound (225 g) firm tofu

½ cup (110 g) dried split mung beans, rinsed and drained

¾ cup plus 2 tablespoons (220 ml) water

¼ cup plus 2 tablespoons vegetable oil, plus about 2½ cups (500 to 625 ml) for frying

Sixteen 8½-inch (22 cm) round rice papers or thirty-two 6-inch (16 cm) round rice papers

1 pound (450 g) taro root, grated

5 shiitake mushrooms, soaked in hot water for 15 minutes, drained, squeezed dry, stemmed and finely chopped

2 dried wood ear mushrooms, soaked in hot water for 15 minutes, drained, squeezed dry, stemmed, and finely chopped

½ pound (225 g; 2 medium or 1 large) carrots, grated

One 3-inch (7.5 cm) piece of leek (white part only), finely chopped

2 garlic cloves, finely chopped

¼ cup roughly chopped cilantro

1 teaspoon salt

¾ teaspoon freshly ground black pepper

Everyday Table Sauce (page 49)

1 head butter or romaine lettuce, broken into large palm-sized pieces

About ½ cup cilantro sprigs

About ½ cup Thai basil leaves

About ½ cup mint leaves

Prepare the Mushroom Powder.

Cut the block of tofu into ⅓-inch-thick (1 cm) slices. Place the slices on a paper towel or a clean dish towel and pat dry.

Put the mung beans in a small pot with the water and bring to a simmer over medium-high heat. Cover, reduce the heat to low, and cook for 15 minutes, until the beans are soft. Uncover and spoon into a large bowl to cool.

Place a paper-towel-lined tray next to the stove. Heat ¼ cup of the oil in a large skillet over medium-high heat. Add the tofu slices and cook for 2 to 3 minutes before carefully

continues

turning over. Cook for another 2 minutes, until evenly golden brown on both sides. Transfer to the paper-towel-lined tray to drain.

Add half of the grated taro to the pan and use chopsticks, tongs, or a spatula to spread over the entire bottom in one even layer. Cook, without stirring or moving, for 2 to 3 minutes. Use a spatula or tongs to flip the taro. Cook for another couple of minutes. The surface should be golden brown and slightly crispy while some of the interior will remain a touch soft. Remove and place on the paper-towel-lined tray. Add 2 tablespoons of the oil to the pan and heat. Repeat with the remaining taro.

Cut the tofu into ⅛-inch-thick (0.5 cm) slices and add to the bowl with the mung beans.

Add the mushrooms, carrots, leek, garlic, taro, cilantro, salt, mushroom powder, and black pepper to the large bowl. Use your hands to mix the filling evenly, squeezing the ingredients together (the cooked mung beans and taro will help bind the ingredients). The filling, kept refrigerated in a well-sealed container, can be made up to 1 day before rolling.

Place a large shallow bowl filled with warm water next to a cutting board. Dip the rice paper round into the water and immerse fully for 5 seconds to moisten completely. Remove and lay flat on the cutting board. Add ¼ cup of the filling to the center lower third of the paper. Use your fingers to make a tight 4-inch (10 cm) log of filling, leaving 2 inches (5 cm) empty on each side. If using small rice papers, use 2 table-spoons of filling and leave 1¼ inches (3 cm) empty on each side. Fold the bottom of the rice paper over the ingredients with a little pressure to slightly tighten the roll. Fold in both sides of the paper, trying to keep each folded edge straight and perpendicular to the bottom of

the roll (this helps to produce beautiful-looking spring rolls). Roll into a tight cylinder and place seam side down on a plate or tray. As you prog-ress, do not stack the rolls as they may stick and tear. Repeat with the remaining rice papers until the filling is used up.

Arrange a wire rack over a baking sheet and a plate lined with paper towels close to the burner you will use to fry the spring rolls.

Before you fry the rolls, make the Everyday Table Sauce.

Pour oil to a depth of ¾ inch (2 cm) (2 to 2½ cups; 500 to 625 ml) into a large skillet or to a depth of about 1 inch (2.5 cm) into a wok and heat over medium-high heat to 325°F (177°C) on a deep-fry thermometer or until you touch the bottom of the wok with a wooden chop-stick and small oil bubbles come up the side of it within 2 seconds.

One at a time, carefully slip in some spring rolls, seam side down to prevent them from open-ing, into the oil. Ensure they're not touching and the pan is not crowded. (If parts of the rolls start to stick together, leave them be and care-fully turn over when necessary. You can gently pry them apart outside of the pan and away from the hot oil.) You will need to cook them in two or three batches. Cook for 4 to 5 minutes, until the bottom is light golden brown in color, and turn the spring rolls over with tongs. Cook for another 4 minutes, or until entirely golden brown. Remove from the oil and place on the paper-towel-lined plate for a minute or so and then transfer on the rack-lined baking sheet. Repeat until the rest of spring rolls are fried.

Arrange the lettuce leaves and herbs on a plate.

To eat, grab a piece of lettuce and add some sprigs of herbs to the center. Place a golden spring roll on top and wrap the lettuce around it. Dip into the table sauce.

TO PREPARE THE SPRING ROLLS IN ADVANCE

Up to several hours in advance fry them about two-thirds of the way, until they're turning a pale golden color, then transfer them to the rack to cool. Just before serving, reheat the oil and refry them until completely golden. Alternatively, fry once until completely golden brown and reheat until warm in a 300°F (150C) oven. They won't be as crispy as when they come straight from the hot oil.

TO FREEZE THE SPRING ROLLS

Fry them two-thirds of the way, as described above. Place them, not touching, on a tray, freeze, and store them for up to a month, in zippered plastic bag or a tightly sealed container in the freezer. When ready to serve them, reheat your oil and fry them, from frozen, until completely golden.

Note:

In Việt Nam fried spring rolls are made using round wrappers, made from rice flour or in combination with tapioca flour, whereas square spring roll wrappers, made of wheat flour, are used in other Asian countries. If you prefer using wrappers made from wheat, seek out TYJ brand. These wrappers do not require a quick presoak in water. Follow the directions on the package for how to seal the spring rolls. Fry them until completely golden brown and then reheat them in a warm oven (a second frying is not necessary). Freeze spring rolls with these wrappers unfried and fry them from frozen.

Rice paper drying on bamboo racks.

CRISPY HALF-MOON PILLOWS

BÁNH GỐI CHAY

In the French colonial part of Hà Nội, I came across a vendor making these crispy fried snacks. I was so eager to try them I almost caused an accident trying to reach her stall. When I got there, I watched a young woman deep-fry half-moon-shaped pillows in the shade of a dracontomelon tree. She handed me one, freshly fried. I wrapped it with herbs and a large piece of lettuce, then dipped it in the spicy sauce. The outside was crispy and flaky, the inside filled with creamy tofu, shredded jicama, and finely chopped mushrooms. It was heavenly. The young woman, named Thuy, was helping her mother and sister-in-law between her college classes. She asked if I wanted to learn how to make them. I returned one morning and watched her sister-in-law assemble them. Thuy explained that the most important step is to squeeze out as much moisture as possible from the jicama and tofu so the dumplings can fully crisp.

These snacks get their Vietnamese name (*bánh gối*) because they resemble a decorative pillow with pleated edges.

Makes about 45 dumplings using 4-inch (10 cm) round dumpling wrappers

FROM THE PANTRY/MAKE AHEAD

2 teaspoons Mushroom Powder (page 36)

---

1 tablespoon vegetable oil plus about 3 cups for frying (750 ml)

½ pound (225 g) meatless ground crumbles or ground seitan (1¼ cup packed)

1 small carrot, coarsely grated (⅔ cup packed)

⅓ pound (150 g) jicama, coarsely grated (1 cup)

¾ pound (340 g) firm or extra-firm tofu, drained and lightly mashed

3 medium dried shiitake mushrooms, soaked in hot water for 15 minutes, drained, squeezed dry, stemmed, and finely chopped

2 dried wood ear mushroom, soaked in hot water for 15 minutes, drained, squeezed dry, stemmed, and finely chopped (¼ cup)

1 small bundle (25 g) cellophane noodles, soaked in hot water for 20 minutes, drained, squeezed dry, and roughly chopped into 1-inch (2.5 cm) pieces (about ½ cup)

1 tablespoon vegetarian mushroom-flavored stir-fry sauce

1 teaspoon salt

1 teaspoon freshly ground black pepper

⅓ cup roughly chopped cilantro

1½ packages 4-inch (10 cm) round Shanghai-style dumpling wrappers

Everyday Table Sauce (page 49) or Soy Chile Dipping Sauce (page 51)

1 head romaine or butter lettuce, broken into large palm-sized pieces

½ cup cilantro sprigs

½ cup Thai basil leaves

Prepare the Mushroom Powder.

Heat 1 tablespoon of the oil in a skillet over medium heat. Add the meatless ground crumbles and leave untouched for a minute or two to brown. Throughout the next 5 to 8 minutes, stir occasionally to break up any large chunks. When most of it is lightly browned, transfer to a plate to cool.

Add the carrot to a large bowl. Place the jicama on the middle of a clean dish towel. Bring the edges together and, over a sink, twist around it to squeeze and expel any water. Add it to the bowl. Scoop the mashed tofu onto the middle of the dish towel. Gradually twist and squeeze around it to expel any water. When the water falling from the towel changes from a stream to droplets, deposit it into the bowl. Add the mushrooms, cellophane noodles, vegetarian stir-fry sauce, mushroom powder, salt, black pepper, and chopped cilantro. Use your hands to break up any large pieces of the meatless ground and add to the bowl. Stir to mix everything together evenly. The filling, kept refrigerated in a well-sealed container, can be made up to 1 day before forming the half-moon pillows.

Set a small bowl filled with cold water and a small pastry brush next to a clean cutting board. Lay a dumpling wrapper on the cutting board. Spoon 2 teaspoons of the filling into the center. With the damp brush or your finger, moisten the upper edge. Bring the opposite edges together and, beginning from one end, pinch them closed. As you move toward the other end, press out any air and squeeze the edges together around the plumpness of the filling. (See Notes.)

To pleat the dumplings: With the damp brush or your finger, moisten the upper sealed edge of one side of the dumpling. Hold the dumpling in your left hand with the moistened rounded edge facing up. Pinch the corner of it with your index finger on top and thumb underneath. Use your thumb to guide and fold the corner over by about ¼ inch (6 mm) toward the center of it. With your thumb now on top and index finger underneath, pinch the corner against the top of the dumpling. For the next pleat, pinch the rough corner, created by the fold, again with your index finger on top and thumb underneath. Use your thumb to guide and fold the corner over by about ¼ inch (6 mm) toward the center. Gently pinch the corner, not the pleat, against the dumpling with your thumb. Repeat, making about 10 more pleats (12 in total) until you reach the other end. When you can't make another pleat, tuck and pinch the corner to the underside of the dumpling.

To crimp the dumpling with a fork: Because the edge of the dumpling is not folded, there is room for more filling. Place 1 tablespoon of filling in the center of a wrapper. Fold and seal into a half-moon shape as described above. Press the back of the tines of a fork along one side to crimp the sealed edge.

Lay the pleated or crimped dumplings on a large plate or tray. Repeat until all the filling is used up. (See Notes.)

continues

Prepare the Everyday Table Sauce or Soy Chile Dipping Sauce.

To fry the dumplings, place a paper-towel-lined plate and a wire-rack-lined baking sheet next to the stove. Pour 3 cups (750 ml) vegetable oil into a wok or quart (1 liter) of oil into a large pot. Heat the oil over medium-high heat until the temperature of a deep-fry thermometer reads 325°F (163°C) or until you touch the bottom of the wok or pot with a wooden chopstick and small oil bubbles immediately form on the surface around the chopstick. Working in batches, being careful not to splash yourself with hot oil, add some dumplings to the oil without crowding them. Deep-fry the dumplings, turning them over with tongs, chopsticks, or a spider every 1½ minutes, for 5 to 7 minutes, or until golden brown and blistered. Use tongs or a spider to remove them from the oil and transfer to the paper-towel-lined plate. Gently turn them over onto the paper to blot away any excess oil and transfer to the wire-rack-lined tray. Fry the remaining dumplings. The dumplings can be fried up to an hour ahead of time, kept at room temperature, and reheated until warm in a 300°F (150°C) oven.

Serve the dumplings alongside a plate of the lettuce leaves and herbs and the dipping sauce in a medium bowl with a spoon.

To eat, grab a palm-sized leaf of lettuce and add some herbs sprigs in the center. Place the crispy fried dumpling pillow on top and wrap the lettuce around it. Dip into the sauce and use the spoon to drizzle some more sauce into the dumpling if needed.

Notes:
- When shaping the half-moon pillows individually lay out four or five wonton wrappers at one time and spoon some of the filling onto each one. Then, one by one, wet the edges and pleat them. To make the work go more quickly you may want to gather an extra pair of hands. If so, try to lay out eight wrappers at one time, spooning the filling onto each one before moistening and pleating the edges.
- To freeze the dumplings, place them, not touching, on a parchment-lined tray and into the freezer. Once frozen, transfer to a zippered plastic bag. Keep frozen for up to a month. To cook, deep-fry from frozen and increase the cooking time by a minute or two.

SUBSTITUTION

Kohlrabi or zucchini can be substituted for the jicama. Grated zucchini should be placed in a colander, salted lightly, and left to sit for at least 15 minutes, then gently squeezed, before you wrap it in a clean dish towel.

BÁNH MÌ SANDWICH

BÁNH MÌ CHAY

French colonists may have introduced baguettes and pâtés to Việt Nam, but it was the Vietnamese who combined these ingredients into the world's greatest sandwich. After savoring many bánh mì throughout the country. I'm convinced that the tastiest ones are prepared at the stalls dotting Hội An. I spent a morning at one of the more famous stalls, Bánh Mì Phương, learning the subtleties involved in making a superlative bánh mì.

Three key components help set the gold bánh mì standard: the type of bread, the layering of ingredients, and the ability to resist using more than one main filling (despite a common urge to go overboard). While Phương, the stall's owner, gets her bread from the baker next door, you can buy a freshly baked, grocery store baguette with a thin crust and light fluffy crumb and make out just fine. Italian ciabatta, Cubano rolls, Mexican bolillo rolls, or Portuguese *papo secos* rolls also work well. Phương gently warms her baguettes in a wooden box by the heat of slowly burning embers. You can warm your baguettes in a 300°F (150°C) oven for few minutes.

Assembling the sandwich is all about layering flavors and textures. Start with the sauces and spreads, then the pickles, vegetables, and herbs, followed by the main filling and a toasty topping to finish. This specific order of layering produces the harmony of flavors so crucial to an extraordinary sandwich.   **Makes one 6-inch (15 cm) baguette, sliced in half lengthwise**

FROM THE PANTRY/MAKE AHEAD

Five-Spice-Glazed Tofu (page 69)

1 generous tablespoon Nutty Mushroom Pâté (page 46)

⅓ cup Pickled Carrots and Daikon (page 47) or Quick Pickled Carrots (page 48), drained

Toasted Sesame Seeds (page 33)

½ teaspoon chile garlic paste or thinly sliced mild fresh long red chiles

⅓ cup assorted herbs: coriander, mint, Thai basil, Vietnamese coriander

Scallions, thinly sliced and mixed with the herbs or cut into 6-inch lengths and thinly sliced lengthwise

Thin slices small (Kirby or Persian) cucumber (or cut an English cucumber into 5-inch lengths and thinly slice lengthwise)

2 or 3 slices ripe fresh plum tomato

continues

2 to 4 teaspoons Bánh Mì Sandwich Super Sauce (page 51) or soy sauce or Maggi Seasoning

1 tablespoon regular or eggless mayonnaise

One 6-inch Vietnamese-style baguette

Prepare the Five-Spice-Glazed Tofu, Nutty Mushroom Pâté, pickles, and Toasted Sesame Seeds.

As you prepare the remaining ingredients, preheat the oven to 300°F (150°C). When the filling and garnishes are ready, warm the baguette in the oven for a few minutes.

Slice the baguette in half lengthwise, but not all the way through, leaving the opposite side uncut (so that it's attached like opening a book).

Drizzle some Bánh Mì Super Sauce (or regular soy sauce or Maggi seasoning) along one of the cut sides of the bread. Spread mayonnaise and pâté along the inside top and bottom of the baguette. Arrange herbs, scallion, and then cucumber and tomato slices, and finally some carrot daikon pickles along the length of the bottom. Layer a slice or two of the tofu on top. Spoon over a little bit of chile sauce or some chile slices. Drizzle a teaspoon or two more of the Bánh Mì Super Sauce over the filling. Sprinkle on some sesame seeds. Hold two chopsticks together or use a dinner knife and press the sandwich filling down into the bread. Close the sandwich and cut crosswise in half or eat whole.

SUBSTITUTIONS

For the main filling substitute one of the following:

- Stir-Fried Tofu with Lemongrass and Chile (page 73), Tofu Skin Sausage (page 44) in thin slices, Bright Green Herby Omelet (page 237) or a plain fried egg, or Stewed Jackfruit with Vietnamese Coriander (page 249).
- Add one or a combination of toppings; Crispy Fried Shallots (page 37); Tofu Skin Chips, (page 42) crumbled into smaller pieces; cellophane noodles tossed with toasted, ground rice thinh (page 39).

OPPOSITE Bánh Mì Sandwich with Five-Spice-Glazed Tofu

SPICY LEMONGRASS MUSHROOM MINCE

HẾN XÀO XẢ ỚT CHAY

Bursting with lemongrass and chile, this mushroom mince is a variation on a dish traditionally made with small river clams. Ideal as an hors d'oeuvre—scoop it up with rice crackers to eat—and simple to make, the mushrooms are finished with crumbled nori, roughly chopped peanuts, cilantro, and a hefty squirt of lime. **Makes 1 cup; serves 4 as an hors d'oeuvres or a light snack**

FROM THE PANTRY/MAKE AHEAD

2 Toasted Sesame Rice Crackers (page 55)

___

1 stalk lemongrass

1 tablespoon vegetable oil

1 fresh red Thai bird chile, finely chopped

2 shallots, finely chopped, or ¼ cup finely chopped white onion

½ pound (225 g) button or portobello mushrooms, finely chopped

½ teaspoon sugar

¼ teaspoon salt, or more as needed

1 tablespoon plus 1 teaspoon vegetarian mushroom-flavored stir-fry sauce

2 sheets nori, torn and crumbled into small pieces with your hands

Freshly ground black pepper

1 lime, cut into wedges

2 tablespoons roughly chopped cilantro

3 tablespoons roasted unsalted peanuts, roughly chopped

Prepare the Toasted Sesame Rice Crackers.

Cut off the tough root end and trim 2 to 3 inches from the top of the lemongrass. Peel away two or three outer layers of the lemongrass and discard. Finely chop the lemongrass stalk.

Heat the oil in a medium skillet or wok over medium heat. Add the shallots and lemongrass and stir-fry until the lemongrass is fragrant and the shallots begin to soften. Add the chile, mushrooms, sugar, and salt and cook, stirring occasionally, for about 5 minutes, or until all of the liquid released from the mushrooms has evaporated. Stir in the mushroom-flavored vegetarian stir-fry sauce and crumbled nori. Stir-fry for another minute and turn off the heat. Add a few generous grinds of black pepper over the top, mix, and taste. Adjust the seasoning, if needed, with a pinch of salt or a squeeze of lime juice. Stir in the cilantro and peanuts and transfer the mushrooms to a serving bowl to serve warm or at room temperature.

Break a small piece from the rice cracker, spoon some of the lemongrass chile mushrooms on top, and enjoy.

GREEN MANGO RICE PAPER RIBBONS

BÁNH TRÁNG TRỘN CHAY

Every day, late in the afternoon, mobile cart vendors set up shop around Hồ Con Rùa, or Turtle Lake, a busy roundabout in Sài Gòn's third district. University and high school students soon congregate, ready to enjoy green mango rice paper ribbons, a newly popular street food best washed down with a glass of sugarcane juice.

One day in the midst of this after-school ritual I came upon a vendor who'd set up a tray with fifteen containers of ingredients. She tossed two big handfuls of thin rice paper ribbons into a large bowl. Then, quickly moving from container to container, she added pinches of shredded green mango, aromatic herbs, crunchy peanuts, and crispy shallots. She drizzled a spicy lime soy dressing over the top and gently massaged it all by hand. After portioning the food into small plastic bags, she handed me one with a pair of wooden chopsticks. Each bite burst with tangy, tart, hot, and sweet flavors.

My version uses five-spice tofu in place of the traditional meat or seafood.

Assuming you've got pantry basics on hand, this snack is quick to make. Just avoid the temptation to scale up the recipe or make it too far ahead; it's best served quickly and in made-to-order quantities. Also, rice paper tends to shatter when exposed to air for a while, so open the package just before you're ready to cut the rice paper into ribbons. **Serves 2**

FROM THE PANTRY/MAKE AHEAD

¼ cup thinly sliced store-bought five-spice tofu or ½ recipe homemade (page 69)

2 teaspoons Annatto Seed Oil (page 35)

2 tablespoons, Crispy Fried Shallots (page 37)

1 hard-boiled chicken egg, cut into 6 pieces, or 4 hard-boiled quail eggs, halved (see Note)

1 tablespoon (about 1 lime) fresh lime juice

2 teaspoons soy sauce

2 teaspoons water

1 teaspoon sugar

¼ fresh red Thai bird chile, seeded and finely chopped, or ½ teaspoon chile garlic paste

Six 8½-inch (22 cm) round rice papers

½ cup shredded green mango

2 tablespoons unsalted toasted peanuts, crushed

2 tablespoons thinly sliced scallion (about 1)

½ cup loosely packed mixed herb leaves (cilantro, basil, mint, Vietnamese coriander)

continues

Prepare the Five-Spice-Glazed Tofu, Annatto Seed Oil, Crispy Fried Shallots, and hard-boiled egg.

In a small bowl, stir together the lime juice, annatto seed oil, soy sauce, water, sugar, and chile until the sugar is fully dissolved.

Lay three rice papers over each other, lining up the woven, rattanlike pattern if possible. Working above a large shallow bowl, use scissors to cut along the lines of the bamboo pattern to make long ½-inch-wide (1.3 cm) ribbonlike noodles and let them fall into the bowl. (The rice paper breaks less when you cut along the lines of the pattern.) Repeat with the remaining three rice papers.

Drizzle the dressing over the rice paper ribbons and gently massage for 30 to 45 seconds, or until they're limp and lose their crispness. Add the green mango, tofu, egg, peanuts, shallots, scallions, and herbs to the bowl.

Toss gently and divide evenly between two small plates and serve with chopsticks.

Note:
Vegans can omit the hard-boiled eggs and slightly increase the tofu.

OPPOSITE Green Mango Rice Paper Ribbons (*bottom*) and Grilled Rice Paper with Mushroom Pâté, Egg, and Sriracha (*top*; page 120)

GRILLED RICE PAPER WITH MUSHROOM PÂTÉ, EGG, AND SRIRACHA

BÁNH TRÁNG NƯỚNG CHAY

Bánh tráng nướng is a sheet of rice paper lightly grilled over coals until partially crisp, then topped with pâté, scallions, and a spoon of raw egg. It's grilled a second time until the egg is cooked and the rice paper fully crisp, and finished with a fiery sriracha drizzle. Some vendors even assemble it like a pizza and sprinkle cheese on top. Apparently it originated in the hill town of Đá Lạt before making its way 190 miles southwest to Sài Gòn. Currently, the epicenter of grilled rice paper vendors in Sài Gòn is Hồ Con Rùa, or Turtle Lake. Vendors in cities like Huế and Hà Nội are starting to make their own versions. Like the Green Mango Rice Paper Ribbons (page 117), I've modified the street version that normally includes meat and/or seafood, by using Nutty Mushroom Pâté to make it vegetarian.

Using the oven is the most foolproof method. But once you get a hang of the timing and know what the rice paper looks like at the initial and final toasting, or if the weather allows, you can grill it over a hot charcoal barbecue (avoid gas barbecues—the flames tend to catch and burn the edges of the rice paper). **Serves 6**

FROM THE PANTRY/MAKE AHEAD
Nutty Mushroom Pâté (page 46)

Twelve 8½-inch (22 cm) round rice papers

12 scallions, finely chopped

3 to 4 large eggs, stirred together in a small bowl

Sriracha chile sauce

Prepare the Nutty Mushroom Pâté.

Position one rack in the middle level of the oven and a second rack on the level below (which should be the lowest level). Turn the oven light on and set your oven to broil at high heat. Place a round of rice paper directly on the middle-level rack. Within 12 to 15 seconds the rice paper will crisp up, turn white, and become a little wavy. Immediately and carefully remove it with your hands or tongs and set aside on a plate. Repeat with the remaining rice papers. This first part can be done an hour or so in advance.

Place a fine-mesh wire rack on a baking sheet and place a broiled sheet of rice paper on the rack. (If the rice paper with the pâté/egg mixture is placed directly on the baking sheet, it will stick and will not retoast.) In a small bowl, stir together 1 tablespoon each of nutty mushroom pâté, scallion, and scrambled egg. Spoon it onto the rice paper and use the back of the spoon to gently spread it as evenly as possible. Don't worry if you can't spread it completely to the edge.

Place the baking sheet in the oven on the lowest rack. After 1 to 1½ minutes, the edges of the rice paper will start to turn golden brown. During the next minute, in spots, the center part will toast and also turn golden brown. When this has happened (about 2½ minutes in total), remove the tray from the oven and transfer the broiled rice paper to a plate.

Cool briefly, about 30 seconds, to crisp up and drizzle a little bit of Sriracha sauce over top. Fold in half and eat with your hands. Repeat until all the filling is used up.

Note:
The longer your broiler is in use, the hotter it gets and the quicker the rice paper toasts and turns golden brown. The total broiling time may decrease to about 2 minutes. Similarly, if your oven does not heat consistently, you may need to adjust the level of the racks or timing of broiling.

TRANSLUCENT MUNG BEAN DUMPLINGS

BÁNH BỘT LỌC CHAY

You know those glorious steamed dumplings at a Chinese dim sum restaurant where the filling peeks through the translucent wrapper? These dumplings give the same impression, but you don't need to be a dim sum chef to make them.

From the late eighteenth to the middle of the twentieth century, Huế's royal court and upper and middle classes served elegant, refined small dishes during multicourse banquets. The elite could express their social rank through their chef's artistry, and these dumplings featured prominently. They're typically made two ways. One version, served at more formal occasions, wraps the dough and filling in thin, tube-shaped banana leaves. The other, more common version, and the recipe I'm sharing here, is for the attractive half-moon-shaped dumplings popular at many local markets and restaurants in Huế. Dumplings like these may have a sophisticated pedigree, but the technique for assembling them is forgiving enough that even my kids help me make them.

Prepare the filling in advance, as you'll want it ready to go as soon as your dumpling dough is ready to shape. (It's easier to shape the dough while it's still warm.)

Glistening with shallot oil and garnished with thinly sliced scallions, dumplings like these are best eaten warm or at room temperature with spicy soy sauce. **Makes about 20 dumplings**

FROM THE PANTRY/MAKE AHEAD

1 tablespoon Crispy Fried Shallots (page 37)

¼ cup Fragrant Shallot Oil (page 38)

½ cup Soy Chile Dipping Sauce (page 51),
   including the chile

FOR THE FILLING

¼ cup (1.5 ounces; 50g) dried split mung beans

1 dried wood ear mushroom

1 tablespoon Fragrant Shallot Oil or
   neutral-flavored vegetable oil

¼ teaspoon salt

OPPOSITE Translucent Mung Bean Dumplings with Soy
Chile Dipping Sauce

continues

FOR THE DOUGH

2 cups (8 ounces; 227 g) tapioca flour, plus a little more for dusting

½ cup (125 ml) boiling water

FOR GARNISH

½ cup Soy Chile Dipping Sauce

⅓ cup thinly sliced scallion, green part only

3 tablespoons Fragrant Shallot Oil

Make the Crispy Fried Shallots, Shallot Oil, or Quick Scallion Greens Oil (see below), and dipping sauce.

To make the filling: Place the mung beans in a bowl, cover by at least 1 inch (2.5cm) of water, and soak overnight (or cover with hot water and soak for 2 hours).

Pour hot water over the wood ear mushroom and leave to soak for 20 minutes.

Drain the mung beans and evenly spread them into a cheesecloth- or parchment-lined bamboo steamer or other type of steamer basket. Steam for 10 to 15 minutes, until pale yellow and fully tender. Remove from the steamer and cool to room temperature.

Drain the mushroom, cutting off any hard bits, and finely chop. Measure to verify you have about 2 tablespoons.

Place the cooled mung beans, wood ear mushroom, crispy shallots, 1 tablespoon shallot oil, and salt in a food processor. Pulse until well blended. Set aside.

To make the dough: Place the tapioca flour in a medium bowl and make a well in the center. Pour the just-boiled water over the flour (hot or lukewarm water won't properly hydrate it)

and use a wooden spoon to mix. Turn out onto a clean counter and knead for a few minutes, until smooth and malleable, like play dough. If you find the dough is too wet, sprinkle a tablespoon or two of tapioca flour onto the work surface and knead it into the dough. The dough should be a little tacky but not so much that it sticks to your hands. Return the dough to the bowl, press plastic wrap against it, and let rest for about 10 minutes.

Lightly oil a baking sheet or line a steamer tray with parchment paper (or lightly oiled banana leaves cut to fit your steamer if you have them).

To make the dumplings: Divide dough in half, covering the unused half with plastic wrap to protect it from drying out, and roll the dough into a log ¾- to 1-inch (2 to 2.5 cm) thick. Use a knife to cut the log into 10 even pieces (about ½ ounce; 18 g). Roll the pieces into rough marble-sized rounds. Using your fingers or palm, gently flatten a piece into a 1½-inch (4cm) round and press your thumb into the center to form a dimple. Spoon ½ teaspoon of the filling into the center and fold over into a crescent or half-moon. Pinch the edges together, making sure that when pinched together they're slightly thinner than the center, to seal and form a 2-inch (5 cm) dumpling. Place the dumpling in the steamer tray or on the baking sheet. Repeat until all of the dough or filling is used up. Arrange dumplings in the steamer, making sure they don't touch each other.

Return the water to a boil and carefully place the steamer on top. Cover and steam for about 8 minutes, or until the dumplings are translucent.

Transfer to a serving platter. Spoon on some of the Soy Chile Dipping Sauce, drizzle the dumplings with some shallot oil, and sprinkle with the scallion greens.

FREEZING AND REHEATING THE DUMPLINGS

If you plan to make the dumplings in advance and then reheat them before serving, immediately place fully steamed dumplings into a bowl of ice water for several minutes. Drain well and transfer to a parchment-lined plate or tray that will fit in your fridge or freezer. Cover tightly with plastic wrap and place in the refrigerator or freeze for several hours and transfer the individual dumplings to a zippered plastic bag and put back in the freezer for up to 2 weeks. To serve, steam dumplings, straight from the fridge or freezer, until filling is warm.

VARIATION

As you become more proficient in making these dumplings, be imaginative and try out other fillings. Just be sure that the ingredients are precooked and any excess moisture is eliminated. If not, the dumplings may easily break or become soggy. Or use the filling from Steamed Flat Rice Dumplings (page 219)

SUBSTITUTION:
QUICK SCALLION GREENS OIL

If you don't have any shallot oil on hand, make a quick scallion greens oil. Thinly slice the green parts of a bunch of scallions (about ½ cup). Heat ¼ cup vegetable oil in a small saucepan over high heat. When the oil is hot and starts to shimmer, turn the heat off and carefully stir in the scallion greens. Cool and transfer to a small bowl or small glass jar. Refrigerate for a couple of days.

4

VIBRANT SALADS

OPPOSITE Ingredients for
"Twelve Predestined Affinity" Salad (page 149)

Vietnamese salads electrify with their bold colors
and bright, vibrant flavors. Raw seasonal vegetables or green unripe fruits
explode with freshness, crispness, and texture. Clear, tangy dressings,
often made without oil, deliver further hits of hot, sour, salty, and
sweet in a remarkable feat of equilibrium. Add in punchy herbs, crispy
shallots, roasted peanuts, or sesame seeds and you're gilding an already
spectacular lily.

Called *nộm* in the North and *gỏi* (sometimes *trộn*) in the center and
South, Vietnamese salads derive their impeccable freshness from the close
proximity many Vietnamese have to the sources of their produce. Many homes
in Việt Nam have fruit trees on their property, so kitchen cooks can easily
pluck green-yellow pomelos (Palate-Cleansing Pomelo Salad, page 139); oval
mangoes (Tart and Spicy Green Mango Salad, page 134); young, spiky jackfruits
(Young Jackfruit Salad, page 137); or cone-shaped banana blossoms (Banana
Blossom Salad, page 143) straight from the branches. Urbanites who don't
have this luxury head to their local market to buy pre-shredded produce from
specialty vendors.

Outside Việt Nam, look for green unripe young fruits, like papaya or mango, at grocers that serve Asian or Latin American customers. Even seasonal Western vegetables will sub in well, so consider the recipes in this chapter both accessible and flexible.

Advance prep pays dividends here, as do tools like Japanese mandolines and julienne peelers, should you have them. (If you don't, a sharp knife works just fine.) To make salads ahead of time, shred and slice vegetables, mix the dressing, and pick herbs up to a day before serving. Place the main ingredients in a serving bowl, scatter the herbs over the top, then tightly wrap the bowl with plastic and store in the fridge until needed. Keeping your pantry stocked with crispy shallots, roasted peanuts, or sesame seeds is smart too, as these final flourishes lend huge textural impact. Right before serving, toss everything together.

Serve these salads as refreshing hors d' oeuvres or as a light meal (when garnished, for example, with sliced tofu). For larger groups, turn to the "Twelve Predestined Affinity" Salad (page 149) or Green Papaya Salad (page 131). Both will wow (and feed) crowds.

TOOLS AND TIPS FOR MAKING
FRUIT AND VEGETABLE MATCHSTICKS

If your knife skills aren't chef quality, don't despair. Several tools make quick work of the matchstick cut so common to Vietnamese salads, spring rolls, soup garnishes, and pickles. They're inexpensive and widely available in both Western kitchen supply stores and Asian groceries. Here are some tips for how to use them safely and effectively.

USING A JAPANESE MANDOLINE

A Japanese mandoline is my matchstick-cutting tool of choice. There's a bit of a learning curve, but stick with it and soon you'll be matchsticking like a pro. I'm partial to the Benriner brand, but whichever brand you buy, please read the safety precautions on the box or instructional insert carefully before using. No matter how skilled you become, always, *always* use the protective guard that comes with the slicer.

Turning the knob on the mandoline adjusts the thickness of the cut, producing slices as thin as $1/90$ inch to as thick as $1/5$ inch (0.3 mm to 5 mm). In general, I prefer a thickness of about $1/8$ inch (3 mm) for fruit and vegetable matchsticks.

Of the three interchangeable blades that come with most mandolines, only the medium and coarse blades make matchsticks suitable for salads and pickles. With some vegetables, you may need to first use the mandoline to produce thin slices, then finish cutting the matchsticks with a sharp knife.

A few final tips:

- Move the fruits or vegetables smoothly and with good control. Work slowly to reduce the risk of slippage. Periodically stop and check your cuts to verify their thickness, turning the knob and adjusting the setting as necessary.

- When working with irregular-shaped foods like carrots, cut them first into 2-inch (5 cm) lengths, then trim one side flat. (The flat side will go against the mandoline's blade, with the guard between the vegetable and your hand.). Before slicing large vegetables like kohralbi, jicama, and cabbage, trim them to the width of the mandoline. When you've sliced down to a small nub of fruit or vegetable, stop using the mandoline and finish slicing with a knife. (Or save the bits for snacking or vegetable stocks.)

- Once you've cut the fruit or vegetable into thin slices, neatly stack several slices and cut them with a knife into 2-inch (5 cm) matchsticks. If they're not completely uniform, don't worry. It's nice to see the occasional irregular hand-cut shape.

USING A JULIENNE PEELER

Large Asian grocers and online retailers also carry julienne peelers. The Kiwi Pro Slice julienne peeler (my pick) is equipped with a large stainless steel blade with a wavy edge. When you peel a vegetable or unripe fruit in short, shallow strokes using light pressure, you create thin strips of julienne vegetables or fruits perfect for the recipes in this book. Applying greater pressure produces crinklier cuts.

GREEN PAPAYA SALAD

NỘM ĐU ĐỦ CHAY

This northern Vietnamese salad features thin strips of crispy green papaya marinated in a sweet and sour dressing, topped with lemony herbs and crushed peanuts. Look for unripe green papayas year-round at Southeast Asian grocers and red, yellow, and purple carrots from the farmers' market. Tender kohlrabi also works particularly well here. For a light meal, top with thin slices of Five-Spice-Glazed Tofu (page 69). **Serves 4 to 6**

FROM THE PANTRY/MAKE AHEAD

3 tablespoons Crispy Fried Shallots (page 37)

———

1 medium (1¼ pounds; 570 g) hard, green unripe papaya

1 medium (¼ pound; 112 g) carrot or 1 cup drained Pickled Carrots and Daikon (page 47)

FOR THE DRESSING

¼ cup plus 2 tablespoons (90 ml) rice vinegar

3 tablespoons sugar

1 tablespoon soy sauce

1 teaspoon salt

2 garlic cloves, minced

1 fresh red Thai bird chile, seeded and finely chopped

⅓ cup roughly chopped Vietnamese balm (or a combination of mint and Thai basil or lemon basil)

⅓ cup roughly chopped cilantro

3 tablespoons roasted unsalted peanuts, roughly chopped

Prepare the Crispy Fried Shallots.

Peel the papaya, cut off the top end, and slice it in half lengthwise. Scrape out the tiny unripe white seeds and thin layer from the interior with a spoon. Shred using a Japanese mandoline or julienne peeler. You should have about 6 cups. Place in a colander and quickly rinse with lukewarm water. Drain well, squeeze dry in a clean dish towel, and transfer to a large bowl. Peel and cut the carrot into matchsticks and place over the papaya.

Put the rice vinegar, sugar, soy sauce, salt, garlic, and chile into a small bowl and stir until the sugar is fully dissolved. Taste. It should be tart, a touch sweet, and mildly spicy. Adjust the balance of flavors by adding a touch more sugar or chile to taste.

Pour the dressing over the papaya and carrot and mix well. Marinate for about 10 minutes, occasionally massaging and tossing the salad. Toss in the Vietnamese balm and cilantro, and half of the peanuts and fried shallots and mix well. Lift out the salad, leaving most of the dressing in the bottom of the bowl, and mound

continues

it onto a shallow serving bowl or plate. Drizzle a spoon or two of dressing over the top if you like. Sprinkle the remaining peanuts and shallots over the salad just before serving.

VARIATION

KOHLRABI AND CARROT SALAD

Select two young tender kohlrabi that are each approximately the size of a baseball (about ¾ pound in total). Peel the kohlrabi and cut into matchsticks (there is no need to give the kohlrabi matchsticks a quick rinse). Proceed with rest of the recipe, reducing the marinating time to 5 minutes.

Note:
If a large green papaya is all you can find, add the extra matchsticks for an additional firm bite to Rainbow Rice Paper Rolls (page 95), make into a quick pickle (page 48) and use in a bánh mì sandwich, or cut into bite-sized chunks and add to the Curried Vegetable Stew with Baguette (page 253).

OPPOSITE Kohlrabi and Carrot Salad

TART AND SPICY GREEN MANGO SALAD

GỎI XOÀI

I make this salad often because it's extraordinarily delicious. Fully mature green mangoes sold at Asian or Latin grocers are harvested for their crisp texture and sweet-tart flavor. They're optimal. Mangoes sold at supermarkets are often significantly underripe, and these underripe mangoes are great to use here. Select mangoes that are hard and firm and do not give when pressed with your thumb. If not using them immediately, refrigerate to prevent them from ripening and softening. Finally, taste a piece of mango before making the dressing. Mangoes vary widely in flavor, and you'll want a handle on its baseline sweetness before adjusting the lime, sugar, and vinegar in the dressing. **Serves 4**

FROM THE PANTRY/MAKE AHEAD

2 tablespoons Crispy Fried Shallots (optional, page 37)

_____

2 unripe green mangoes (1½ pounds; 700 g), peeled and cut into matchsticks

¼ pound (113 g) jicama, cut into matchsticks (1 cup)

FOR THE DRESSING

3 tablespoons sugar

3 tablespoons water

2 tablespoons rice vinegar

1 teaspoon soy sauce

1 tablespoon plus 1 teaspoon fresh lime juice

½ teaspoon salt

1 fresh red Thai bird chile, seeded and finely chopped

1 garlic clove, finely chopped

1 cup Thai basil leaves, large leaves roughly cut or torn

⅓ cup mint leaves, large leaves roughly cut or torn

2 to 3 tablespoons roasted unsalted peanuts, roughly chopped

Prepare the Crispy Fried Shallots, if using.

Place the green mango and jicama matchsticks in a medium bowl.

Spoon the sugar, water, rice vinegar, soy sauce, lime juice, and salt into a small bowl. Stir to fully dissolve the sugar. Mix in the chile and garlic. Taste and adjust the seasoning if needed. Toss the herbs into the bowl and pour the dressing over the mango and jicama. Mix well.

Place the salad in a serving dish and garnish with the peanuts and crispy shallots, if using. (Add another tablespoon of chopped roasted peanuts if not using crispy fried shallots.)

How to Cut a Green or Unripe Mango into Matchsticks

Use a vegetable peeler or sharp paring knife to peel the skin from the mangoes. Resist the urge to use a box grater to grate the mangoes since it yields shreds that are too short and too thin. To cut the mango into matchsticks, use one of the following options.

USING A JAPANESE MANDOLINE

Mangoes can sometimes be fibrous. I prefer to use the flat blade on a mandoline, instead of using one of the interchangeable blades, to cut the mango into consistent even slices. Then I cut them into matchsticks with a knife.

Cut a thin slice of mango from each of the two large, rounded sides. Place one flat side down on the surface of a Japanese mandoline and see if the mango fits onto the sliding surface; if the mango is wider than the sliding surface, trim off several slices from one of the other narrow sides. Shave one of the large sides into four or five 1/8- to 1/4-inch (3 to 6 mm) slices or until you reach the large flat stone in the mango's center. Repeat with the other large side and two remaining narrower sides.

Stack four or five mango slices at a time and cut them lengthwise into long, 1/8- to 1/4-inch-wide (3 to 6 mm) matchsticks until all the slices are cut up.

HAND-CUTTING USING A KNIFE

Create a flat surface by trimming off several slices from one of the narrow sides of the mango. Turn the mango onto this flat side, against the cutting board to act as a stable base, and cut one of the large sides into 1/8- to 1/4-inch (3 to 6 mm) slices until you reach the large flat stone in the mango's center. Turn the mango around and slice the other large side. Turn the mango onto one of its flat surfaces and cut the remaining narrow side. Stack four or five mango slices at a time and cut them lengthwise into long, 1/8- to 1/4-inch-wide (3 to 6 mm), matchsticks until all of the slices are cut up.

YOUNG JACKFRUIT SALAD

GỎI MÍT CHAY

Young green jackfruit is a superb conductor of flavor, even more so when shredded, as the shreds soak up loads of dressing. Canned young unripe jackfruit in brine is readily available at Asian grocers, and increasingly at supermarkets, and makes a fine substitute. Just read labels carefully and avoid canned ripe jackfruit that contains sugar syrup, which is intended for dessert. Light and refreshing, this salad makes an ideal predinner bite when spooned atop toasted rice crackers and paired with beer, cocktails, or fruity white wine.   **Serves 3 or 4 as part of a multidish meal**

FROM THE PANTRY/MAKE AHEAD

1 tablespoon Toasted Sesame Seeds (page 33)

2 tablespoons Crispy Fried Shallots (page 37)

1 or 2 Toasted Sesame Rice Crackers (page 55)

One 17-ounce (482 g) can young green jackfruit (see photo on page 307) in water (drained weight 280 g)

1 tablespoon vegetable oil

¼ pound (112 g) oyster mushrooms, trimmed and cut into bite-sized pieces (1¼ cup)

¼ teaspoon salt

¼ teaspoon freshly ground black pepper

½ medium carrot, cut into matchsticks (½ cup)

½ small white onion, thinly sliced

⅓ cup roughly chopped Vietnamese coriander leaves

2 tablespoons roughly chopped cilantro

2 tablespoons roughly chopped mint

FOR THE DRESSING

3 tablespoons sugar

¼ cup water

2 tablespoons rice vinegar

1 teaspoon soy sauce

1 tablespoon plus 1 teaspoon fresh lime juice

½ teaspoon salt

½ fresh mild long red chile, seeded and finely chopped, or 1 fresh red Thai bird chile for more heat

1 garlic clove, finely chopped

Prepare the Toasted Sesame Seeds, Crispy Fried Shallots, and Toasted Sesame Rice Crackers.

Drain the jackfruit, rinse well, and gently squeeze out any excess water. Cut or pull apart into bite-sized strips or shreds, discarding any hard sections, and place in a large bowl.

OPPOSITE Young Jackfruit Salad with toasted rice cracker

continues

Heat the oil in a large skillet over medium-high heat. Add the mushrooms, ¼ teaspoon salt and pepper, stirring to coat the mushrooms lightly with oil. Cook for 2 to 3 minutes, without shaking the pan or stirring, to brown the mushrooms. Give them a quick stir and cook for another 2 minutes, again without stirring. Push the jackfruit to one side of the bowl and spoon the mushrooms into the empty side to cool.

Make the dressing: Spoon the sugar, water, rice vinegar, soy sauce, lime juice, and ½ teaspoon salt into a small bowl. Stir to fully dissolve the sugar. Add and mix the chile and garlic into the dressing. Taste and adjust the seasoning if needed.

Toss the carrot, onion, Vietnamese coriander, cilantro, and mint over the jackfruit. Pour the dressing into the bowl and mix well. Scoop the salad, leaving most of the dressing in the bowl, onto a serving dish. Spoon half of the dressing, or to taste, over the salad. Decoratively sprinkle the toasted sesame seeds and crispy shallots over the top.

To eat, break off a bite-sized piece of the rice cracker and spoon a small amount of the salad on top.

PALATE-CLEANSING POMELO SALAD

GỎI BƯỞI CHAY

Sweeter than grapefruits, pomelos work beautifully in salads, especially when paired with tart green mango. Although I might normally lean toward cucumber or jicama in a salad like this one (and both would be excellent), my trusted vegetable vendor in Hà Nội prefers green mango in this salad, and as soon as I made it her way I knew why. Refreshing and slightly spicy, this salad complements more intense dishes such as Soy Ginger Glazed Eggplant (page 247) and Five-Spice-Glazed Tofu (page 69).   **Serves 4 as part of a multidish meal**

FROM THE PANTRY/MAKE AHEAD

2 tablespoons Crispy Fried Shallots (page 37)

1 Toasted Sesame Rice Cracker (page 55)

—

3 tablespoons vegetable oil

¼ pound (112 g) firm tofu, cut into ¼-inch-thick (6 mm) slabs, patted dry on paper towel

1 (1½ pounds; 650 g) ripe pomelo (see Note)

½ cup unripe or green mango, cucumber, jicama, apple or bean sprouts

1 tablespoon plus 1 teaspoon sugar

2 tablespoons fresh lime juice

1 tablespoon plus 2 teaspoons soy sauce

1 tablespoon water

1 garlic clove, finely chopped

1 fresh red Thai bird chile, seeded and finely chopped

⅓ cup mint leaves, larger leaves torn

3 tablespoons cilantro leaves, roughly chopped

2 tablespoons roasted unsalted peanuts, roughly chopped

Prepare the Crispy Fried Shallots and Toasted Sesame Rice Cracker.

Place a plate lined with paper towel next to the stove.

Heat the oil in a small skillet over medium-high heat. Carefully add the tofu slices, cooking for 2 to 3 minutes before carefully turning them over. Cook for another 2 minutes, until evenly golden brown on both sides. Transfer to the paper-towel-lined plate to drain and cool.

Cut into ⅛-inch (0.5 cm) strips.

Cut about ¾ inch (2 cm) off each end of the pomelo and discard. Score the pomelo rind by cutting it vertically, about ¾ inch (2 cm) deep, from end to end. Repeat to get five or six segments. At one of the ends of the pomelo, use a small paring knife to cut around the perimeter about ½ inch (1.5 cm) from the edge of the rind, roughly where the pulp and rind meet. Dig your fingers between the rind and the flesh and pull the scored rind away. Repeat until all of the rind is removed and you're left with the fruit with a white pithy membrane clinging to it.

continues

At one of the ends where the segments come together put your thumbs into the center dimple and pry the fruit into two parts. Use your fingers to pull the individual segments apart and to peel off any white membrane that remains (a small paring knife may come in handy to scrape away some of the membrane). Over a large bowl, pull or break each segment into small bite-sized pieces and place, along with the green mango, into the bowl.

Spoon the sugar, lime juice, soy sauce, and water into a small bowl. Stir to fully dissolve the sugar. Add and mix the garlic and chile into the dressing. Taste and adjust the seasoning if needed.

Pour the dressing over the fruit and mix well. Add the tofu, mint, cilantro, peanuts, and crispy shallots and toss lightly.

Transfer to a shallow bowl or serving platter and serve immediately. To eat, break off a bite-sized piece of the rice cracker and spoon a small amount of the salad on top.

Note:
You can substitute grapefruit for the pomelo, but set the grapefruit segments into a colander set over a bowl for 5 to 10 minutes to drain any excess liquid. Cut the segments into large bite-sized pieces and prepare the salad as described (drink the juice as an extra treat).

Pomelos in the street

OPPOSITE Palate-Cleansing Pomelo Salad made with ruby red grapefruit

BANANA BLOSSOM SALAD

NỘM HOA CHUỐI/GỎI BẮP CHUỐI

My son says that banana blossoms are magical, and he's right. In Việt Nam, cooks cut them into thin curls that twist around bean sprouts and fresh herbs with enchanting aesthetic results. Tossing them with a bright dressing creates an alluring salad.

Preparing a banana blossom is similar to preparing an artichoke. First, peel off the tough outer leaves to expose the pale leaves underneath. Trim away the pale yellow buds close to the base. (These are actually immature bananas-to-be.) Transfer the sliced leaves to a bowl of acidulated water (fresh lime juice works best) to inhibit browning.

While fresh banana blossoms are available year-round at Asian grocers, if you can't find them, substitute three-quarters of a green cabbage and one-quarter of a red cabbage for a superb Vietnamese-style coleslaw.

Serves 4 to 6 as part of a multidish meal

FROM THE PANTRY/MAKE AHEAD

Toasted Sesame Seeds (page 55)

Crispy Tofu Skin Strips (page 43) or thin slices of fried tofu (page 60) (optional)

———

¼ cup fresh lime juice

1 (about 1¼ pounds; 570 g) fresh young banana blossom

FOR THE DRESSING

¼ cup rice vinegar

1 or 2 tablespoons fresh lime juice

3 tablespoons sugar

2 tablespoons soy sauce

1 teaspoon salt

1 garlic clove, minced

½ fresh mild long red chile, seeded and finely chopped

1 cup (3 ounce; 80 g) bean sprouts

1 small carrot, cut into matchsticks (about 1 cup)

⅔ cup roughly chopped Vietnamese coriander or Thai basil

3 tablespoons roasted unsalted peanuts, roughly chopped

Prepare the Toasted Sesame Seeds and the Crispy Tofu Skin, if using.

Fill a large bowl with 6 cups cold water and ¼ cup lime juice and place near a cutting board.

Peel off several outer layers (two to three for a small blossom and up to five for a very large blossom) of dark petals from the banana

OPPOSITE Banana Blossom Salad

continues

blossom until you reach the inner petals that are whitish yellow in color near the stem and then halfway up become light purple and tightly cling around each other at the tip. Reserve one or two petals for presentation if desired. Cut the banana blossom in half lengthwise. Lay both halves cut side down on a cutting board. Beginning from the narrow tip slice as thinly as possible using a sharp knife or Japanese mandoline, occasionally transferring the slices to the acidulated water to prevent any immediate discoloration. Briefly pause when you reach about 4 inches from the bottom of the stem or when you see some small bits of cut immature banana buds on the cutting board. Peel away the remainder of the petals and discard any of the small bunches of buds. Stack three or four petals on top of each other, thinly slice, and transfer to the acidulated water. Repeat with the remaining petals and the other half. (You can slice the banana blossom up to a couple of hours in advance. If you plan to do so, press several layers of strong paper towel or a clean dish towel against the banana blossom slices to keep them submerged to limit discoloration.)

Make the dressing: Place the rice vinegar, 1 tablespoon of the lime juice, the sugar, soy sauce, salt, garlic, and chile in a small bowl and stir until the sugar is fully dissolved. Taste, adding another tablespoon of lime juice if you want more tang. Adjust the flavoring to your preferred balance of sweet, salty, and spicy. Set aside.

If you see a few small bits of banana flowers floating on the top of the water, don't worry. But if there is a lot, carefully skim off as much as you can. Lift the sliced banana blossom out of the acidulated water, pat dry with a clean dish towel, and place in a large shallow bowl. Add the bean sprouts, carrot, Vietnamese coriander, half of the peanuts and sesame seeds. Drizzle the dressing into the bowl and toss to mix well. Place a reserved banana petal or two on a serving platter, if desired, and nicely arrange the salad in the petals. Sprinkle the remaining peanuts and sesame seeds over the top. Garnish with either shreds of crispy tofu skin or thin slices of fried tofu, if using.

CUCUMBER AND SHREDDED TOFU SKIN SALAD

GỎI DƯA CHUỘT ĐẬU HŨ KY

Whenever I make this simple salad of cucumber, tofu skin, and Vietnamese coriander, I can't stop eating it. If there's any left after the meal (which is rare, trust me), I'll continue to pick at it as I tidy the kitchen. Crumbled tofu skin sticks, also called *dried bean curd sticks*, lend this salad a meaty, toothsome quality. (You'll find them at well-stocked Chinese grocery stores.) Just plan ahead as it takes a few hours to rehydrate them. Or substitute sautéed oyster mushrooms. You can even split the difference as I often do, using half tofu skin and half sautéed mushrooms.   **Serves 4 as part of a multidish meal**

FROM THE PANTRY/MAKE AHEAD

2 teaspoons Fragrant Shallot Oil (page 38) or vegetable oil

Three 1-foot-long (31 cm) tofu skin or dried bean curd sticks (1½ ounces; 45 g)

1 teaspoon soy sauce

½ cup thinly sliced sweet onion, such as Vidalia or Walla Walla

¼ English cucumber or 3 small (Kirby or Persian) cucumbers (½ pound; 225 g)

3 tablespoons rice vinegar

1 tablespoon sugar

½ teaspoon salt

¼ cup packed Vietnamese coriander leaves

½ fresh red mild long chile, seeded and thinly sliced

Pinch of freshly ground black pepper

1 tablespoon roasted unsalted peanuts, roughly chopped

Prepare the Fragrant Shallot Oil, if using.

Place the tofu skin sticks in a casserole dish (snap them, keeping them in long lengths, if too long for the dish). Fill the dish with hot water and lay a small-mesh rack or a large stainless-steel spoon (something that won't float) across them to keep them submerged.

Quick Soak Method: Place the casserole dish in a 200°F (95°C) oven for 1 to 1½ hours.

Long Soak Method: Or soak at room temperature for at least 8 hours before you plan to prepare the salad.

The tofu skin sticks are ready when they are a lighter color and there are no dried parts at the core of the sticks when you cut through them.

Drain, cut off, and discard any tough parts (this tends to be the thin curved part at one end that touched the stick or rack when drying). Cut the sticks into 2-inch (5 cm) lengths.

continues

Gently squeeze out any excess water and pat dry with a clean dish towel. Pull apart into shreds or cut three or four times lengthwise—if using looser tofu skin sticks, tear them into about ¼-inch-wide (6 mm) strips—and place in a small bowl. You should have about ¾ cup. Toss with the soy sauce.

Soak the onion in a bowl of ice water for 10 minutes.

Cut the cucumber in half lengthwise. Use a small spoon to scrape out and discard the seeds. Cut on a diagonal into ¼-inch (6 mm) slices and place in a large bowl. Or slice small cucumbers crosswise into ¼-inch (6 mm) coins.

In a small bowl, mix together the rice vinegar, sugar, shallot oil, and salt. Stir to fully dissolve the sugar.

Drain the onions and press lightly with the towel to remove any excess moisture. Add to the cucumber along with the tofu skin strips, Vietnamese coriander, and chile. Pour the dressing over the salad and toss well. Mound the salad onto a serving dish and sprinkle black pepper and peanuts over the top.

VARIATION

EARTHY OYSTER MUSHROOM AND CUCUMBER SALAD

Replace the tofu strips with bite-sized pieces of ½ pound (225 g) trimmed oyster mushrooms. Cook the mushrooms in a tablespoon of vegetable oil over medium-high heat for a couple of minutes, stirring occasionally to color lightly before adding the soy sauce. Cool before mixing with the rest of the ingredients.

Cucumbers, fresh red Thai bird chiles, and limes

COOLING BITTER MELON APPLE SALAD

GỎI MƯỚP ĐẮNG

In the last few years, stylish vegetarian restaurants serving modern dishes have started popping up in Việt Nam's larger cities. A young chef from one such a restaurant in Hà Nội taught me how to make this cooling salad combining translucent slices of raw bitter melon and tart apple, all tossed in a hot and sweet dressing. For those new to bitter melon, here's your ideal point of entry. **Serves 3 or 4 as part of a multidish meal**

FROM THE PANTRY/MAKE AHEAD

1 teaspoon Toasted Sesame Seeds (page 33)

1 tablespoon Crispy Fried Shallots (page 37)

1 Toasted Sesame Rice Cracker (page 55)

1 medium dried wood ear mushroom

1 tablespoon dried hijiki or wakame seaweed

1 small or ½ large (¼ pound; 125g) bitter melon

¼ tart green apple, cut into matchsticks (unpeeled)

2 inches (5 cm) carrot, cut into matchsticks or ¼ cup Pickled Carrots and Daikon (page 47)

1½ inches (4 cm) English cucumber or ½ small (Kirby or Persian) cucumber, thinly sliced (⅓ cup)

1 shallot, thinly sliced

1 tablespoon finely chopped fresh red mild long chile or red bell pepper

2 tablespoons roughly chopped Thai basil

1 tablespoon roasted unsalted peanuts or unsalted cashews, roughly chopped

FOR THE DRESSING

¼ tart green apple, roughly chopped

1½ fresh red Thai bird chile, seeded and roughly chopped

3 tablespoons sugar

1 tablespoon plus 1 teaspoon soy sauce

1 teaspoon salt

2 garlic cloves, roughly chopped

1 tablespoon fresh lime juice

Prepare the Toasted Sesame Seeds, Crispy Fried Shallots, and Toasted Sesame Rice Cracker.

Place the mushroom and seaweed in a bowl and cover with hot water. Soak for 15 minutes or until soft and pliable.

Cut the bitter melon in half crosswise. (If using a large bitter melon, cut it crosswise slightly less than in the middle and use the smaller piece. Cut it in half lengthwise and scrape out the seeds and spongy membrane.) Use a small spoon or your fingers to push and scrape out the seeds and spongy inner membrane. Use

continues

a Japanese mandoline or sharp knife to slice into paper-thin rounds (or half-moons if using a large bitter melon). Soak in a bowl of ice water as you prepare the rest of the ingredients.

Cut out the mushroom's small chewy center and discard. Cut the mushroom thinly into 1-inch (3 cm) lengths. Measure out 2 tablespoons and place in a medium mixing bowl. Squeeze any excess water from the seaweed and thinly slice. Add to the bowl. Toss the apple matchsticks, carrot, cucumber, sliced shallots, 1 tablespoon chile, and Thai basil over the top.

Make the dressing: Place the roughly chopped apple, roughly chopped chile, sugar, soy sauce, salt, garlic, and lime juice in a blender and blend until pureed. Transfer to a bowl or small glass jar.

Drain the bitter melon slices into a colander and pat dry with paper towels or a clean dish towel before adding to the rest of the ingredients.

Spoon 3 tablespoons of the dressing (store the remainder in the fridge for up to 5 days to use for another salad) into the bowl and toss well to coat all of the bitter melon slices evenly. Transfer to a serving dish and garnish with the toasted sesame seeds, crispy shallots, and the peanuts. To eat, place a small portion of the salad on morsels of rice cracker.

"TWELVE PREDESTINED AFFINITY" SALAD

(NỘM) THẬP NHỊ NHÂN DUYÊN

The English translation of Vietnamese dishes on restaurant menus can be both funny and confusing. Out of sheer curiosity, I often order dishes like Fried Bumps or Princess Frog Legs, which is how I chanced upon this particular salad. Called "Twelve Predestined Affinity" on the menu of a popular vegetarian spot in Huế, this salad of artistically arranged vegetable mounds, crispy noodles, leafy herbs, and a lemongrass and lime dressing tempted me as much with its lofty name as with its promising flavors.

Because it stands up well, you can make the salad several hours before serving. Put the moist vegetables (and fruit) in the bottom of a mixing bowl and the firmer, drier vegetables on top. Save the dressing for the serving time, drizzling it on at the last minute. **Serves 4 to 6 as part of a multidish meal**

FROM THE PANTRY/MAKE AHEAD

2 teaspoons Toasted Sesame Seeds (page 33)

¼ pound (112 g) firm tofu, drained

1 cup (250 ml) vegetable oil

½ cup (2 ounces; 60 g) fresh egg noodles or 1 scant cup fried chow mein noodles

FOR THE DRESSING

2 tablespoons fresh lime juice

2 tablespoons soy sauce

1 tablespoon sugar

1 lemongrass stalk, bottom third finely chopped

1 garlic clove, finely chopped

1 fresh mild long red chile, seeded and finely chopped

½ cup (2 ounces; 60 g) fresh pineapple matchsticks

½ cup (2 ounces; 60 g) cucumber matchsticks

½ cup (2 ounces; 60 g) lotus stem or root-let matchstick (packed in brine, drained, rinsed, cut in half crosswise, and quartered lengthwise) or celery matchsticks

½ cup (2 ounces; 60 g) jicama matchsticks

½ cup (2 ounces; 60 g) carrot matchsticks

¾ cup (2½ ounces; 75 g) thinly sliced or shredded red cabbage

1 small handful (1½ ounces; 45 g) bean sprouts, rinsed and drained

½ cup packed (40 g) mixed herbs: Vietnamese coriander or cilantro, Thai basil, mint

2 tablespoons roasted unsalted peanuts, roughly chopped

continues

Prepare the Toasted Sesame Seeds.

Cut the tofu into rectangles 1½ by 3 or 4 inches (4 cm by 7.5 or 10 cm) and about ⅓ inch (1 cm) thick.

Use paper towel to pat dry to remove any excess moisture.

Place a large plate lined with paper towel next to the stove.

Heat the oil in a wok or medium pot over medium-high heat. (If using prefried chow mein noodles, omit this step and panfry the tofu in 3 tablespoons of oil.) After a couple of minutes, when the oil is hot, carefully add the tofu. Fry for a couple of minutes, until golden, and then flip over and fry for another couple of minutes. Remove with a spider or slotted spoon and drain on the paper-towel-lined plate. Set aside to cool.

Allow the oil to reheat for 15 to 20 seconds. Carefully drop half of the fresh noodles into the hot oil. Use a spider or slotted spoon to gently push and stir them below the surface a few times during the first 20 seconds. At that point the sizzling sound should begin to subside and the noodles will look puffy. Flip the mass of noodles and cook for another 10 seconds or so. Remove with the spider or slotted spoon and drain on the paper-towel-lined plate. Repeat with the remaining noodles and set aside.

Cut the tofu into thin strips. Lightly squeeze the cooled noodles to break them into smaller pieces.

Make the dressing: Spoon the lime juice, soy sauce, and sugar into a small bowl and stir until the sugar is fully dissolved. Add the lemongrass, garlic, and chile. Allow the dressing to stand as you prepare the rest of the ingredients. Taste and adjust the seasonings if needed.

Add the salad ingredients to a large bowl in the following order: pineapple, cucumber, lotus stem, jicama, carrot, cabbage, bean sprouts, and tofu.

Right before serving, sprinkle the herbs and pour dressing over the top. Toss to mix well. Garnish with the toasted sesame seeds, the peanuts, and the chow mein noodles for a burst of crunch. Serve immediately.

SEASONAL SUBSTITUTIONS

For red cabbage: thinly sliced Napa cabbage, radicchio, Belgian endive, or kale

For jicama: matchsticks of kohlrabi, broccoli stems, or daikon

For lotus stems: matchsticks of celeriac, or thinly sliced chard stems

For cucumber: matchsticks of sweet or tart apples or thinly sliced green, red, or yellow bell peppers

OPPOSITE "Twelve Predestined Affinity" Salad

LIGHT SOUPS

OPPOSITE Seasonal vegetables for sale
by a temporary vendor at a market in Hà Nội.

Việt Nam's broth-based soups (*canh*) are light, clear, energizing, and economical. Vietnamese cooks retain and season the water in which a meal's vegetables are cooked, jump-starting a soup's stock, garnishing it with a vegetable or two and a fresh herb. In the past, broth was a typical "beverage" at Vietnamese meals as one didn't normally sip water or other drinks when eating. Today you'll still see diners tip some broth into their rice bowls at the end of a meal to gather up any flavors and remnants, leaving nothing to waste. This practice is especially common among members of the older generation.

The soups in this chapter are easily adapted for Western-style eating. Make the Light Vegetable Stock (page 30) first and you'll have a head start on the recipes that follow. The Savoy Cabbage Tofu Parcels in Broth (page 159) and the Hot and Sour Tamarind Soup (page 161) are my favorite ways to begin a special meal. If you're looking for more substantial soups that can be meals on their own, see Chapter Six: Bowls of Noodles.

CLEAR BROTH SOUP
WITH TOFU AND LEAFY GREENS

CANH RAU

Clear broth soups like this one arose from times of necessity and frugality. Historically, Việt Nam experienced periods of famine, most recently following the Vietnam War, forcing cooks to come up with practical recipes that retain flavor and fill hungry bellies. Using this recipe as a template, rotate vegetables and herbs according to the season and strive for a balance of bitter, sweet, earthy, and sharp flavors. (I've given you some suggestions to get you started.) Whether sipped throughout a basic rice meal or whenever you're feeling unwell, this soup provides great comfort with relative ease.

Serves 4 or 5 as part of a multidish rice meal

FROM THE PANTRY/MAKE AHEAD

1 quart (1 liter) vegetable cooking water or Light Vegetable Stock (page 30)

1 to 2 teaspoon Fragrant Shallot Oil (page 38) (optional)

½ teaspoon Mushroom Powder (page 36)

½ pound (225 g) firm tofu, cut into 1-inch (2.5 cm) cubes

Pinch of sugar

½ teaspoon salt

Generous handful leafy greens (see options below), stemmed and very roughly chopped

Freshly ground black pepper

1 teaspoon sesame oil (optional)

2 tablespoons roughly chopped Chinese celery leaves

Prepare the Light Vegetable Stock, the Fragrant Shallot Oil, if using, and the Mushroom Powder.

Bring the vegetable stock to a boil in a medium pot over medium heat. Add tofu, sugar, salt, and ½ teaspoon mushroom powder and simmer for a couple of minutes. Toss in the leafy greens and simmer for another minute or two, until tender. Taste and adjust the salt. Twist a few grinds of black pepper into the soup and drizzle a teaspoon or two of shallot oil or the sesame oil, if desired. Ladle a scant cup of soup into small soup bowls, garnish with some Chinese celery leaves, and serve with a rice meal. Gradually sip the soup throughout the meal, leaving some to tidy up your rice bowl and to finish the meal with.

continues

SUBSTITUTIONS AND OPTIONS

· For the Tofu: daikon, carrot, chayote, kohlrabi, pumpkin, squash, zucchini, mushrooms—for denser vegetables, cut into ¼-inch (1.3 cm) slices; for tender ones cut into bite-sized chunks).

· Leafy green varieties: Water spinach, regular spinach, red amaranth, watercress, chrysanthemum greens, mustard greens, chard, green cabbage.

· Herb varieties: Cilantro, scallions, chives, Chinese chives, sorrel, Thai basil.

Peeled beets, carrots, chayote, and daikon for soup are sold at markets throughout southern Việt Nam.

MAGENTA BEET TOFU SOUP

CANH CỦ DỀN

One morning I hitched a ride on a small tour bus from Sài Gòn to the Củ Chi tunnels, the vast underground system built by the Việt Cộng during the Vietnam War. The bus stopped near a fantastical-looking building—the main temple of the Cao Đài religion—in the city of Tây Ninh, an hour or so northwest of Sài Gòn. Cao Đài followers believe that the Supreme Being founded Cao Đài as a way to integrate all of the great religions into a single new faith. I followed white-robed men and women (and some elders in blue, red, or yellow) into the building to observe the noon service. The vast hall exploded in color, with dragon-wrapped pillars, carved windows, and a nine-foot globe of the All-Seeing Eye (the sacred symbol of Cao Đài).

After the service, some of the female elders invited me to join them for their vegetarian lunch. We ate this deeply satisfying soup, tinted magenta from sweet, earthy beets. **Serves 4 as part of a multidish meal**

FROM THE PANTRY/MAKE AHEAD

1 quart (1 liter) vegetable cooking water or Light Vegetable Stock (page 30)

½ teaspoon salt, or to taste

1 medium beet (¼ pound; 112 g), quartered, and sliced ⅛ inch (0.5 cm) thick

½ medium carrot (¼ pound; 112 g), sliced ⅛ inch (0.5 cm) thick

½ chayote or kohlrabi (¼ pound; 112 g), halved and sliced ⅛ inch (0.5 cm) thick

¼ pound (112 g) firm tofu, cut into 1-inch (2.5 cm) cubes

⅛ teaspoon freshly ground black pepper

1 tablespoon roughly chopped cilantro or Chinese celery

Prepare the Light Vegetable Stock, if using. Pour the vegetable stock and salt into a medium pot and bring to a boil over medium-high heat. (If using vegetable cooking water, you most likely will have already added some salt to it, so do not add the full ½ teaspoon of salt.) Add the beet and carrot, partially cover with a lid, and cook for about 4 minutes. Toss in the chayote and cook for another 2 to 3 minutes, or until all of the vegetables are tender. Add the tofu and black pepper and simmer for a minute. Check the seasoning and adjust if necessary. Sprinkle the cilantro over the soup and serve immediately.

VARIATION

To bring a nice background flavor of ginger to the soup, add two ⅛-inch (0.5 cm) slices of ginger to the stock with the vegetables.

SAVOY CABBAGE TOFU PARCELS IN BROTH

CANH BẮP CẢI CUỐN

On a trip to Hội An, my daughter, father-in-law, and I took a class at the popular Morning Glory cooking school, operated by chef Trịnh Diễm Vy. Ms. Vy, famous throughout Việt Nam, described how this soup is typically one of the first dishes a new bride in the country's central region makes for her in-laws. Once simmered, the soup would reveal the extent (or absence) of her culinary skills. If the young bride could produce harmony in the bowl, the thinking went, she could also do so in the home. My daughter loved that the two cabbage rolls symbolize husband and wife. I've adapted the soup's original shrimp mousse filling to make this vegetarian one instead. Adding sesame oil right before serving gives the soup an intoxicating aroma.

Serves 4 as a starter or part of a multidish meal

FROM THE PANTRY/MAKE AHEAD

1 quart plus 1 cup (1.25 liter) Light Vegetable Stock (page 30)

¼ teaspoon Mushroom Powder (page 36)

FOR THE TOFU SEAWEED FILLING

½ pound (225 g) medium-firm or firm tofu

1 small bundle (1 ounce; 25 g) cellophane noodles, soaked in hot water for 20 minutes, drained, squeezed dry, and roughly chopped into ½-inch lengths (½ cup packed)

2 medium dried shiitake mushrooms, soaked in hot water for 15 minutes, drained, squeezed dry, stemmed, and finely chopped (2 tablespoons)

1 dried wood ear mushroom, soaked in hot water for 15 minutes, drained, squeezed dry, stemmed, and finely chopped (2 tablespoons)

1 tablespoon dried seaweed (cut wakame or hijiki), pounded into a powder using a mortar and pestle or an electric spice grinder to get 1½ teaspoons of seaweed powder

2 scallions, greens and whites separated—greens finely chopped; whites thinly sliced for garnish

½ teaspoon salt

¼ teaspoon freshly ground black pepper

———

10 scallions or chives

10 savoy or green cabbage leaves

½ medium carrot, cut into thin rounds (⅓ cup)

½ teaspoon salt

2 tablespoons cilantro leaves, whole

Freshly ground black pepper

Sesame oil

OPPOSITE Savoy Cabbage Tofu Parcels in Broth

continues

Prepare the Light Vegetable Stock if using, and the Mushroom Powder.

Prepare the filling: Roughly cut the tofu into large cubes and place in the center of a clean dish towel. Gather the cloth up and, over the sink or a bowl, gradually twist it around the tofu to make a rough ball. As you do this some water will drip from the cloth. Squeeze the tofu a few times to expel more water. Unwrap the cloth and check that the tofu is a little moist but not wet. Transfer the tofu to a medium bowl. You should have about ¾ cup packed of squeezed tofu.

Add the cellophane noodles, mushrooms, seaweed powder, chopped scallion greens, ½ teaspoon salt, black pepper, and ¼ teaspoon mushroom powder to the bowl and mix thoroughly.

Trim off the roots from the whole scallions and cut the scallions at a point about 2 inches (2.5 cm) from the root end, just below the part where they turn from light green to dark green. Reserve the scallion greens. (Set aside the scallion whites for another use.)

Pour the vegetable stock into a medium pot and bring to a boil. Set a large bowl of ice water next to the stove. Add the cabbage leaves to the vegetable stock, gently push the leaves under the surface of the water, and boil for 2 minutes. Carefully remove with tongs or a spider and plunge into the ice water. Add the scallions to the stock and boil for 10 seconds. Turn off the heat and transfer the scallion greens to the bowl of ice water. After a few minutes, when both the cabbage and scallion greens are cool, remove from the water and drain well. Gently squeeze out the water and spread both cabbage leaves and scallion greens out on a clean dish towel to dry.

Lay a whole cabbage leaf, with the smooth side facing up and the bottom stem pointing toward you, on a cutting board. Trim the bottom part of the leaf off, where the tough midrib is, so the leaf becomes a rough rectangle 6 inches (15 cm) wide and 4½ to 5 inches (11.5 to 12.5 cm) long.

Lay a blanched scallion green flat next to the cabbage leaf.

Place approximately 2 tablespoons of tofu mixture centered over the bottom third of the cabbage leaf. Lift the bottom edge of the cabbage leaf over the filling and roll over once into a tight cylinder. Fold in the sides of the leaf to make a roll 2½ to 3 inches long, and roll over one more time.

Gently lift the cabbage roll onto the middle of the scallion. Tie the scallion, using two quick knots, to secure the roll. Use a knife or scissors to trim any long ends of the scallion if need be. Place the tied roll on an open part of the cutting board or on a plate. Repeat with the remaining cabbage leaves and filling.

Add the cabbage leaf rolls, carrots, and salt to the stock and simmer gently, partially covered, over medium to medium-low heat for about 8 minutes, or until the carrot slices are fully tender.

Carefully transfer two cabbage rolls into each of four bowls and evenly divide the carrot slices among them. Sprinkle the scallion whites and cilantro leaves over cabbage rolls and ladle on enough broth to just cover the rolls. Use a pepper mill to grind some pepper and add a few drops of sesame oil to each bowl.

To eat, take alternate sips of the broth and small bites from the roll (lift a roll with a spoon or chopsticks and take a small bite out of it).

HOT AND SOUR TAMARIND SOUP

CANH CHUA CHAY

Think of this southern recipe as a chunky Vietnamese minestrone. The first time my wife tasted it she devoured four bowls, and it's easy to see why. Tart tamarind invigorates a broth already bright with fresh pineapple, sweet tomato, and citrusy rice paddy herb.

Find the bright green taro stem (*bac hà*) and rice paddy herb at Asian grocers. If you can't find them, substitute celery for the taro stem and either red perilla or Thai basil for the rice paddy herb. Serve alone as an appetizer or bulk it up with a bit of cooked rice for a one-bowl meal.

Serves 4 as a main course or 6 as a starter or part of a multidish meal

FROM THE PANTRY/MAKE AHEAD

1 quart plus 1 cup (1.25 liters) Light Vegetable Stock (page 30) or water

1½ teaspoons Annatto Seed Oil (page 35)

2 tablespoons Crispy Fried Shallots (page 37)

———

¼ cup (60 g) tamarind pulp or 1¼ cups Tamarind Liquid (page 41)

1 cup boiling water

¼ pound (100 g) okra, thinly sliced ¼ inch thick on a diagonal (1cup)

⅛ pound (56 g) oyster mushrooms, cut or torn into bite-sized pieces (1 cup)

½ cup (65 g) drained canned bamboo shoots, rinsed and thinly sliced

1 ounce (30 g) taro stem peeled and thinly sliced on a diagonal (½ cup) or celery

½ cup (75 g) fresh pineapple cut into ¼-inch-thick (6 mm) pieces

2 plum tomatoes, each cut into 8 pieces

2 tablespoons sugar

1½ teaspoons salt

½ pound (225 g) firm tofu, cut into 1-inch (2.5 cm) cubes

1 cup bean sprouts

FOR GARNISH

2 scallions, thinly sliced

2 tablespoons roughly chopped rice paddy herb or red perilla or Thai basil

2 tablespoons roughly chopped cilantro

½ teaspoon freshly cracked black pepper

1 lime, cut into wedges

2 fresh red Thai bird chiles, thinly sliced

Prepare Light Vegetable Stock, if using; Annatto Seed Oil, and Crispy Fried Shallots.

Roughly break the tamarind pulp apart into small chunks and place in a medium bowl. Add 1 cup of boiling water. Mash with a wooden spoon or spatula and leave to soften for 15 minutes. Use your fingers to separate the fibers and seeds from the pulp. Place a fine-mesh

continues

strainer over another medium bowl and pour in the tamarind water and pulp. Use a wooden spoon, spatula, or your hands to rub the tamarind fibers against the strainer. Pour ¼ cup more hot water over the tamarind to dissolve any remaining pulp. Discard the fibers and set aside the strained liquid.

Place the vegetable stock or water and tamarind liquid in a large pot and bring to a boil. Add the okra, mushrooms, bamboo shoots, and taro stem and cook for 3 minutes. Add the pineapple, tomatoes, sugar, and salt and bring back to a boil. Reduce the heat and simmer for another 3 minutes. Add the tofu, bean sprouts, and annatto seed oil, and simmer for another minute. Taste. The broth should not be too tart but should have a nice balance between sweet and sour. Adjust the salt and sugar if needed.

Divide the scallions, rice paddy herb, and cilantro equally among four bowls. Ladle some soup along with tofu and vegetables into each bowl. Sprinkle some crispy shallots and a scant ⅛ teaspoon of black pepper over each bowl of soup. Pass a plate of lime wedges and sliced chiles for each diner to add to taste.

If serving as a main course, serve in large bowls alongside a bowl of steamed rice or warm, cooked vermicelli rice noodles. Allow diners to add several spoonfuls of rice or a small portion of noodles to their bowls.

OPPOSITE Hour and Sour Tamarind Soup

SQUASH AND SWEET POTATO COCONUT MILK SOUP

CANH BÍ ĐỎ HẦM DỪA

I spent a chilly winter morning assisting the Buddhist nuns in the kitchen at a small nunnery outside Huế. Their kitchen pantry included produce from their kitchen garden and small greenish pumpkins donated by a vegetable vendor at the nearby market. That day the nuns prepared a creamy soup with pumpkins, green bananas, coconut milk, and boiled peanuts. I've replaced the raw peanuts with cooked navy beans and the green bananas with orange-fleshed sweet potatoes. Chunks of winter squash (butternut, buttercup, kabocha, and red kuri) would all work well as stand-ins.   **Serves 4 to 6 as part of a multidish meal**

FROM THE PANTRY/MAKE AHEAD

2 cups (500 ml) Light Vegetable Stock (page 30) or water

---

1 pound (454 g) squash or pumpkin, cut into 1-inch (2.5 cm) cubes (2 cups)

1 pound (454 g) sweet potato (cut into 1-inch (2.5 cm) cubes (2 cups)

One 13.5-ounce can unsweetened coconut milk

¾ cup drained canned navy or cannellini beans, rinsed (see Note)

1 teaspoon sugar

½ teaspoon salt

Freshly ground black pepper

2 tablespoons roughly chopped cilantro leaves

2 scallions, thinly sliced (optional)

Prepare the Light Vegetable Stock, if using.

Place the squash, sweet potato, coconut milk, stock or water, navy beans, sugar, and salt in a medium pot. Bring to a boil over medium-high heat, reduce the heat to medium, and simmer, partially covered, for 10–15 minutes, or until both vegetables are soft, tender, and just starting to fall apart. Cover and let the soup sit for 5 to 10 minutes to develop flavor further and to thicken slightly. Taste and adjust with a pinch or two of salt, if needed. (If you want to add more body to the soup, scoop out a third of the vegetables and beans and mash them in a small bowl before returning to the soup.)

Ladle portions into small soup bowls and garnish with a generous pinch of freshly ground black pepper, cilantro, and scallion, if using.

OPPOSITE Squash and Sweet Potato Coconut Milk Soup

continues

Note:

Shelled raw peanuts are a good source of protein for vegetarians, but I've opted to replace them with cooked navy beans since raw peanuts are sometimes hard to come by (sold mainly at Asian grocers). If you want to make the soup with peanuts, partially precook them before starting the soup. Place ½ cup of shelled and skinned raw peanuts in a medium saucepan and cover with water by at least a couple inches. Simmer for 20 minutes or more, or until they're a little chewy (older peanuts take longer to get to this stage).

VARIATION

Add two teaspoons of finely chopped ginger with the ingredients at the start of cooking.

Green bananas (see recipe on page 167) hanging from a bicycle handle.

GREEN BANANA TOMATO TOFU SOUP

CANH ĐẬU PHỤ CHUỐI XANH CHAY

This northern countryside soup, an adaptation of a soup my friend Linh and her mother Quyên serve at their small vegetarian restaurant in Hà Nội, is quite popular. (See page 181 for their Tomato and Creamy Tofu Noodle Soup.) Blanching starchy, unripe bananas in turmeric-infused water removes both bitterness and stickiness before the banana is simmered in a flavorful, colorful turmeric tomato stew. For even more texture, add a cubed, sautéed portobello mushroom. Remember, green bananas are not the same as plantains. If you can't find them, use sweet potato, but squirt in some lime juice at the end to balance the extra sweetness. Serve it as part of a rice meal or, as Linh does, over a bowl of rice vermicelli noodles.

Serves 4 as one-dish meal or 4 to 6 as part of a multidish meal

FROM THE PANTRY/MAKE AHEAD

1 quart (1 liter) Light Vegetable Stock (page 30)

2 tablespoons Tamarind Liquid (page 41)

½ teaspoon Mushroom Powder (page 36)

———

4 tablespoons vegetable oil

½ pound (225 g) firm tofu, cut into 1-inch (3 cm) cubes, patted dry with paper towel

4 teaspoons ground turmeric

2 green bananas (about ¾ pound; 350 g)

¼ cup thinly sliced shallots

2 plum tomatoes, each cut into 8 pieces

2 teaspoons sugar

1 teaspoon salt

4 wild betel leaves, stemmed, halved, and thinly sliced

1 small handful perilla leaves, stemmed and thinly sliced

Prepare the Light Vegetable Stock, Tamarind Liquid, and Mushroom Powder.

Place a plate lined with paper towel next to the stove. Heat 3 tablespoons of the oil in a large skillet over medium-high heat. Add the tofu and panfry on each side for about 2 minutes (for a total of 8 minutes), until lightly golden brown. Transfer to the paper-towel-lined plate.

Place 2 teaspoons of the turmeric and 3 cups of water into a small pot.

Cut off the top of each banana. Using a paring knife, lightly score the skin, from top to bottom, only just enough to go through the skin. Repeat three or four more times. Lightly cut the peel, again only enough to go through the skin, around the middle of the banana. Use your fingers or paring knife to loosen a section of the skin and peel it sideways. Don't worry if a

continues

little skin remains stuck to the banana. Cut the banana into three equal lengths, then cut each piece into four even sticks.

Add the banana to the pot of turmeric water and bring to a boil over high heat. Turn off the heat and let the bananas sit in the water for a couple of minutes before draining, Discard the water.

Heat the remaining tablespoon of oil in a medium pot over medium heat. Toss in the shallots and cook for 3 minutes, until soft and translucent. Add the remaining 2 teaspoons of turmeric, the banana sticks, and mushroom powder, and stir-fry for 30 seconds. Pour in the vegetable stock, tamarind liquid, the tomato pieces, the sugar, and the salt and bring to a simmer. Simmer gently, adjusting the heat if necessary, for 10 minutes. Toss in the tofu cubes and sliced wild betel leaves and simmer for another 5 minutes. Taste and adjust the seasoning. Stir in the perilla leaves and serve.

TO SERVE WITH NOODLES
Place a handful of warmed cooked rice vermicelli noodles in a bowl. Spoon some bananas, tofu, tomato, and herbs on top. Ladle a cup or so of broth over the top.

OPPOSITE Midday prayer service for Cao Đài followers inside the Holy See in Tây Ninh (see page 157)

6

BOWLS OF NOODLES

OPPOSITE A busy lunch time on a full-moon day at
a vegetarian Bún Bò Huế vendor at Đông Ba market in Huế.

Phở may be Việt Nam's best-known culinary export, and legendary the world over for its one-bowl nourishment, but that's hardly the end of the story. There are many other phenomenal noodle dishes equally worth discovering. At all times of day, bowls of noodles are available on any street corner in Việt Nam, where they're traditionally eaten for breakfast. (Of course, they also make a satisfying lunch or dinner.) At mealtimes it's common to see diners of all ages at their neighborhood noodle stall hunched over a large bowl, chopsticks in hand, slurping noodles and fragrant broth. Whether it's Star Anise Cinnamon Scented Pho Noodle Soup (page 175) or a regional specialty such as Fragrant Lemongrass Huế-Style Noodle Soup (page 179), a bowl of noodles provides year-round comfort.

Most of the dishes in this chapter are meant to be eaten as a complete meal and are served with both chopsticks and a large spoon. The majority are "wet dishes," meaning the noodles are served in boiling broth. A few, however, are "dry dishes," meaning the noodles are quickly sautéed or tossed with a light sauce instead.

If you find your bowls are too shallow or not large enough to accommodate the noodle recipes that follow, seek out those of a more generous size at Asian grocers.

A few more notes: The ingredient list and instructions for some noodle recipes may appear daunting at first, but cooking a noodle soup isn't hard. It's even easier when you keep homemade vegetable stock (page 30 or 31) in the fridge or freezer, so try to make some when time allows.

Depending on the dish, Vietnamese noodles may be made from rice, tapioca, or wheat and egg. Rice noodles, or even brown rice noodles, may be substituted in all the recipes in this chapter for those who avoid gluten.

Finally, when it comes to green garnishes, the list of options is long. Western greens such as chard, arugula, or (broccoli rabe) perform well, as do as a combination of cilantro, Thai basil, and mint. Don't feel boxed in by the Asian greens referenced in the recipes. They're there to show you what's traditional, but substitutes are perfectly fine. And the final garnishing of a noodle bowl is a highly individual affair. Each diner uses whatever garnishes—whether bursts of lime juice, slivers of fiery chiles, squirts of soy sauce, a dab of fermented tofu, smatterings of herbs—best suit his or her palate and individual preference.

STAR ANISE CINNAMON SCENTED PHO NOODLE SOUP

PHỞ BÒ CHAY

What sets a mediocre dish apart from an outstanding one isn't always skill. Sometimes it's a commitment to slowing down and giving a recipe the time it needs to be fully realized. Give two cooks the exact same ingredients and the one that follows a time-honored technique will always produce better-tasting results than the cook who rushes.

Two spectacular bowls of vegetarian phở (pronounced like *feu*, the French word for fire) forced me to pause, midbowl, to consider why I felt so compelled to drink every last drop of broth. While many vegetarian Vietnamese cooks rely on powdered vegetable stock and MSG for flavor, both of these soups were prepared using freshly made stocks. The cooks from each kitchen— one in Sài Gòn and one in Cần Thơ—had coaxed flavor and umami from gently simmering root vegetables and mushrooms. They both employed the longstanding technique of fire-roasting and charring unpeeled shallots and chunks of ginger, which mellows the aromatics and intensifies the broth's richness. Cinnamon, star anise, and cloves infuse the broth with warm spiciness. Several years ago the cooks in the Cần Thơ restaurant started adding miso to their broth. Doing so noticeably heightened the broth's flavor, so I've followed suit in my version here.   **Serves 4 as a one-dish meal**

FROM THE PANTRY/MAKE AHEAD

2 quarts (2 liters) Rich Vegetable Stock (page 31)

1½ tofu skin sticks, rehydrated, cut into 2-inch (5 cm) lengths, and fried (Crispy Tofu Skin Sticks, page 43)

FOR THE BROTH

6 shallots or 1 small onion, unpeeled

2 inches (5 cm) ginger, unpeeled

2 tablespoons soy sauce

1 tablespoon red miso

3 whole star anise pods

One 3-inch (7 cm) cinnamon stick

3 whole cloves

1 teaspoon salt

OPPOSITE Star Anise Cinnamon Scented Pho Noodle Soup

continues

¼ pound (112 g) carrot, cut into ½-inch (1.25 cm) rounds (about ¾ cup)

¼ pound (112 g) daikon, cut into ½-inch (1.25 cm) (about ¾ cup)

¼ pound (112 g) oyster mushrooms, torn or cut into bite-sized pieces (about 2 cups)

FOR THE BOWLS

½ pound (225 g) dried medium or large flat pho rice noodles

½ small white onion, sliced paper-thin, soaked in ice water for 15 minutes, and drained

4 scallions, white parts cut into 4-inch lengths and thinly sliced lengthwise, green parts thinly sliced crosswise

6 culantro leaves, thinly sliced

¾ cup cilantro sprigs, coarsely chopped

Freshly ground black pepper

GARNISH

1 fresh red mild long chile or 2 fresh red Thai bird chiles, thinly sliced

1 lime, cut into 6 wedges

Prepare Rich Vegetable Stock and Crispy Tofu Skin Sticks.

Char the shallots and ginger by placing on the grate of gas burner set to medium heat. (A small stainless steel wire cooling rack placed over the grate of the gas burner prevents the ginger and shallots from falling into the burner.) Let one side of the shallot and ginger char and then rotate or turn over to char the other parts. Do this for about 10 minutes, or until the shallots and ginger have softened and most of the surface area is charred. (Alternatively, heat the oven to 425°F (220°C) and place the shallots and ginger on a baking sheet. Roast for about 30 minutes, turning occasionally, or until

browned and softened.) Set aside the shallots and ginger until cool enough to handle. Peel away and discard any of the burned shallot skin. Use a spoon or a paring knife to scrape off the charred ginger skin. Rinse the shallots and ginger under running water to loosen and remove any small burned pieces. Cut the ginger into 3 pieces and use the back of a chef's knife to lightly smash each piece. Place them in a 3-quart (3-liter) pot.

Add the vegetable stock, soy sauce, miso, and spices to the pot and bring to a boil. Reduce the heat to the lowest setting and cover to let the flavors infuse for about 20 minutes. Taste and adjust the seasoning with salt if needed.

In a large bowl of hot tap water, soak the noodles for 15 to 20 minutes, or until soft and pliable. Drain.

Meanwhile, prepare and assemble any of the garnishes for the noodle bowls. Soak the onions in ice water. Mix the scallion greens, culantro, and cilantro in a small bowl. Place the scallion whites in a small bowl or plate. Set aside.

Place a fine-mesh strainer over a large bowl and strain the broth. Return to the pot, cover, and increase the heat to medium. Add the carrots and daikon and cook for 5 minutes. Toss in the tofu stick and mushrooms and cook for another 5 minutes, or until the vegetables are fully tender.

Bring a large pot of water to a boil. Place a quarter of the noodles in a fine-mesh strainer. Dunk in the water untangle with tongs or chopsticks, and cook for about 15 seconds. Remove the strainer and quickly shake it to let any excess water drip back into the pot. Place the noodles in one of four serving bowls.

Repeat with the remaining noodles in three batches.

Evenly divide the carrot, daikon, tofu skin, and mushrooms among the four bowls. Decoratively place some sliced onion, scallion whites, and a small handful of the scallion greens, cilantro, and culantro mix over the noodles. Grind a generous pinch of black pepper over the top.

Ladle about 1¾ cups (440 ml) of very hot broth over the noodles and serve with chile and lime for diners to add themselves.

VARIATION

If you want to gild the lily, blanch one or two whole lengths of scallion whites with each portion of noodles and, as a good friend noted on his blog, lay them like "big scallion tadpoles on the surface of the broth."

SOUTHERN-STYLE GARNISH

Sprinkle the soup with sliced whites and greens of scallion. Serve the soup alongside a plate of bean sprouts, stems of Thai basil, cilantro, and whole culantro leaves. Pull off herb leaves from the stems or tear the culantro leaves into two or three pieces and gradually add to the bowl, along with the bean sprouts, as you eat the soup.

Soup spoons drying in the sun

Wooden chopsticks

FRAGRANT LEMONGRASS HUẾ-STYLE NOODLE SOUP

BÚN BÒ HUẾ CHAY

Huế (pronounced *Hway*) is known for its royal past. It was Việt Nậm's capital during the Nguyễn dynasty from 1802 to 1945. Today the city is known as much for its atmospheric rain showers as for its marvelous noodle soup (*bún bò Huế*).

Cycling one morning outside the walled imperial citadel, I sought shelter from a sudden storm at the central market. Damp and hungry, I wandered through the maze of goods and into a crowded soup stall. Behind the counter a mother and her daughters hurried to meet the considerable demand. One of the daughters blanched thick rice noodles while her mother portioned tofu and vegetables. All were then drowned in a broth fragrant with lemongrass and earthy mushrooms. A sunlit cloud descended upon the stall as the mother set a bowl before me.   **Serves 4 as a one-dish meal**

FROM THE PANTRY/MAKE AHEAD

2 quarts Rich Vegetable Stock (page 31)

1½ tofu skin sticks, rehydrated, cut into 2-inch (5 cm) lengths, and fried (Crispy Tofu Skin Sticks, (page 43)

1 tablespoon plus 1 teaspoon Annatto Seed Oil (page 35)

4 (¼-inch; 6 mm) slices Tofu Skin Sausage (page 44), each cut in half (optional)

Lemongrass Chile Satay (page 54) (optional but recommended) or 1 fresh red mild long chile or 2 fresh red Thai bird chiles, thinly sliced

———

½ pound (225 g) firm tofu, cut into 1½-inch (4 cm) cubes

3 tablespoons vegetable oil

⅓ pound (2 or 3; 150 g) large king oyster mushrooms, cut into ½-inch (1.3 cm) bite-sized pieces (about 1½ cups)

FOR THE BROTH

3 stalks fresh lemongrass, white part of 1 stalk finely chopped, the other 2 stalks each cut into 3 pieces lengthwise and the thicker bottom part lightly bruised with the back of a knife

¼ pound (112 g) carrot or butternut squash, cut into ½-inch-thick (1.25 cm) pieces (¾ cup)

¼ pound (112 g) chayote or kohlrabi, peeled and cut into 1-inch (3 cm) chunks (¾ cup)

½ plum tomato, diced

¼ cup fresh pineapple in bite-sized chunks or bamboo shoot matchsticks

2 tablespoons soy sauce

1 tablespoon red miso

¼ teaspoon dried chile flakes or chile garlic paste

1 teaspoon salt

continues

OPPOSITE Fragrant Lemongrass Huế-Style Noodle Soup

14 ounces (400 g) large dried round bun bo Huế rice noodles or ½ pound (225 g) large dried flat Pho rice noodles

FOR THE BOWLS

½ small white onion, sliced paper-thin and soaked in ice water for 15 minutes

¾ cup cilantro leaves

¾ cup Thai basil leaves

1½ cups (2½ ounces; 75g) bean sprouts

1 cup thinly sliced banana blossom, soaked in acidulated water and drained (see pages 143–44), or green or red cabbage, finely shredded)

Freshly ground black pepper

FOR GARNISH

1 lime, cut into 6 wedges

1 cube fermented tofu

Prepare Rich Vegetable Stock, Crispy Tofu Skin Sticks, Annatto Seed Oil, Tofu Skin Sausage, and Lemongrass Chile Satay.

Place the tofu on a plate lined with paper towel or a dish towel to remove excess moisture.

Place a plate lined with paper towel next to the stove. Heat the oil in a large skillet over medium-high heat. Add the tofu and panfry on each side for about 2 minutes, until lightly golden brown. Transfer to the paper-towel-lined plate.

Add the mushroom to the skillet and cook for 2 minutes without stirring. Turn over and cook for another minute or two, until lightly browned. Transfer to the paper-towel-lined plate.

Heat the annatto seed oil in a heavy pot over medium-high heat. Add the chopped lemongrass, briefly stir-frying until fragrant, about 20 seconds. Toss in the carrot, chayote, and

mushrooms and cook for a minute. Pour in the vegetable stock, bruised lemongrass, tomato, pineapple, soy sauce, miso, chile flakes, and salt. Increase the heat and bring to a boil. Reduce the heat to the lowest setting, cover, and let the flavors infuse for about 20 minutes.

Meanwhile, in a large bowl of hot tap water, soak the noodles for 15 to 20 minutes, or until soft and pliable. Drain. Prepare and assemble any of the ingredients for the noodle bowls. Set aside.

Check the doneness of the carrot and cha-yote. They should be tender and fully cooked. If not, increase the heat and simmer, uncov-ered, until tender. The broth should be citrusy, slightly spicy, and have a sweet tang. Adjust the seasoning, keeping in mind that you'll add a touch of salty, fermented tofu and chile as garnish. Remove any large pieces of lemongrass, if desired. Add the tofu and tofu skin sticks.

Bring a large pot of water to a boil. Place a quar-ter of the noodles in a fine-mesh strainer. Dunk in the water, untangle with tongs or chopsticks, and cook for about 15 seconds. Remove the strainer and quickly shake it to let any excess water drip back into the pot. Place the noodles into one of four serving bowls. Repeat with the remaining noodles in three batches.

Evenly divide the mushrooms, vegetables, tofu, and tofu skin sticks among the four bowls. Place two ¼-inch (6 mm) pieces of tofu skin sausage over the top and garnish with some banana blossom, thinly sliced onion, bean sprouts, herbs, and a generous pinch of freshly ground black pepper. Ladle about 1¾ cups (440 ml) of hot broth over the noodles and serve. Each diner can taste and then adjust the seasoning by adding a touch of lemongrass chile satay (or thinly sliced fresh red chile—1 long mild red chile or 2 Thai bird chiles), ½ teaspoon or more of fermented tofu, and a squirt of lime.

TOMATO AND CREAMY TOFU NOODLE SOUP

BÚN RIÊU CUA CHAY

Make this divine noodle soup in late summer and early fall when tomatoes are plump, ripe, and juicy. My friend Linh and her mother, Quyên, serve this soup at their small vegetarian restaurant in Hà Nội. They pour a stock sweet with tomatoes and musky with annatto seed oil over thin rice noodles and garnish it with herbs and bean sprouts. Creamy tofu appears twice: as lightly fried cubes and in fluffy clouds floating on the broth's surface.

Quyên showed me how to make the tofu curds. She adds an acidic liquid (typically using a liquid by-product from fermented rice wine called *dấm bỗng*, but rice vinegar or lime juice will do) to fresh soy milk and stock. It acts as a coagulant, producing cloudlike curds. Fresh soy milk—seek it out in Asian grocers—makes thicker curds, but I've adapted her technique using commercial soy milk with excellent results. This soup is on the sour side. If you like, add a touch of sugar to soften its tang. **Serves 4 as a one-dish meal**

FROM THE PANTRY/MAKE AHEAD

1 quart (1 liter) Light Vegetable Stock (page 30)

1 tablespoon Annatto Seed Oil (page 35)

¼ cup Crispy Fried Shallots (page 37)

Lemongrass Chile Satay (optional, page 54)

1 teaspoon Mushroom Powder (page 36)

¾ pound (340 g) small dried rice vermicelli noodles (*bun*)

¼ cup vegetable oil

½ pound (225 g) firm tofu, cut into 1-inch (3 cm) cubes and patted dry with paper towel

¼ cup thinly sliced shallots (about 2; 45 g)

2 plum tomatoes, each cut into 8 pieces

2 tablespoons tomato paste

2 tablespoons soy sauce

1 teaspoon sugar

1 teaspoon salt

3 cups (750 ml) unsweetened plain organic soy milk, fresh or boxed

3 tablespoons (45 ml) rice vinegar or fresh lime juice

FOR GARNISH

1½ cups (2½ ounces; 75 g) bean sprouts

4 scallions, thinly sliced

6 red perilla sprigs, torn or roughly chopped

6 Vietnamese balm sprigs, torn or roughly chopped

Small handful of cilantro, roughly chopped

Freshly ground black pepper

1 lime, cut into 6 wedges

continues

Prepare Light Vegetable Stock, Annatto Seed Oil, Crispy Fried Shallots, Lemongrass Chile Satay, if using, and Mushroom Powder.

Soak the noodles in a large bowl of hot tap water for 15 to 20 minutes, or until soft and pliable. Drain.

Place a plate lined with paper towel next to the stove.

Heat 3 tablespoons of the oil in a large skillet over medium-high heat. Add the tofu and panfry on each side for about 2 minutes (for a total of 8 minutes), until lightly golden brown. Transfer to the paper-towel-lined plate.

Heat the remaining tablespoon of oil over medium heat in a 3-quart (3-liter) pot. Cook the ¼ cup raw shallots, stirring regularly, for 4 to 5 minutes, until soft. Pour in the annatto seed oil and allow it to heat up for 10 to 20 seconds. Toss in tomatoes, tomato paste, soy sauce, sugar, salt, and mushroom powder and cook for a minute or two. Pour in the vegetable stock, and increase the heat to medium-high, and bring to a simmer.

In a separate small pot, bring the soy milk to a simmer over medium-high heat. When it begins to simmer gently, reduce the heat to low and add the vinegar in a slow, steady stream while stirring lightly with a slotted spoon. Once all the vinegar has been added, stop stirring to allow curds to develop over a minute or two.

Give a quick light stir to see that the soy milk has separated a bit and soy curds have risen to the surface. Use the slotted spoon to carefully transfer the soy milk curds, trying not to break them up too much, to a small plate. When you've removed all of the curds, pour the soy milk into the pot with the vegetable stock.

Add the fried tofu cubes and adjust the heat to produce a gentle simmer.

Bring a large pot of water to a boil. Place a quarter of the noodles in a fine-mesh strainer. Dunk in the water, untangle with tongs or chopsticks, and cook for about 15 seconds. Remove the strainer and quickly shake it to let any excess water drip back into the pot. Place the noodles in one of four serving bowls. Repeat with the remaining noodles in three batches.

Divide the bean sprouts and scallions among the four bowls. Ladle about 1¾ cups (440 ml) of hot broth over the top trying to evenly divide the tofu and tomato pieces. Carefully spoon an even amount of soy curds into each bowl. Sprinkle herbs, 1 tablespoon crispy fried shallots, and a generous pinch of freshly ground black pepper over the top of each bowl. Serve immediately and encourage diners to adjust the seasoning by adding a touch of the lemongrass chile satay or some sliced fresh red Thai bird chile slices and a squirt of lime if desired.

OPPOSITE Tomato and Creamy Tofu Noodle Soup

HOT AND SOUR THAI-STYLE NOODLE SOUP

BÚN THÁI CHAY

Younger Vietnamese favor this Thai-inspired *tom-yum*-like soup with its hot and sour broth fragrant with lemongrass and wild lime leaf. Crisp bean sprouts, bright mustard greens, and aromatic Thai basil add a fresh finish. This soup is a uniquely Vietnamese introduction to Thai flavors. I even tried one version garnished with golden nuggets of fresh pineapple. Although not essential, they were such a sweet, welcome surprise that I've included them in my version.   **Serves 4 as a one-dish meal**

FROM THE PANTRY/MAKE AHEAD

2 quarts (2 liters) Light Vegetable Stock (page 30)

2 teaspoons Annatto Seed Oil (page 35)

¼ cup Tamarind Liquid (page 41)

¼ cup Crispy Fried Shallots (page 37)

¼ cup vegetable oil

¼ cup thinly sliced shallots (about 2; 45g)

2 garlic cloves, finely chopped

1 inch (2.5 cm) ginger, roughly chopped

1 inch (2.5 cm) galangal, roughly chopped

2 lemongrass stalks, outer 2 layers peeled off, thinly sliced

2 fresh red Thai bird chiles, cut in half lengthwise

6 fresh wild lime leaves, leaves lightly torn

¾ pound (340 g) small dried rice vermicelli noodles

½ pound (225 g) firm tofu, cut into 1-inch (3 cm) cubes and patted dry with paper towel

2 plum tomatoes, each roughly cut into 1-inch (2.5 cm) cubes

¼ pound (112 g) fresh oyster or cremini mushrooms, cut into halves or quarters, depending on size (about 1 cup)

2 tablespoons soy sauce

1 tablespoon sugar

1 teaspoon salt

FOR GARNISH

¼ pound (112 g) Asian mustard greens, spinach, or arugula, stems trimmed, roughly chopped into bite-sized pieces (3 to 4 cups)

3 cups (⅓ pound; 150 g) bean sprouts

1 cup thinly sliced banana blossom, soaked in acidulated water and drained (See pages 143–44), or green or red cabbage, finely shredded

6 Thai basil sprigs, stemmed and roughly chopped

¼ cup (1½ ounces; 45 g) fresh pineapple in small bite-sized chunks

1 fresh red Thai bird chile, thinly sliced

1 lime, cut into 6 wedges

Prepare Light Vegetable Stock, Annatto Seed Oil, Tamarind Liquid, and Crispy Fried Shallots.

Heat 1 tablespoon of the vegetable oil and the annatto seed oil in a pot over medium-high heat. Add the shallots, garlic, ginger, galangal, and lemongrass and cook for 1 minute. Add the chiles, wild lime leaves, and vegetable stock and bring to a boil. Partially cover, reduce the heat to medium-low, and simmer gently for 20 minutes.

In a large bowl of hot tap water, soak the noodles for 15 to 20 minutes, or until soft and pliable. Drain.

Place a plate lined with paper towel next to the stove.

Heat the remaining 3 tablespoons of vegetable oil in a large skillet over medium-high heat. Add the tofu and panfry on each side for about 2 minutes (for a total of 8 minutes), until lightly golden brown. Transfer to the paper-towel-lined plate.

Place a fine-mesh strainer over a large bowl and strain the broth. Return the broth to the pot and increase the heat to medium-high. Add the tofu, tomatoes, mushrooms, soy sauce, tamarind liquid, sugar, and salt and simmer for 5 minutes. Taste. It should be a wonderful balance of sour, salty, and spicy hot. Adjust the flavor with sugar and salt if necessary. (Remember that diners can add more chile or lime juice later on.)

Bring a large pot of water to a boil. Place a quarter of the noodles in a fine-mesh strainer. Dunk in the water, untangle with tongs or chopsticks, and cook for about 15 seconds. Remove the strainer and quickly shake it to let any excess water drip back into the pot. Place the noodles in one of four serving bowls. Repeat with the remaining noodles in three batches.

Top each bowl with mustard greens, bean sprouts, and banana blossom. Place a few pieces of pineapple around the noodles. Sprinkle some basil over the top and ladle about 1 ¾ cups (440 ml) of the broth into the bowls. Sprinkle crispy fried shallots over the top. Serve immediately, with chile and lime for diners to add themselves.

WILD MUSHROOM AND LEAFY GREENS NOODLE SOUP

BÚN NẤM CHAY

Perched high on a hill overlooking the gentle Perfume River is Thiên Mụ, Huế's oldest and most famous monastery. There boys as young as six live, study, and train to become monks.

As I walked around the complex, a teenage monk approached me, eager to practice his English. Upon learning I was a chef, he offered to give me a tour of the monastery's kitchen and then to join him for an early evening meal. I was confused, as most monks finish eating by midday.

I returned later to find the tables in the dining area set for a meal and was directed to an empty seat with some teenage monks. Across the table I noticed a touch of white and blue peeking from under the collar of a couple of the monk's robes. I soon learned there was an important match that evening for which the monastery soccer team needed extra sustenance. (I'd seen the jerseys hanging from a clothesline earlier in the day. Now I understood why.)

This umami-filled noodle soup, full-flavored with mushrooms, watercress, and bright green morning glory (water spinach) is inspired by that evening's meal. Use at least three types of mushrooms—chanterelles, maitake, or even morels are fantastic if you can get them—for optimal texture and flavor. And mix bitter greens such as rapini (broccoli rabe), mustard leaves, turnip tops with sweeter leaves like chard, spinach, or kale. Aim, as always, for balance. **Serves 4 as a one-dish meal**

FROM THE PANTRY/MAKE AHEAD

1 quart plus 3 cups (1.75 liters) Rich Vegetable Stock (page 31)

Four ¼-inch (6 mm) slices Tofu Skin Sausage (page 44), cut in half (optional)

½ teaspoon Mushroom Powder (page 36)

———

2 inches (5 cm) ginger, peeled, cut into 3 pieces, and lightly smashed with the back of a chef's knife

2 tablespoons soy sauce

1 tablespoon red miso

1 teaspoon salt

½ pound (225 g) firm tofu, cut into 1½-inch (4 cm) cubes, drained and patted dry with paper towel or a clean dish towel

3 tablespoons vegetable oil

⅓ pound (about 2; 150 g) king oyster mushrooms, cut lengthwise into sixths or eighths

¼ pound (2 or 3; 113 g) small bok choy, cut into quarters

3 cups assorted mushrooms (oyster, fresh shiitake, shimeji or button), stemmed and cut into bite-sized pieces

1 medium carrot, cut into matchsticks (about 1 cup)

4 cups assorted leafy greens such as watercress and water spinach, tough stems removed and roughly cut into 3-inch-wide (7.5 cm) pieces

1 package (200 g) enoki mushrooms, root end trimmed, remaining length cut in half

4 to 5 Chinese celery stems, leaves and tender stalks cut into 1-inch (2.5 cm) lengths (½ cup)

4 scallions, cut into 2-inch (5 cm) lengths

¾ pound fresh (340 g) or ½ pound (225 g) dried egg noodles

A few pinches of freshly ground black pepper

FOR GARNISH (OPTIONAL)

2 fresh red Thai bird chiles, thinly sliced

Soy sauce or a smidge of fermented tofu

Prepare Rich Vegetable Stock and Tofu Skin Sausage, if using, and Mushroom Powder

Pour the vegetable stock, ginger, soy sauce, miso, salt, and mushroom powder into a 3-quart (3-liter) pot and bring to a boil. Reduce the heat to the lowest setting and cover to allow the ginger to infuse for about 15 minutes. Taste and adjust the salt if needed.

Place a plate lined with paper towel next to the stove. Heat the vegetable oil in a large skillet over medium-high heat. Add the tofu and panfry on each side for about 2 minutes (for a total of 8 minutes), until lightly golden brown. Transfer to the paper-towel-lined plate.

Bring a large pot of water to a boil.

Uncover the broth and scoop out and discard the ginger. Increase the heat to medium, bringing the broth to a simmer before adding the tofu and king oyster mushrooms to cook for 2 minutes. Toss in the bok choy and mixed mushrooms (except enoki) and simmer for another couple minutes. Add the carrot and leafy greens and simmer for another minute. Stir in the enoki mushrooms, celery, and scallions. Cover and simmer for a final minute, or until the leafy greens are limp.

Add the noodles to a pot of boiling water and cook for 2 to 3 minutes for fresh, 3 to 4 minutes for dry, until firm and chewy, but tender. Drain and divide among four large soup bowls.

Use a large spoon, chopsticks, or tongs to remove and evenly divide the tofu and vegetables among bowls. Lay a portion of tofu skin sausage on top, if using. Ladle 1½ cups (375 ml) or more of the broth over the top. Grind a generous pinch of black pepper over each bowl.

Allow each diner to add some chile slices for heat or a few squirts of soy sauce (or fermented tofu) for extra seasoning.

TASTY RICE NOODLE BOWL

BÚN CHAY

As spring dawns, I long to spend more time outdoors. I seek dishes that are easy and light without sacrificing flavor. This one-bowl meal is flexible and forgiving. Simply cook some rice noodles, slice some vegetables, drizzle some spicy sauce over it all, and stir. Embellish it, if you like, with slices of aromatic Five-Spice-Glazed Tofu (page 69), wedges of roasted squash (page 236), or chunks of warm spring rolls (page 107).   **Serves 4 as a light one-dish meal**

FROM THE PANTRY/MAKE AHEAD

1 cup Pickled Carrots and Daikon (page 47) or Quick Pickled Carrots (page 48)

⅓ cup Crispy Fried Shallots (page 37)

1 tablespoon plus 1 teaspoon Fragrant Shallot Oil (page 38)

¾ cup (180 ml) Everyday Table Sauce (page 49) or Soy Chile Dipping Sauce (page 51)

—

½ pound (225 g) dried rice vermicelli noodles

2 cups thinly sliced lettuce greens (Boston, Bibb, leaf, or romaine lettuce)

1 cup seeded English cucumber, matchsticks

1 cup (50 g) bean sprouts

½ cup green mango, matchsticks (optional)

MAIN TOPPING

Choose one, or two if you wish: Sautéed Squash with Basil and Peanuts (see page 236); ½ recipe Five-Spice-Glazed Tofu (page 69), cut into strips; ½ recipe Stir-fried Tofu with Lemongrass and Chile (page 73); Stir-Fried Water Spinach (page 231)

A small handful of a combination of at least two (or all) herbs—cilantro, mint, Thai basil, Vietnamese balm, perilla leaves—torn or roughly chopped

¼ cup roasted unsalted peanuts, roughly chopped

Prepare the pickles; Crispy Fried Shallots, Fragrant Shallot Oil, and your chosen sauce.

Bring a large pot of water to a boil. Drop in the noodles and use chopsticks or tongs to untangle and loosen them. Boil until tender, 3 to 5 minutes, then drain in a colander set in the sink and immediately flush with cold water. Squeeze gently four or five times to get rid of any excess water. Give the colander several shakes sideways and up and down to release any extra water from the noodles. Gently fluff the noodles a couple of times over the next 20 to 30 minutes to dry further.

Toss the lettuce, cucumber, pickles, bean sprouts, and green mango, if using, in a large bowl and divide among four bowls.

Place a portion of noodles in each bowl. Distribute your chosen topping(s) over the noodles and drizzle with 3 tablespoons of your chosen sauce and 1 teaspoon shallot oil. Garnish with the herbs, peanuts, and crispy shallots. Toss the noodles with all of the ingredients several times before eating.

OPPOSITE Tasty Rice Noodle Bowl with Taro Root Mung Bean Spring Rolls (page 188)

Serving a Meal as a Hot Pot

A popular way to feed many mouths is to serve a meal in the style of a hot pot or steamboat (*lẩu*). Here's how it works: Fill a communal pot with simmering broth and set it on a portable burner in the middle of a table, surrounded by tender vegetables, cubes of tofu, and slices of seitan. Your guests will add their preferred ingredients to the pot to cook or reheat. Meanwhile, place cooked rice or thin egg noodles into your bowl; when the vegetables are tender, transfer them to your bowl and ladle in some of the broth. Encourage others to follow your lead. Season with dabs of fermented tofu, chiles, a squirt of lime, and fresh herbs. The broth gains depth of flavor as more ingredients are added to the pot.

Part of the joy when eating a meal in this style is its convivial nature. It's impossible not to chat excitedly with your tablemates as everyone waits for their ingredients to cook. (It's kind of like fondue, at least conceptually.) Groups of friends in Việt Nam often eat this way when dining out.

When I dined with a large group of monks or nuns, five to eight of us would sit around a table and eat in this hot pot style. Eating like this promotes community, yes, but it's also highly economical.

At monasteries these meals are eaten in complete, mindful silence. That's not to say there's no communication. On the contrary: A knowing glance reveals who needs more broth ladled into his or her bowl or a plate of garnishes passed.

To serve a meal as a hot pot, use either the Hot and Sour Thai-Style Noodle Soup (page 184) or the Wild Mushroom and Leafy Greens Noodle Soup (page 186) as a starting point. A European fondue pot and burner are too small, so seek out a portable burner or electric hotplate from the housewares section of Asian markets.

To ensure quick, even cooking, cut dense vegetables like carrots or daikon into matchsticks (or grate them). Cut cabbages, mushrooms, and leafy greens into bite-sized pieces. Precook other dense vegetables (potatoes, squash) until just tender and add to the broth to warm through.

VERMICELLI NOODLES WITH FRESH TURMERIC, TOFU, AND CHINESE CHIVES

BÚN XÀO NGHỆ

In this simple recipe from the center of Việt Nam, fresh turmeric transforms plain white rice noodles into a lively bright yellow tangle, while snippets of Chinese chives add notes of garlic. You can use dried turmeric if you must, but when fresh the root's flavor and aroma are unquestionably superior. With its tan skin hiding a bright orange interior, fresh turmeric resembles ginger but with thinner, nubbier "fingers." Find it in well-stocked grocery stores and Asian markets.

Be warned, though: Turmeric stains easily. Wear an apron (and use your least favorite cutting board) when working with it, and if you do find yourself fighting a stain, a generous squirt or scrub of cut lemon works wonders at removing it. **Serves 4 as a light meal or 4 to 6 with 2 or 3 other dishes**

½ **pound (225 g) dried vermicelli rice noodles**

¼ **pound (112 g) firm tofu, cut into ¼-inch-thick (0.5 cm) slices and 1½-inch (4 cm) lengths**

1 **tablespoon plus 2 teaspoons soy sauce**

½ **teaspoon plus a couple pinches sugar**

2 **tablespoons vegetable oil**

¼ **pound (112 g) oyster or button mushrooms, cut into bite-sized pieces (1 cup)**

2 **scallions, thinly sliced on a diagonal**

½ **fresh red mild long chile or green cayenne or jalapeño chile, thinly sliced**

2 **tablespoons roughly chopped peeled fresh turmeric or 2 teaspoons ground turmeric mixed with 2 tablespoons water**

½ **cup Chinese chives in 1½-inch (4 cm) lengths**

¼ **teaspoon salt**

¼ **teaspoon freshly ground black pepper**

Soak the noodles in hot water for 15 to 20 minutes, until soft and pliable. Drain.

Place the tofu in a small bowl and toss with 2 teaspoons of the soy sauce and a pinch of sugar. Marinate for about 10 minutes.

Put the fresh turmeric, ½ teaspoon sugar, and salt in the bowl of a mortar and pestle and pound to a paste. Add a tablespoon of water. (Alternatively, place the turmeric, sugar, and a tablespoon of water in a blender and puree to a paste.) If using ground turmeric, mix it with the sugar, salt, and water in a small bowl.

Heat the oil in a large skillet or wok over medium-high heat. Add the tofu slices and stir-fry for a minute. Add the mushrooms,

continues

scallions, and chile and stir-fry for 45 seconds to a minute. Stir in the turmeric paste and cook for 20 seconds. Toss in the chives and stir-fry for another 20 to 30 seconds. Add the noodles, the remaining tablespoon of soy sauce, a pinch of sugar, and the salt and pepper. Stir to untangle and to color the noodles evenly. Stir-fry until the noodles are hot. (If at any point you find the ingredients are sticking to the pan, add a splash or two of hot water.) Transfer to a serving platter or evenly distribute among four dinner plates.

A basket of orange-yellow fleshed turmeric

STIR-FRIED NOODLES WITH ASPARAGUS, SHIITAKE MUSHROOMS, AND TOFU

PHỞ / MÌ XÀO CHAY THẬP CẨM

Stir-fried noodle dishes (*phở xào* in the North and *hủ tiếu khô* in the South) are essentially noodle soups minus the broth. On a shopping excursion to my treasured vegetable vendor in Hà Nội, I spotted plump asparagus and a basket overflowing with fresh shiitakes. Inspiration started there and continued with soaked and stir-fried rice noodles, tofu, vegetables, herbs, roasted peanuts, and spicy chiles. This recipe serves two. If scaling it up, stir-fry in batches for two people and repeat as necessary. **Serves 2 as a one-dish meal**

FROM THE PANTRY/MAKE AHEAD

1 tablespoon Tamarind Liquid (page 41) (optional)

½ teaspoon Mushroom Powder (page 36)

¼ pound (112 g) medium or large dried rice pho noodles

2 tablespoons soy sauce

2 tablespoons water

1½ teaspoons cornstarch

1 teaspoon sugar

2 tablespoons vegetable oil or Fragrant Shallot Oil (page 38)

2½ ounces (75 g) firm tofu, cut into ¼-inch-by-½-inch (6 mm by 1.25 cm) sticks (½ cup)

1 garlic clove, minced

¼ pound (112 g) asparagus, woody ends discarded and spears cut diagonally into ¼-inch-thick (6 mm) slices (½ cup)

2 ounces (60 g) green cabbage, cut into 1-inch (2.5 cm) pieces (½ cup)

2 ounces (60 g) fresh shiitake mushrooms, stemmed and cut into bite-sized pieces (1 cup)

½ teaspoon salt

2 scallions, cut into 1-inch (2.5 cm) pieces (¼ cup)

1 cup bean sprouts (1.8 ounces; 50 g)

2 tablespoons roughly chopped cilantro

2 tablespoons roughly chopped Thai basil

Freshly ground black pepper

FOR GARNISH

2 tablespoons roasted unsalted peanuts, crushed, or 2 teaspoons Toasted Sesame Seeds (page 33) or a handful of Tofu Skin Chips, crushed (page 42) (optional)

½ lime, cut into 3 wedges

½ fresh mild long red chile or ½ fresh red Thai bird chile, thinly sliced, or ¼ teaspoon Lemongrass Chile Satay (page 54) or chile garlic paste

continues

Make the Tamarind Liquid, if using, and the Mushroom Powder.

Place the rice noodles in a large bowl, cover with hot water, and soak for 15 to 20 minutes, until soft and pliable. Drain.

Stir the tamarind liquid, soy sauce, water, cornstarch, and sugar together in a small bowl until the sugar is fully dissolved.

Place a plate lined with paper towel next to the stove. Heat the oil in a large skillet or wok over medium-high heat. Add the tofu and cook undisturbed for about 2 minutes, then turn over and cook for another 1½ minutes, until golden brown. Transfer the tofu with tongs or a slotted spatula, trying to leave as much oil in the skillet, to a paper-towel-lined plate.

Add the garlic and stir-fry for 10 seconds. Toss in the asparagus and cabbage and stir-fry for 1 minute. Add the mushrooms, salt, and mushroom powder and stir-fry for another minute. Toss in the scallions and bean sprouts and stir-fry for 45 more seconds. Untangle the noodles, toss into the skillet or wok, and stir-fry for another 30 seconds. Stir the soy sauce mixture, then drizzle it over the noodles and stir-fry until the noodles are hot and lightly coated with sauce. Remove the skillet or wok from the heat and sprinkle half of the herbs over the top and toss. Divide between two dinner plates and garnish with the remaining herbs and the peanuts, or sesame seeds.

VARIATIONS

STIR-FRIED NOODLES WITH MIXED VEGETABLES
(PHỞ / MÌ XÀO CHAY THẬP CẨM)

While various combinations of vegetables can be used for this dish, it's most important to make sure the total amount of vegetables is 2 to 2½ cups. Briefly blanch denser vegetables such as carrots, broccoli, and cauliflower in boiling water until just tender. Cut tender vegetables like bell peppers or celery into ¼-inch (6 mm) or thinner slices and stir-fry.

CRISPY EGG NOODLES

Remove the tofu from the skillet or wok, lower the heat to medium, and add a tablespoon of vegetable oil. Add ½ pound (225g) cooked egg noodles (from ¼ pound dried egg noodles) and spread to cover the bottom of pan evenly. Panfry undisturbed for 4 to 5 minutes, or until crispy and golden. As they cook they will stick together in one mass. Turn the noodles with a wide spatula or by thrusting the skillet upward in a smooth, fast motion so the mass of noodles flies and flips up in front of you, landing in the pan (as for flipping pancakes). Drizzle another tablespoon of oil around the edges of the pan and panfry the other side for 5 minutes or so. Slide the panfried noodles onto a cutting board and cut in half with a sharp knife or scissors and divide between two plates. Stir-fry the vegetables, adding the sauce near the end, and divide over the crispy noodles.

The tables are set, ready to serve a hot and sour mushroom hot pot (see pages 184 and 190) with pumpkin flowers and local greens, to celebrate the Abbot's birthday at the Zen Buddhist Temple in Mỹ Khánh.

GRAINS OF RICE

OPPOSITE Rice terraces along the hillsides outside Sa Pa

Once you get away from the bustling modern cities and into the Vietnamese countryside, time seems to stand still both in the villages and in the patchwork fields of small family rice paddies. Male farmers guide water buffalo through knee-deep mud to plough their paddies. Female family members follow, wearing conical hats (*nón lá*) to shield their faces from the bright sun as they transplant individual rice seedlings into the paddies. Soon those paddies will be carpeted in various shades of green, from deep emerald to yellow-green. In the distance, children cycle to and from school along the dikes that separate larger paddies. Scenes like these occur daily in a country where rice farming remains the main agricultural activity and traditional farming methods persist.

Rice is central to the Vietnamese diet. A meal is simply incomplete without it in some form or other. Endlessly versatile, it can be savory or sweet, ground to a powder, transformed into noodles or translucent wrappers, fermented to make rice vinegar or rice wine, or simply steamed.

Other chapters in this book include rice in the form of wrappers or noodles. This chapter, however, focuses on dishes that use rice as a grain or in flour form. When rice is served as the heart of a family meal, the Vietnamese turn to steamed, fragrant, long-grain white jasmine rice (*gạo thơm*). Glutinous (sticky) rice (*gạo nếp* when raw and *xôi* when cooked) may be eaten alone for breakfast or as a late afternoon snack when mixed with a touch of sugar and grated coconut (page 201). Use either whole rice, broken rice, or leftover rice to make a Silky Rice Porridge (page 203), a wholesome, one-dish meal. Or try the crispy crepelike *bánh xèo* (page 217). Made from a batter of soaked, ground mung beans, plain rice flour, a pinch of turmeric, and some coconut milk, the crepes are filled with bean sprouts, scallions, and cilantro, then wrapped with herbs and lettuce and dipped into Everyday Table Sauce (page 49).

STICKY RICE WITH MUNG BEAN POWDER AND CRISPY SHALLOTS

XÔI XÉO CHAY

Whenever I travel, I try to find one of the local breakfast staples for my first meal, a practice that helps ease me into my new surroundings. In Việt Nam, that means finding the nearest sticky rice street vendor. Thế was one such vendor, as her stall was just a short walk from my house in Hà Nội. Soon I became a regular, and whenever she'd see me approaching, she'd start portioning my order: a mound of plump steamed sticky rice, tinted light yellow with turmeric and plopped into the center of a large piece of banana leaf. She'd liberally drizzle rich shallot oil over the top and garnish it with steamed mung beans and crispy shallots. Each bite offered rich, buttery flavors with a hint of sweet grassiness from the rice. To keep it vegetarian, Thế would omit the customary dried pork floss and spoon some ground toasted sesame seeds (*muối vừng*) on the side in its place.

Sticky rice is simple to make and can be eaten at any time of day. I tend to eat it with my kids after school, as a snack or light meal, or serve it to friends late at night when I host a party. Thế taught me the importance of planning ahead as the rice and mung beans both need a good soak before cooking. Soaking improves the flavor, makes each grain of rice more tender, and shortens the cooking time.   **Serves 4 as a light meal or snack**

FROM THE PANTRY/MAKE AHEAD

½ cup Crispy Fried Shallots (page 37)

2 tablespoons Fragrant Shallot Oil (page 38)

Ground Sesame Seed Salt (optional but recommended; page 34)

———

2 cups (13 ounces; 400 g) short-grain glutinous rice

⅛ teaspoon ground turmeric

½ cup (113 g) dried split mung beans

½ teaspoon salt

Place the rice and turmeric in a large bowl and the mung beans in a medium bowl and cover each by at least 2 inches with room-temperature water. Soak the rice for at least 6 hours and the mung beans for at least 2 hours. (Alternatively, use hot tap water and soak each for 2 to 3 hours.)

Prepare the Crispy Fried Shallots, Fragrant Shallot Oil, and Ground Sesame Seed Salt, if using.

continues

Fill the bottom of a steamer pot or wok with several inches of water and bring to a boil over high heat.

Drain the rice and rinse until the water runs clear. Shake the strainer from side to side, and briefly up and down, to remove any excess water from the rice.

Dampen a piece of cheesecloth the size of a dish towel or an 18-inch (45cm) square and line a 10-inch (25 cm) steamer basket so that some of the cloth hangs over the sides. Pick up a third of the rice with your hands and gently scatter in an even layer over the cloth. Repeat two more times until all of the rice is in the cheesecloth. Drape the sides of the cheese-cloth toward the center of the basket to make a loosely covered package.

Drain the mung beans and shake the strainer from side to side, and up and down, to remove any excess water. Dampen a second piece of cheesecloth 18 inches square (45 cm) and lay over the rice bundle. Pour the mung beans into the center, pressing loosely to shape them into a rough square. Drape the sides of the cheesecloth toward the center of the basket to make a loosely covered package.

Cover and set the steamer basket into a pot or wok so that it fits tightly and no steam escapes around the edges.

Steam for 15 minutes. Uncover and allow the steam to dissipate to prevent burning yourself. Lift the mung bean package from the steamer onto a plate. Unwrap the rice package and, using chopsticks or a fork, stir some rice from the edges toward the center before spreading it into an even layer (see Note). Give the rice a quick stir one more time and taste the rice to gauge its doneness. Close the rice package. Unwrap the mung bean package and taste to see if the mung beans are tender and fully cooked. If done, spoon onto a plate to cool. If not, bundle up the package and return to the steamer for 5 minutes. Check the water level in the pot or wok (add very hot tap water if necessary). Re-cover the steamer and steam the rice for another 5 to 10 minutes, or until it's shiny and tender. Gently fluff the rice before serving.

Place the cooled mung beans into the bowl of a mortar and pestle or small food processor. Quickly pound or pulse until the beans are ground and fluffy.

Serve the rice warm (not hot). Scoop a generous cup of rice onto a small plate. Drizzle a couple teaspoons of shallot oil over the top. Sprinkle a large spoon of ground mung beans, a generous pinch of crispy fried shallots, and a teaspoon of sesame salt, if using, over the top or on the side. Eat the rice with your hands or a small spoon.

Note:
Gently stirring the rice with chopsticks is an easy option, but I learned a nonchopsticks option. After the steam dissipates, lift the steamer basket from the pot or wok and unwrap the rice. Grab the two closest corners, one in each hand, and lift them up toward you. As that happens some of the rice from the edges will fall into the center. Repeat this a couple more times using different corners of the cloth. Fold the cloth back together again, return the steamer basket to the pot or wok, and finish steaming the rice.

SWEETENED STICKY RICE WITH SHREDDED COCONUT

XÔI DỪA

Folding sweetened coconut cream into sticky rice during the last few minutes of cooking perfumes the rice and ensures it will absorb maximum coconut flavor. Freshly shredded coconut and toasted sesame seeds deliver a sparkling, nutty finish. This dish is a popular breakfast item in Việt Nam, but I prefer it for dessert, sometimes dressed up with ripe mango, pineapple, or papaya. **Serves 4 as a snack**

FROM THE PANTRY/MAKE AHEAD

Toasted Sesame Seeds (page 33) or Ground Sesame Seed salt (page 34)

---

2 cups (13 ounces; 400 g) short-grain glutinous rice

½ teaspoon salt

½ cup (125 ml) unsweetened coconut cream

3 tablespoons sugar

¼ teaspoon vanilla extract

1 cup freshly shredded coconut

Place the rice in a large bowl and cover with room temperature water by at least 2 inches. Soak the rice for at least 6 hours. (Alternatively, soak in hot tap water for 2 to 3 hours.)

Prepare the Toasted Sesame Seed or Ground Sesame Seed Salt.

Fill the bottom of a steamer pot or wok with several inches of water and bring to a boil over high heat.

Drain the rice and rinse it until the water runs clear. Shake the strainer from side to side, and briefly up and down, to remove any excess water from the rice.

Dampen a piece of cheesecloth the size of a dish towel or an 18-inch (45 cm) square and line a 10-inch (25 cm) steamer basket so that some of the cloth hangs over the sides. Pick up a third of the rice with your hands and gently scatter in an even layer over the cloth. Repeat two more times until all of the rice is in the cheesecloth. Drape the sides of the cheesecloth toward the center of the basket to make a loosely covered package. Cover and set the steamer basket into the pot or wok so it fits tightly and no steam escapes around the edges. Steam for 20 minutes.

Mix the coconut cream, sugar, and vanilla in a small bowl.

Uncover the pot and allow the steam to dissipate to prevent burning yourself. Unwrap the package and drizzle half of the coconut cream mixture over the top of the rice. Using chopsticks or a fork, stir some rice from the edges

continues

toward the center before spreading it into an even layer. Drizzle the rest of the coconut cream and sprinkle half of the grated coconut over the rice, give it a quick stir one more time, and taste the rice to gauge its doneness. Close the rice package. Check the water level in the pot or wok (add very hot tap water if necessary). Re-cover the steamer and steam the rice for another 5 to 10 minutes, or until it's shiny and tender. Gently fluff the rice before serving.

Spoon a generous cup of warm (not hot) rice onto a small plate. Sprinkle some freshly grated coconut, and toasted sesame seeds or sesame salt over the top. Eat the rice with your hands or a small spoon along with a few slices of tropical fruit.

Garnishes for Sticky Rice (*clockwise from left*): steamed mung beans, crispy fried shallots, pork floss (not vegetarian), toasted sesame salt, shallot oil

SILKY RICE PORRIDGE

CHÁO

This rice porridge (*cháo*) may be the simplest recipe in this cookbook. It comforts and warms the soul, much like a soothing risotto. You may be familiar with its Korean, Cantonese, or Hindi name: *jook*, *congee*, or *kanji*. In Việt Nam it's associated with Vietnamese mothers or grandmothers, who often prepare it to heal an ailing family member or to feed a large crowd.

There's almost nothing to it. Throw raw (or even cooked) rice and water (or stock) into a pot, allowing them to simmer gently together until the rice breaks down and releases its silky starch. You can make the porridge thicker or thinner according to the weather or personal preference, simply by varying the proportion of rice to liquid. (Cold weather often demands thicker, more stick-to-your-ribs fare.)

Consider this basic recipe a blank canvas. The two *cháo* recipes that follow offer guidance on garnishes and ways to add creative touches.

Serves 4 as a one-dish meal

2 inches (2.5cm) ginger, peeled and cut into four ¼-inch (6 mm) slices

¾ cup (150 g) long-grain or broken white jasmine rice

½ teaspoon salt

For a thick, porridge consistency: 2 quarts (2 liters) Light or Rich Vegetable Stock (page 30 or 31) or water

For a thin soupy consistency: 2½ quarts (2.5 liters) vegetable stock or water

Place the rice in a heavy 4-quart (4-liter) pot and cover with cold water. Stir to release some starch and any impurities. Wait for the rice to settle and then drain all of the cloudy water. Repeat.

Add the salt and pour in the amount of stock required based on the consistency you would like. Bring to a boil and reduce the heat to medium-low or low so that the stock is happily simmering away (the bubbles should quickly come to the surface, but not so fast that it's boiling). Stir, making sure to scrape free any rice grains that may have stuck to the bottom of the pot. A thin layer of foamy starch will rise to the surface, but there is no need to skim it. You want to keep it to maintain a silky consistency.

FOR A THICK CONSISTENCY

Simmer the rice for 15 minutes, remove from the heat, and cover. Allow the grains to absorb liquid for about 10 minutes before adding any

continues

garnishes. You may need to add some more stock or water if you want to maintain a loose consistency and prevent it from becoming too thick.

FOR A SOUPY CONSISTENCY

Simmer the rice for 45 minutes to 1 hour, stirring occasionally. After 25 minutes of cooking it will soften and start to break down. As the rice continues to cook it will break down further, almost melting into the liquid, resulting in a soupy, porridgelike consistency.

FOR BROWN RICE

Increase the cooking time to 25 minutes for a thicker consistency or to 1¼ hours to 1½ hours for a thinner consistency.

RICE PORRIDGE MADE WITH LEFTOVER COOKED RICE

A quick shortcut to make cháo is to use leftover rice. To serve four people, use a ratio of 1 cup (150g) leftover cooked rice to 3½ cups (825 ml) or more stock or water. Bring it to a simmer and cook it until the rice starts to break down.

Note:

As the rice sits, it continues to absorb liquid. So if you make it in advance or eat it as leftovers, you will need to thin it out with a touch of water or stock.

Fresh watercress (see recipe on page 205) for sale in the main market in Đà Lạt.

MIXED MUSHROOM RICE PORRIDGE WITH BITTER GREENS

CHÁO NẤM

The city of Tây Ninh sits about 55 miles (90 km) northwest of Sài Gòn. It's the only city in Việt Nam where the number of vegetarian restaurants far outnumbers nonvegetarian restaurants, due in large part to its seat as the center of worship for followers of the Cao Đài religion (see page 157). Its adherents eat vegetarian meals anywhere from six days a month to full-time.

One evening, I'd just finished observing the six o'clock mass in the fantastical temple that serves as the main focal point of the Cao Đài religious complex. I exited through the southern gate and, to my left, saw a series of signs with the words *cơm chay*, meaning "vegetarian restaurant." I parked my motorbike in front of the first one and walked in. The server (the cook's wife) informed me that they were serving only mushroom rice porridge that evening and that her husband, Hùynh, was in the process of preparing it. She guided me back to the outdoor kitchen, which was nothing more than two propane burners on the ground.

On one of the burners, a large cauldronlike pot bubbled with rice porridge. Hùynh placed a wok on the other burner, squatted, and stir-fried fleshy mushrooms until tender. He stirred these into the rice porridge, adding chopped watercress along with it.

I've based this soul-satisfying recipe on that meal. I like it best with at least three types of mushrooms for maximum flavor and textural interest. If you like, you can also add mild greens such as kale, spinach, or chard or heartier ones like dandelion or turnip greens. **Serves 4 as a one-dish meal**

continues

FROM THE PANTRY/MAKE AHEAD

Rich Vegetable Stock (page 31) (optional)

1 tablespoon Toasted Sesame Seeds (page 33)

¼ cup Crispy Fried Shallots (page 37)

1 teaspoon Mushroom Powder (page 36)

Silky Rice Porridge recipe (page 203), preferably made with Rich Vegetable Stock

———

3 tablespoons vegetable oil

½ pound (225 g) firm tofu, cut into 1-inch (3 cm) cubes, patted dry on paper towel or a clean dish towel

1 medium carrot, cut into ¼-inch (6 mm) cubes (½ cups)

4 cups (½ pound/225 g) assorted whole fresh mushrooms (oyster, shiitake, shimeji, enoki), torn or cut into bite-sized pieces

1 teaspoon plus a pinch of salt

2 tablespoons soy sauce

2 handfuls watercress or other bittersweet green such as arugula, very roughly chopped

2 teaspoons finely chopped ginger

3 scallions, thinly sliced

2 tablespoons roughly chopped cilantro

Freshly ground black pepper

1 fresh red mild long red chile or two fresh red Thai bird chilies, thinly sliced, or chile garlic paste

Make Rich Vegetable Stock, if using; Toasted Sesame Seeds; Crispy Fried Shallots, and Mushroom Powder. Prepare the rice porridge as directed in the recipe.

Place a paper-towel-lined plate next to the stove. Heat the oil in a large skillet over medium-high heat. Add the tofu and cook for about 2 minutes on each side (about 8 minutes in total), until lightly golden brown. Transfer to the paper-towel-lined plate.

Add the carrot, mushrooms, and a pinch of salt to the skillet and cook, stirring often, until a little darkened and tender, about 5 minutes. Transfer to a small bowl and set aside.

When the rice porridge has reached your desired consistency, add the sautéed mushrooms, mushroom powder, soy sauce, and 1 teaspoon salt. Simmer, stirring occasionally, for a few minutes. Stir in the watercress and simmer for a minute, until wilted. Taste and adjust the seasoning with salt if needed.

Ladle about 1¾ cups of rice porridge into four individual serving bowls. Sprinkle the ginger, scallions, cilantro, crispy shallots, sesame seeds, and a couple generous grinds of black pepper on top. Serve alongside sliced chiles or chile paste.

OPPOSITE Mixed Mushroom Rice Porridge with Bitter Greens

RICE PORRIDGE WITH SQUASH, KIDNEY BEANS, AND CORN

CHÁO THẬP CẨM

I first encountered this soothing dish in the hill town of Đà Lạt, about 190 miles northeast of Sài Gòn. It was a full moon day, a day when devout Mahayana Buddhists change their diet (and street food vendors their menus) to a vegetarian one. The vendor served me a steaming bowl of rice porridge dotted with tiny jewels of corn and scarlet kidney beans. A smattering of cilantro, scallions, and bits of crispy tofu skin gleamed on top. I dabbed on some fresh chile paste and gave it all a squeeze of lime juice, realizing several bites later how Tex-Mex-like these flavors and textures were.

Once back in my own kitchen and bent on re-creating it, I added some squash, chipotle pepper salsa for some smoky heat, and a few crumpled tortilla chips for the crispy tofu skin. *Thập cẩm* means "mixed," so this flexible dish is designed to be garnished with whatever you crave or have on hand.

Serves 4 as a one-dish meal

FROM THE PANTRY/MAKE AHEAD

Light Vegetable Stock (page 30)

A handful or two of Tofu Skin Chips (page 42)

Silky Rice Porridge recipe (page 203), preferably made with Light Vegetable Stock

———

½ pound (225 g) butternut or acorn squash or pumpkin, cut into ½-inch (1 cm) cubes (1½ cups)

¾ cups drained canned kidney beans or ⅓ cup dried kidney beans, soaked, cooked separately, then drained (see Note)

¾ cup corn kernels, from 1 ear (use the cob when making the stock, if you like)

3 scallions, thinly sliced

2 tablespoons roughly chopped cilantro

1 fresh red mild long red chile or 2 Thai bird chiles, thinly sliced, or chile garlic paste

1 lime, cut into wedges

Make the Light Vegetable Stock, if using, and the Tofu Skin Chips. Prepare rice porridge according to the recipe.

About 15 minutes before the estimated end of the cooking time for the rice porridge, add the squash, kidney beans, and corn to the pot. Cook until the rice has reached your preferred consistency and the squash is tender. Taste and adjust the seasoning with salt if needed.

Ladle 1¾ to 2 cups of the porridge into each of four bowls. Top with a generous sprinkling of scallions, cilantro, and a few tofu skin chips. Encourage diners to enhance the seasoning with a squeeze of lime and some chopped chile or chile paste.

Note:

You can add the soaked and drained kidney beans at the beginning with the rice, instead of cooking them separately, but they will turn the porridge a purple-gray color (the same thing will happen with black beans).

Clockwise from bottom left: split green mung beans, skinned yellow mung beans, brown rice, white rice, kidney beans, and peanuts behind Hà Nội's Đồng Xuân market.

CRUNCHY LEMONGRASS MUSHROOM RICE BOWL

CƠM HẾN CHAY

This rice bowl, a specialty of Huế, is robust, spicy, and highly textured. Tropical aromas will perfume your kitchen as you sauté lemongrass, chile, and mushrooms; the scent alone merits making this recipe. Both nori and fermented tofu add a briny complexity, and toasted peanuts, rice crackers, and tofu skin chips give it crunch. Serve over fresh or day-old rice (warm or at room temperature) or even with some cooked vermicelli rice noodles instead.

Serves 4 as a light one-dish meal

FROM THE PANTRY/MAKE AHEAD

3 cups (450g) cooked rice

2½ cups (625 ml) Light or Rich Vegetable Stock (page 30 or 31)

⅓ cup Crispy Fried Shallots (page 37)

1 Toasted Sesame Rice Cracker (page 55), broken into small bite-sized pieces

A handful of Tofu Skin Chips (page 42), crushed into smaller pieces

1 recipe Spicy Lemongrass Mushroom Mince (page 116)

2 teaspoons to 1 tablespoon (½ to 1 cube) fermented tofu

2 teaspoons soy sauce

2 teaspoons vegetarian mushroom-flavored stir-fry sauce

Salt

1 or 2 lime wedges

1 star fruit, cut into matchsticks, or ½ tart green apple, peeled, cut into matchsticks, and squeezed with fresh lime juice

1 cup thinly sliced banana blossom (see pages 143–44) or shredded green cabbage

½ cup mint and Vietnamese coriander or cilantro leaves, roughly chopped

2 tablespoons roasted unsalted peanuts, whole or (2 teaspoons) Toasted Sesame Seeds (page 33)

Lemongrass Chile Satay (page 54) or chile garlic paste

Prepare the rice, Light or Rich Vegetable Stock, Crispy Fried Shallots, Toasted Rice Cracker, and Tofu Skin Chips. Stir-fry the Spicy Lemongrass Mushroom Mince as directed in the recipe.

Bring the vegetable stock to a boil in a small saucepan over medium heat. Reduce the heat to low and whisk in a teaspoon each of the fermented tofu, soy sauce, and the vegetarian mushroom-flavored stir-fry sauce. Taste and

OPPOSITE Crunchy Lemongrass Mushroom Rice Bowl

continues

adjust the seasoning with more fermented tofu, soy sauce, and salt until it has a balanced briny flavor. I find a small squeeze of fresh lime juice is sometimes what's needed for a final balance of flavors. Keep warm over low heat.

Mound about ¾ cup of room-temperature or warm rice into four bowls. Scoop a scant ¼ cup of the spicy lemongrass mushroom mince over the top. Spoon small mounds of star fruit, banana blossoms, herbs, crispy shallots, roasted peanuts or sesame seeds, a few pieces of toasted rice cracker, and a generous pinch of tofu skin chips around the rice and mushrooms. Pour about ⅓ to ½ cup warm broth over the mushrooms. You want just enough broth to moisten the rice but not so much that it becomes a soup. To eat, stir everything together, taste, and adjust the heat with the lemongrass chile satay or chile garlic paste.

Rice for sale along an alleyway in Hà Nội.

GOLDEN CRISPY RICE SHELL

COM CHÁY

In this recipe, precooked or leftover rice is used to make a layer of crispy rice that is then torn into bite-sized pieces and smeared on one side with Caramelized Soy Dipping Sauce (page 215). Or you can use the crispy pieces like crackers to scoop up salads or dip.

Cooks in the countryside prepare rice in a thick, heavy-bottomed iron pot, purposely leaving the pot over the heat for an extended period of time so a crust of toasted rice develops around the bottom and sides. They scoop out the softer rice in the center to serve with the meal, then return the pot to the heat to further toast and crisp the crust. The crust eventually pulls away from the sides of the pot, making it easy to lift out a rough, pot-shaped "shell." Eager family members fight over this delicacy.

Nowadays, those living in urban areas tend to use electric rice cookers, which cannot produce this cherished treat. Restaurants serving country-style food offer it on their menus, a move both savvy and fittingly nostalgic.

Makes about five 9-inch (23 cm) round crackers

4 to 5 teaspoons vegetable oil

4 cups (600 g) cooked rice, at room temperature

Set a soupspoon in a small bowl of water on the counter next to stove.

Spoon 1 teaspoon of the oil into a seasoned 9-inch (23 cm) cast-iron skillet, tilting the pan to swirl the oil evenly over the bottom and about ½ inch (1.5 cm) or so up the sides of the skillet. Set the pan over medium heat and heat for 20 to 30 seconds. Add 2 cups (300 g) of the rice and flatten it by pressing it with the back of the soupspoon. To prevent the spoon from sticking, occasionally dip it in the bowl of water. Try to spread the rice about 1 inch (2.5cm) up along the side of skillet. Cover with a lid. Depending on how the burners on your stove maintain a consistent heat, you may need to keep the heat at medium or adjust it to medium-low.

Every 5 minutes, rotate the skillet around the burner by a third to evenly distribute the heat on the bottom. After 15 minutes the rice around the edges will turn lightly golden and be just coming away from the side. Use the soupspoon to carefully scrape away as much of the inner soft rice as you can until you hit the crispy layer. Transfer back into the bowl of rice. If the crispy rice shell moves as you scrape

continues

away the rice, use a chopstick or another soupspoon to gently hold it in place. Use tongs, chopsticks, or a spatula to lift the crispy rice shell from the pan and invert it, crispy side up, onto a plate.

Repeat until you have made enough crackers or until you use up all of the rice.

Note:
· You can make these an hour or so in advance and then loosely cover them with a clean dish towel or plastic wrap. I like to sometimes quickly reheat them until warm in a warm oven (200°F; 95C) before serving.
· As you become proficient in making them, try making two at a time in separate cast-iron skillets. You will need to adjust the amount of rice added to the second skillet if not the same size.

Offering incense sticks in front of an altar at a pagoda.

CARAMELIZED SOY DIPPING SAUCE

KHO QUẸT

Kho quẹt is a fine example of the simplicity and ingenuity that rural cooks in the Mekong countryside employed during times of scarcity to stimulate their taste buds with a few bold ingredients. The salinity in fish sauce, with its preservative properties, allowed them to prepare large batches that would stay fresh for weeks or months. In this vegetarian version, soy sauce and sugar are combined with sautéed leeks, shallots, garlic, and radish and slowly simmered until caramelized and thick. Coarsely ground black pepper provides a sharp bite.

Serve *kho quẹt* as an appetizer with a plate of boiled or steamed vegetables or as a light meal with some plain or Golden Crispy Rice Shell and a small bowl of soup. **Makes 1½ cups**

2 tablespoons vegetable oil

15 (10 g) small dried red chiles

1 fresh red Thai bird chile

½ cup (about 4; 70 g) shallots, finely chopped

One 3-inch (7.5 cm; 50 g) piece leek, finely chopped (½ cup)

2 tablespoons minced garlic (about 4 cloves; 30 g)

1 cup (250 ml) light soy sauce

¾ cup (180 g) sugar

One 3-inch (7.5 cm; 70 g) piece daikon radish, cut into ¼-inch (6 mm) cubes (½ cup)

1 tablespoon (8 g) coarsely ground black pepper

Heat the oil in a medium saucepan over medium-high heat. Toss in the dried and fresh chiles and stir-fry for 30 seconds. Scoop out onto a small plate and reserve. Reduce the heat to medium and add the shallots and leek. Cook, stirring regularly, for 3 minutes. Add the garlic and cook for 30 seconds. Return the chiles to the pan and pour in the soy sauce and sugar, stirring to fully dissolve the sugar. When it reaches a simmer, reduce the heat to low to maintain a gentle simmer. After 10 minutes, toss in the daikon and black pepper. Simmer gently for another 15 minutes, or until slightly thickened (it should cling lightly to a spoon instead of quickly running off) and roughly the consistency of maple syrup.

Transfer to a bowl to cool. If you feel that it's too thick, spoon in a tablespoon or two of warm water to loosen it up.

Store in a wide-mouth glass jar in the refrigerator for several weeks. Bring back to room temperature before serving.

CRISPY RICE AND MUNG BEAN CREPES

BÁNH XÈO

I'm a huge fan of Indian dosas, so my first run-in with Vietnamese *bánh xèo* (pronounced "bang say-o") thrilled me as the two foods are quite similar. Bánh xèo is a savory Vietnamese crepe-style dish in which portions of the crepes are bundled around tender lettuce and fresh herbs and dipped into a tangy sauce.

Although bánh xèo are prepared much like French crepes, their lentil-and-rice batter does make them closer to dosas. While I did observe cooks in the kitchen of the Zen Buddhist monastery in Mỹ Khánh make large crepes using a seasoned wok, I prefer using smaller, cast-iron pans the way cooks do in central Việt Nam. Cast iron retains heat better, thus producing crispier exteriors. (You can also use a nonstick frying pan, but don't expect much crispiness.)

You may make the batter up to two days ahead and refrigerate it, covered. Just be sure to stir it well before using as the ground mung beans and rice flour settle over time. **Makes 10 crepes; serves 4 as a main dish**

½ cup (120 g) mung beans

1½ cups (375 ml) water

1 cup (105 grams) rice flour

¼ teaspoon ground turmeric

½ teaspoon salt

¼ cup coconut milk

Double recipe Everyday Table Sauce (page 49)

1 cup thinly sliced scallions

1 cup roughly chopped cilantro

10 tablespoons (150 ml) vegetable oil

2½ cups (125 g) bean sprouts

2 medium heads Bibb or Boston lettuce, leaves separated and torn into palm-sized pieces if needed.

2 cups mixed herbs such as Thai basil, mint, Vietnamese balm, radish or mustard sprouts

Place the mung beans in a bowl, cover with 2 inches (5 cm) of warm water, and soak for at least 1 hour, preferably 2 hours to overnight.

Drain and place in a blender with the water. Blend for 1 minute. Add the rice flour, turmeric, salt, and coconut milk and blend for another minute. Pour through a fine-mesh strainer into a bowl to remove any lumps. Put the batter in the fridge for at least 30 minutes or overnight.

OPPOSITE Crispy Rice and Mung Bean Crepes

continues

Make a double recipe of the Everyday Table Sauce and set aside. (Before serving, portion the sauce into small bowls so that each diner has a bowl to dip the lettuce-wrapped bánh xèo in).

If you're planning to serve all of the bánh xèo at one time, preheat the oven to 300°F (150°C).

Mix together the scallions and cilantro in a small bowl.

Heat 1 tablespoon of the oil in a 10-inch (25 cm) cast-iron skillet over medium-high heat for 2 to 3 minutes for the first crepe. (The pan will be hot for the following crepes, so you'll need to heat the oil for only about a minute. Pour ¼ cup batter into the hot pan, swirling and tilting the pan to evenly distribute it over the bottom. Fry for 1½ to 2 minutes, until it becomes crisp and golden brown. Sprinkle 3 tablespoons of the scallion-cilantro mix and a small handful of bean sprouts over half of the crepe. Cover, turn the heat to medium-low, and continue to cook for 2 minutes.

Uncover the pan and use a spatula to fold the crepe in half. Gently press on it with the spatula and let it cook and crisp up for another 30 seconds. Remove and transfer to a plate and serve immediately (or to a baking sheet and into the oven).

Repeat with the remaining batter and ingredients until each diner is full or the ingredients are all used up (the latter being the case in our house).

To serve, use scissors to cut each crepe into four or five segments. To eat, place a piece of lettuce in one hand, top with a generous pinch of herbs, and add a piece of crepe on top. Roll the lettuce leaf up and dip into the sauce.

VARIATION

TOFU, MUSHROOM, AND BEAN SPROUT FILLING

¾ pound (340 g) firm tofu, cut into 1-by-1½-inch (2.5 by 4 cm) rectangles ½ inch (1.5 cm) thick

¼ pound (113 g) thinly sliced button mushrooms (1 cup)

2½ cups (150 g) bean sprouts

½ cup thinly sliced scallions

———

Cilantro sprigs

Heat 3 tablespoons of oil in an 8-or 9-inch nonstick skillet or seasoned cast-iron pan over medium heat. Add the tofu slices and cook for 3 minutes, until lightly golden. Turn over and cook for another 3 minutes. Remove to a paper-towel-lined plate.

Pour out most of the oil, leaving about a teaspoon in the pan, and lightly sauté the mushrooms for a minute or two. Remove and set aside with the tofu.

When it's time to add the filling, place three pieces of tofu, four slices of mushroom, a tablespoon of scallions, and a small handful of bean sprouts over half of the crepe. Finish cooking as described above, adding cilantro to the mixed herbs, and serve immediately.

STEAMED FLAT RICE DUMPLINGS IN BANANA LEAVES

BÁNH NẬM CHAY

I spent a day learning how to make Huế's famous dumplings in the home of Hoàng Thị Như Huy, a poet and professor who specializes in the culinary culture of Huế. Filled with sautéed mushrooms and carrots and encased in banana leaves, *bánh nậm* are flat steamed rectangular rice dumplings.

These dumplings are but one example of the unique flavors and refined artisanship typical of Huế, the former imperial capital of Việt Nam. The Nguyễn royalty, which ruled from 1802 to 1945, demanded that a wide variety of dishes regularly grace the table. A formal banquet would typically exceed a hundred dishes, while a vegetarian feast might offer twenty-five. To please the king, creative cooks tried to outdo one another, creating dainty dim-sum-style dishes. Some, like these bánh nậm, are still prepared by Huế street food vendors or in homes today.

To eat, open the banana leaves, drizzle chile-infused soy sauce over the warm dumpling inside, split the dumpling in half with the side of a spoon, then lift the slippery delicacy to your mouth.

The dough will stiffen if left too long before the dumplings are assembled. For this reason, Ms. Hoàng suggests making the filling while the flours hydrate and assembling the dumplings while the dough is still warm.

Makes 24 dumplings; serves 4 to 6 as a starter or light snack

FROM THE PANTRY/MAKE AHEAD

2 tablespoons Fragrant Shallot Oil (page 38)

¼ teaspoon Mushroom Powder (page 36)

1 cup finely chopped fried firm or extra-firm tofu (page 60)

FOR THE DOUGH

¾ cup plus 2 tablespoons rice flour

2 tablespoons tapioca flour

¼ tablespoon salt

2¼ cups room-temperature or cold water

Twenty-four 9-by-5½-inch (23 by 13.5 cm) banana leaf rectangles, plus 2 or 3 extra-large pieces of banana leaves to cut for the ties (substitute parchment paper and string for banana leaves)

FOR THE FILLING

2 tablespoons vegetable oil

¾ cup finely chopped carrot

continues

½ cup (about 3) finely chopped fresh wood ear mushrooms

1 tablespoon finely chopped white part of scallion

1 tablespoon soy sauce

½ teaspoon salt

½ teaspoon sugar

½ teaspoon freshly ground black pepper

¼ cup thinly sliced green part of scallion

Prepare the Fragrant Shallot Oil and Mushroom Powder. Cook and finely chop the tofu.

Mix the flours and salt together in a medium bowl. Pour the water into the bowl in a steady stream and whisk thoroughly. Set a fine sieve over a medium saucepan and pour the batter through to strain out any lumps. Cover and let sit for at least 15 minutes for the flours to hydrate fully.

Heat the vegetable oil in a medium skillet over medium-high heat. Add the carrot and cook, stirring occasionally, for 2 minutes Add the mushrooms and white part of scallion and cook for 1 minute. Stir in the tofu, soy sauce, salt, sugar, and mushroom powder. Cook for another couple of minutes, adding a couple tablespoons of water if any ingredients are sticking to the pan. Stir in the black pepper and green parts of scallion. Mix well, remove from the heat, and transfer to a bowl to cool.

Fill the bottom of a steamer pot or wok two-thirds full with water and bring to a boil. Fit a large colander into a medium bowl and set beside the stove.

Using scissors, cut 14 ties that are ⅛ wide and 14 inches long (3 mm by 36 cm) from extra banana leaves (a couple extra in case they break) or kitchen string.

Put half of the banana leaf rectangles into boiling water for 10 seconds and transfer to the colander. Repeat with the remaining banana leaves and thin ties of banana leaves. (Omit if using parchment paper and string.)

Carefully pour out enough water so that the level of water will be slightly below (about ½ inch; 1.5 cm) the bottom of a steamer basket when steaming the dumplings.

Place the saucepan with batter over medium heat and stir steadily using a wooden spoon for about 5 minutes. As it cooks it will thicken slightly to the consistency of pudding and then thicken a touch more similar to pastry cream. A couple of minutes later, when it begins to feel as if it's sticking to the bottom of the sauce-pan, remove it from the heat, stirring for 1 more minute, and drizzle in the fragrant shallot oil (this helps to prevent the dough from sticking to the banana leaves or parchment paper when steamed).

Organize ties of banana leaves (or string) together next to a clean countertop workspace or cutting board. Wipe dry each banana leaf with a clean cloth and stack (or parchment paper, if using) beside your workspace.

Place a banana leaf with the longest side facing you and bright shiny side against the work-space. Spoon 1½ tablespoons of the dough into the center of the leaf. With your fingertips or the back of a spoon, spread it out 2.5 inches (6.5 cm) long. Spoon about 2 teaspoons of filling along the length and center of dough.

Fold the top of the length of leaf 2 inches toward the center, almost covering the filling. Make a ¼-inch (6 mm) fold along the bottom length of the leaf. Fold the bottom length of leaf toward the center, overlapping the folded top part by 1 inch (2.5 cm).

Make a fold backward 2 inches (5 cm) from the left side of package. Make a similar fold from the right side. You should be left with a package that is 5 inches (13 cm) long and 2 inches (5 cm) wide with a folded creased edge running down the middle and two 2-inch (5 cm) flaps on the back of the package.

Use your fingertips to gently press on the package to evenly spread the dough and filling from the center to the edges.

Place the package flap side down on a work surface.

Repeat with another banana leaf. When two packages are folded, put them with the bent flap sides together. Grab a tie and, beginning 1 inch (2.5 cm) from one end, and leaving about 1½ inches (4 cm) of length loose, tighten along the package and tuck each end in between the two packages. If using string, tie a knot 1 inch (2.5 cm) from one of the ends. Wrap about 3 times around the packages, tying a second knot about 1 inch (2.5 cm) from the other end.

Set aside and repeat until all of the filling and banana leaves are used up.

Arrange the tied packages in an even layer in a steamer basket and steam for 8 to 10 minutes. Take one out and open to test doneness. If the dough is translucent and no longer white, it is done.

To serve, open each package and spoon on some Spicy Soy Drizzling Sauce (see below). Cut a bite-sized portion with a spoon and enjoy.

SPICY SOY DRIZZLING SAUCE

3 tablespoons plus 1 teaspoon soy sauce

2 tablespoons water

1 teaspoon sugar

1 fresh red Thai bird chile, roughly cut into 5 pieces

Place the soy sauce, water, and sugar in a small bowl. Stir until the sugar is fully dissolved. Add the chile and serve.

Banana leaves folded in rectangles and filled with rice dumpling filling before steaming.

8

FROM THE MARKET AND GARDEN

OPPOSITE Early morning market shoppers at a "wet"
market on the outskirts of Cần Thơ.

Local "wet" markets, fresh food markets with wet floors and humid surroundings, in Việt Nam are adventuresome mazes—hives of activity perfect for wandering and getting happily lost in. I'd often plan entire days around an early morning or late afternoon visit to a local market.

Châu Long market in the Trúc Bach district of Hà Nội is one of my favorite places to shop. It's dark and damp but filled with character, and you need to keep an eye out for the odd motorcyclist delivering fresh produce from the fields. Once you build up a rapport with the vendors, you're guaranteed not only the freshest, tastiest produce but also a warm welcoming smile with every visit. There's another reason I love this market so much: female vendors have a distinct ritual of exercising that's a joy to watch (I'll often join in). At about 11:30 each morning, the loudspeakers blare Vietnamese pop music, and virtually every vendor rises from her seat and lines up in the aisles to perform her own personal aerobics and dancing routine. I've never seen anything like it.

Rows of vegetable sellers each try to one-up their neighbors, competing, it seems, for whose colorful vegetable piles draw the greatest number of shoppers. Nothing is shrouded in plastic. Everything, especially the greens and fragrant herbs, comes fresh from the fields, all dew-kissed with tiny dirt clumps clinging to their roots.

Daily market sprees are a fixture of Vietnamese life. The practice dates back to a time when refrigeration was less widespread, but it very much continues to this day. Many Vietnamese also grow their own vegetables. In the countryside, families set aside small plots for a seasonal kitchen garden. Ethnic minority farmers in the North intersperse corn between their rice terraces and grow vegetables like runner beans on adjacent patchy slopes. In hilly, wooden areas like the central highlands, foragers harvest delicacies from the forest floor, using their finds in dishes like Bamboo Shoots and Wild Mushrooms with Peanuts and Sesame Seeds (page 241). Even monks and nuns actively meditate by growing fresh foods for their pantries, everything from herbs and vegetables to tea bushes. Urban gardeners with limited access to land devise clever ways of growing vegetables: in the spaces of overturned cinder blocks; up trellises or canopies; or, as I saw at a pagoda in Hà Nội, between the plants of an otherwise ornamental garden.

Located 180 miles (300 km) northeast of Sài Gòn in the South-central highlands, the quaint town of Đà Lạt was once known as the summer retreat for French colonists who wanted to escape the suffocating heat and humidity of Sài Gòn. Thanks to its high altitude, temperate year-round climate, and fertile valleys, it's one of Việt Nam's prime agricultural areas where a wide variety of Vietnamese and temperate Western vegetables such as artichokes, asparagus, beets, and fennel thrive. Vegetables from Đà Lạt are known for their high quality and are therefore often labeled with their point of origin.

Most of the vegetable side dishes that follow are served in private homes, at vegetarian diners (*cơm bình dân*), or at casual restaurants. They're typically served as part of a basic rice meal, along with mock meat or tofu, soup, and plain rice.

Vietnamese vegetable dishes reflect the seasonal rhythms of the farmers' fields. The variety of leafy greens alone is mind-boggling. Water spinach, amaranth, and Chinese broccoli are year-round stalwarts, while pumpkin blossoms and the delicate flower bud clusters of Tonkin jasmine (*hoa thiên lý*) are among the many fleeting, seasonal treats.

Cooks are especially resourceful with sweet potatoes, chayote, and kohlrabi, as both the vegetables and their accompanying leaves are used in many preparations. Come winter, roasted cobs of corn and sweet potatoes are popular roadside snacks, carrying a touch of smoke along with their natural sweetness.

These dishes are delightfully unfussy. Many are best boiled (the water reserved for use in a soup) or steamed and served with a flavorful dipping sauce as a seasoning, or else quickly sautéed with garlic. Some, like Fire-Roasted Tomato, Chile, and Garlic Salsa (page 239), can be served as snacks or hors d'oeuvres. Other recipes here might introduce you to a new method of cooking vegetables you're accustomed to eating raw, like Stir-Fried Romaine Lettuce with Tomatoes and Peanuts (page 234).

While you'll easily be able to find many of the vegetables featured in these recipes at your supermarket or farmers' market, some—like water spinach or Chinese broccoli—will require a visit to an Asian grocer. You can often substitute chard, kale, and zucchini blossoms as well as some vegetables not typically part of the Vietnamese vegetable patch, like Brussels sprouts, parsnips, or Jerusalem artichokes.

Finally, if you have a green thumb yourself, why not grow some herbs or vegetables specific to the Vietnamese kitchen? I've supplied a list of seed companies in the Resources at the back of the book to get you started.

TENDER BOILED VEGETABLES

RAU LUỘC

A plate of simply prepared seasonal boiled or steamed vegetables is a common part of every rice meal. Vegetables are easy and quick to make, highly nutritious, and their clean flavors help balance out rich and spicy dishes.

Robust brassicas such as broccoli, Chinese broccoli (*gai lan*), cauliflower, cabbage, kohlrabi, and daikon radish make frequent appearances, as do sweeter vegetables like carrots, green and long beans, chayote, asparagus, okra, and even pumpkin. Consider including vegetables not traditional to the Vietnamese table that you also love, whether broccoli rabe, heirloom radishes, spring fiddleheads, summer zucchini, and fall turnips and squashes, to name a few. So long as they're at their seasonal peak, they'll shine in straightforward recipes like this one. Don't forget hardy greens like water spinach, watercress, squash or chayote tendrils, and amaranth.

Above all, aim for variety, plus a balance of bitter and sweet. And if you're used to barely boiling your vegetables to al dente, you'll need to push the cooking time a bit longer. In true Vietnamese style, cook the vegetables until they're tender with just the faintest bite remaining. In fact, boil each vegetable separately, if you're willing, to ensure even, consistent doneness. The cooking times that follow are guidelines and will vary depending on the vegetable's age and the thickness of the cut.

Serve with Fermented Tofu, Lemongrass, and Chile Dipping Sauce (page 230), Caramelized Soy Dipping Sauce (page 215), or Everyday Table Sauce (page 49). Or dip them in a quick mix of salt, pepper, and sliced chile, moistened with a squirt of lime. **Serves 4 to 6 people as part of a multidish meal**

continues

Approximately 1 pound of vegetables

Bring a large pot of salted water—1 teaspoon salt per quart (liter) water—to a boil. Add the vegetables and cook them for the suggested times.

Asparagus, cut into 5-inch-long spears: 30 seconds

Broccoli and cauliflower, cut into 2½-inch-long florets: 4 minutes

Carrots, cut into ½-inch-thick slices: 4 minutes

Chinese broccoli and broccoli rabe cut into 2½-inch-long florets: 3 minutes

Fall squashes, cut into ¾-inch-thick slices: 3 to 4 minutes

Kohlrabi, daikon radish, or chayote, cut into ½-inch-thick slices: 3 to 4 minutes

Green and long beans in 3-inch lengths: 3 to 4 minutes

Green cabbage, cut into 2-inch pieces: 2 to 3 minutes

Zucchini, cut into ½-inch-thick slices: 1½ to 2 minutes

Leafy greens (water spinach, watercress, squash or chayote tendrils, amaranth), cut into 3-inch long pieces: 30 seconds to a minute

Start by cooking the vegetables that will take longer first. Test the doneness of each vegetable by removing a couple pieces of vegetables and inserting the tip of a knife, a bamboo skewer, or the side of a spoon to try to cut through. When inserted, the knife tip, skewer, or spoon should go through without much resistance. Have a bite of a piece of vegetable as your teeth are also great judges of the tenderness of a vegetable.

When one kind of vegetable is ready, remove the pieces with a spider or slotted spoon and reserve on a plate. Continue cooking the other vegetables. If you feel the reserved vegetables have cooled too much, throw them in right at the end of cooking the last vegetable to simply warm through. Remove them using a spider or slotted spoon and transfer to a serving dish and serve with a dipping sauce.

Use the cooking broth to quickly assemble a light soup or reserve to use when making a vegetable stock (page 30 or 31).

Note:
It's also common to include a plate of thin slices of cucumbers and tomatoes, in season and at their peak, as part of a simple rice meal.

OPPOSITE Tender Boiled Vegetables (page 227) with Fermented Tofu, Lemongrass, and Chile Sauce (page 230). *Clockwise from top left:* fall squash, asparagus, green beans, carrots, young Chinese broccoli

FERMENTED TOFU, LEMONGRASS, AND CHILE SAUCE

NƯỚC CHẤM CHAO

On the day I showed up late to my friend Linh's vegetarian restaurant in Hà Nội, they'd sold out of their extremely popular Tomato and Creamy Tofu Noodle Soup (page 181). Linh, her sister, her mother, and a family friend, who had brought along this sauce as her contribution, were seated for their staff meal. They offered me a taste, and I was immediately taken with the sauce's robust, cheesy flavor and strong notes of lemongrass and chile. At my request, the family friend generously shared her recipe.

Fermented tofu smells pungent but mellows considerably when heated. Because of its strong, salty flavor, a little goes a long way. Spoon some into a condiment bowl and use as a dip for warm Tender Boiled Vegetables (page 227). (Boiled okra is especially classic.)   **Makes 4 to 6 tablespoons; serves 3**

FROM THE PANTRY/MAKE AHEAD

1 tablespoon Fragrant Shallot Oil (page 38) or vegetable oil

—

2 tablespoons fermented tofu

1 to 3 tablespoons brine from the tofu jar or water

1 lemongrass stalk, root end trimmed, outer 2 or 3 layers peeled away, bottom 2½ inches (6.5 cm) finely chopped (1 tablespoon)

½ fresh red Thai bird chile, finely chopped

1 teaspoon sugar

Juice of ½ lime

Prepare the Fragrant Shallot Oil, if using.

Remove the cubes of fermented tofu with a clean spoon or fork from the bottle. Place them in a small bowl and mash them to a puree with the back of a fork. Thin out the mashed tofu with a tablespoon of brine or water.

Heat the shallot oil in a small saucepan over medium heat. Toss in the lemongrass and chile and stir-fry for 45 seconds to a minute. Reduce the heat and spoon in the mashed tofu and sugar. Rinse the small bowl with a tablespoon or two of water to get as much of the tofu from the bowl. Gently simmer the tofu for a minute. Stir in the lime juice and transfer to a small bowl, making sure you've scraped out as much of the mixture as possible. If you feel the sauce is too thick—it should be the consistency of heavy cream—thin it with some water or brine from the jar.

Serve the sauce warm or at room temperature.

STIR-FRIED WATER SPINACH

RAU MUỐNG XÀO

A Vietnamese rice meal isn't complete without some kind of nutritious leafy green. Most common is water spinach or morning glory (*rau muống*), referred to in Cantonese as *ong choy*. Quickly stir-fry it with garlic, just until it loses its raw edge. Or drape it with creamy, fermented tofu sauce. Peppery watercress (*rau xà lách son)* or red- or purple-veined amaranth (*rau den*), whose cooking juices turn a lovely shade of fuchsia, benefit from the same luxurious treatment. Other seasonal favorites include neglected tender shoots of pumpkin (*rau bí*) and chayote (*rau su su*) with their spiraling antennae and hollow stems. Western spinach, chard, and sweet potato leaves (*yam leaves*) also work well.

Wash leaves and greens well in several changes of water as speckles of grit and sand hide in tiny crevices (including in the hollow stems of water spinach, pumpkin, and chayote). And cook more than you think you might need; greens shrink considerably once prepared. **Serves 4 as part of a multidish meal**

1½ pounds (680 g) water spinach

1 tablespoon vegetarian mushroom-flavored stir-fry sauce

1 tablespoon water

½ teaspoon sugar

2 tablespoons vegetable oil

3 garlic cloves, finely chopped

Trim off the bottom, tougher part (3 to 4 inches; 7.5 to 10 cm) of the water spinach stems and any discolored leaves. Discard the stems or save, cut thinly lengthwise, and use as a soup garnish. Cut the water spinach into 3-inch (7.5 cm) lengths and place in a sink or very large bowl full of cold water to soak for a few minutes. Give it a good aggressive stir with your hands to loosen any dirt. Let it rest for another minute or two to allow the dirt particles to sink to the bottom. Remove from the water and repeat the washing process one or two more times until you don't see any accumulated dirt particles in the water.

Bring a large pot of lightly salted water to a boil over high heat. Toss in the water spinach and blanch until the leaves are wilted (30 to 45 seconds). Drain in a colander and rinse with cold water until cool. Grab a third of the water spinach and press it several times to squeeze out any extra water. Set it aside and repeat a couple more times with the remaining water spinach. You can do this part several hours in advance and refrigerate until ready to stir-fry.

Stir the vegetarian mushroom-flavored stir-fry sauce, water, and sugar together in a small bowl (see Note). Heat the oil in a wok or large skillet set over high heat. Add the garlic and stir-fry for about 10 seconds, or until it's fragrant. Toss

continues

in the water spinach and stir-fry for another 2 to 3 minutes. Add the sauce and cook for another minute. Check the seasoning and adjust with salt if necessary.

Note:
If you like, you can omit adding the sauce and season it with salt or serve it with a dipping sauce (like Everyday Table Sauce, page 49).

VARIATIONS

STIR-FRIED WATER SPINACH WITH FERMENTED TOFU

3 tablespoons fermented tofu
1½ teaspoons brine from the jar
¾ teaspoon sugar

Mash the fermented tofu and mix with the brine. Set aside. Prepare the water spinach as directed, omitting the stir-fry sauce. Stir-fry for a minute or two to heat and stir in the fermented tofu and sugar. Serve immediately.

STIR-FRIED WATERCRESS OR AMARANTH OR SWEET POTATO LEAVES WITH GARLIC OR FERMENTED TOFU

Cut off the bottom inch or two of any tough stalks. Cut watercress (or amaranth/sweet potato leaves) into 3-inch (7.5 cm) lengths. Prepare as described for water spinach with garlic or fermented tofu.

STIR-FRIED CHARD WITH GARLIC OR FERMENTED TOFU

Separate the leaves from the stems of one bunch of chard. Trim the tougher bottom inch or two from the stems and cut them into 1- to 1½-inch (2.5 to 4 cm) lengths. Cut them into thick matchsticks and set aside. Coarsely chop the leaves into large bite-sized pieces. Add the stems to the hot oil and stir-fry for several minutes. Toss in the garlic and leaves and briefly stir-fry. Cover the skillet (or reduce the wok's heat) and cook the leaves until wilted and tender, about 5 minutes. Season with the stir-fry sauce or fermented tofu.

STIR-FRIED PUMPKIN, SQUASH, OR CHAYOTE STEMS WITH GARLIC

Keep watch for these stems, from late July through the early autumn, at the stalls of Hmong and Vietnamese farmers at your local farmers' market. I've also seen them sold at Chinese, Vietnamese, or Korean grocers.

The tip end of each shoot or tendril (3 to 4 inches; 7.5 to 10 cm) is tender enough not to need peeling. But a thin, prickly, fibrous outer layer needs to be removed from the thicker stems, a process that's similar to peeling the thin, tough skin from mature stalks of rhubarb.

Use a paring knife to just cut through the thicker end of a stem (or break it with your hands) and pull the edge of the knife up against the outer surface of the stem to release and peel off any stringy fibers. Pull off any larger fuzzy leaves and discard with the removed fibers. Cut the stems into 2½-inch (6.5 cm) lengths. Wash the tender tips and thicker stems separately and blanch the thicker stems in boiling water for about a minute. Drain the stems and immediately place them in a bowl of ice water until cool. Drain them and pat them dry well on a clean dish towel. Stir-fry them as directed for 3 to 4 minutes.

STIR-FRIED ZUCCHINI BLOSSOMS WITH GARLIC

BÔNG BÍ XÀO TỎI

While visiting a market on the outskirts of Cần Thơ, I came across bright pumpkin flowers nestled among various greens. The precious golden pumpkin blossoms always sell out quickly, so only early shoppers reap the rewards, and I felt especially lucky. I grabbed a bunch, buying them specifically to share with an elderly couple whose home I was renting. Their daughter stir-fried them until wilted, flavoring them simply with papery slices of garlic.

If you're a gardener, take advantage of your pumpkin, squash, and zucchini plants, as they produce an abundance of flowers, all of which can be used in this recipe. Choose bright, unblemished male flowers—they're thinner at the base where they attach to the stem—and leave the female flowers to produce a fruitful harvest. Use these delicate flowers immediately as they're highly perishable or refrigerate in a paper bag. Use within a day or two.

Serves 4 as a part of a multidish meal

30 to 40 (about ½ pound; 225 g) zucchini
    blossoms, stems trim to about 1 inch
    (2.5 cm)

1 tablespoon vegetable oil

3 garlic cloves, thinly sliced

¼ teaspoon salt

Carefully open the blossoms and, using your fingers, snap off the pistil. Quickly rinse with water and gently pat dry with a clean kitchen towel or paper towel.

Heat the oil in a wok or sauté pan over medium-high heat. Add the garlic and stir-fry for 30 seconds. Toss in the zucchini blossoms and salt. Stir gently until the blossoms begin to wilt, about 20 seconds. It's better to be extra cautious and remove them early as opposed to having them become soft and soggy from overcooking.

Quickly transfer to a platter and serve immediately.

STIR-FRIED ROMAINE LETTUCE WITH TOMATOES AND PEANUTS

RAU DIẾP XÀO CÀ CHUA ĐẬU PHỘNG

As a form of active meditation each morning in Buddhist monasteries, monks and nuns clean, do laundry, chop firewood for the kitchen stoves, or tend the kitchen garden. A large monastic community has more space and more helping hands to cultivate a wider variety of vegetables for culinary and medicinal purposes. Smaller, urban monasteries plant easy-to-grow vegetables and herbs in beds that dot their courtyards.

I tasted this warm saladlike dish on a visit to the Bamboo Forest (*Trúc Lâm*) Zen monastery in Đà Lạt. The monks stir-fried freshly harvested lettuce leaves until supple. Right before serving they tossed in sliced tomato and crispy tofu skin, ending with a toasted peanut garnish.

High heat sweetens and transforms lettuce's delicate flavor, intensifying it. This recipe works well with other leafy greens too, among them chard, frisée, watercress, and kale.   **Serves 4 as part of a multidish rice meal**

FROM THE PANTRY/MAKE AHEAD

A handful of Tofu Skin Chips (page 42), roughly broken into 1½-inch (4 cm) pieces

---

1 tablespoon soy sauce

1 tablespoon water

¼ teaspoon sugar

¼ teaspoon salt

1 tablespoon vegetable oil

½ fresh red mild long chile, seeded and thinly sliced, or ½ cup red bell pepper, thinly sliced

1 pound (450 g) hearts of romaine lettuce, cut into 1-inch (2.5 cm) pieces

8 cherry tomatoes, cut in half lengthwise

2 tablespoons roasted unsalted peanuts, roughly chopped

Prepare the Tofu Skin Chips.

Stir together the soy sauce, water, sugar, and salt in a small bowl and set next to the stove.

Heat the oil in a wok or large skillet over high heat. Swirl the oil around the wok, add the chile, and stir-fry for 5 to 10 seconds. Toss in the lettuce and cook until it starts to wilt, about 1 minute. Stir the sauce, swirl it into the wok, and stir-fry for another 30 to 45 seconds. Add the tofu skin chips and tomatoes, toss to mix, and warm through. Remove from the heat and transfer immediately to a serving dish. Garnish with the peanuts and serve.

OPPOSITE Stir-Fried Romaine Lettuce with Tomatoes and Peanuts

SAUTÉED SQUASH WITH BASIL AND PEANUTS

BÍ ĐỎ XÀO ĐẬU PHỘNG

Butternut and kabocha are terrific in this recipe, but red kuri, with its deep orange, dense, and silky-smooth flesh, is especially well suited, and sure to carry you through the dark winter months. I often include this and as part of a Tasty Rice Noodle Bowl (page 188) or as a side for a weeknight rice meal.

Serves 4 as part of a multidish meal or as garnish for a Tasty Rice Noodle Bowl

FROM THE PANTRY/MAKE AHEAD

¼ cup Light or Rich Vegetable Stock (page 30 or 31) or water

1½ pounds (680 g) butternut, kabocha, or red kuri squash

1 tablespoon vegetable oil

1 tablespoon finely chopped garlic

½ teaspoon salt

¼ cup roasted unsalted peanuts, lightly chopped

¼ cup roughly chopped Thai basil

Freshly ground black pepper

Prepare the vegetable stock, if using. Peel and seed the squash. Cut the squash into 1-inch-thick (2.5 cm) bite-sized pieces.

Heat the oil in a wok or large skillet over medium heat. Add the garlic and cook for 1 to 2 minutes, until fragrant and starting to color. Toss in the squash, stock or water, and salt and bring to a simmer. Cover, reduce the heat to medium-low, and cook, stirring every few minutes, for about 12 minutes or until tender (not mushy or falling apart), with 1 or 2 tablespoons of liquid remaining. (If the squash is ready but there's too much liquid, remove the squash, increase the heat, and reduce the liquid.)

Turn off the heat and stir in half of the peanuts and chopped basil. Taste and adjust the salt if necessary. Transfer to a serving bowl and sprinkle a generous grinding of black pepper and the rest of the peanuts and Thai basil over top.

VARIATION

ROASTED WINTER SQUASH WITH BASIL AND PEANUTS

Heat the oven to 375°F (190°C). Place the cut-up squash in a large bowl. Drizzle the oil over it and sprinkle the salt over the top. Spread in one layer on a parchment-lined baking sheet and roast for about 30 minutes, or until tender. Every 10 minutes or so, stir or turn the squash over. When tender, stir in the garlic and cook for several minutes, just long enough for the raw garlic taste to mellow. Remove the baking sheet from the oven and sprinkle a generous grinding of black pepper and all of the peanuts and Thai basil over the top. Transfer to a serving dish.

BRIGHT GREEN HERBY OMELET

TRỨNG GÀ NGẢI CỨU

Early mornings buzz and hum in Vietnamese cities. As motorcyclists speed by on their way to work, women wearing conical hats adopt a different, slower pace, ambling down the sides of streets with bamboo poles balanced across their shoulders. Baskets bob at either end of these poles, some with a portable burner, small frying pan, farm-fresh eggs, and bright green leaves—a sure sign the woman will be making Vietnamese-style omelets. Soon hungry passersby will stop her, and right there on the spot, she'll set up her mobile kitchen, quickly whisk an egg, bind it with a fragrant, thinly sliced herb, and cook it up. Diners will eagerly dip their omelets into salty sauce made with lime and chili.

The herb mugwort (*ngải cứu* in Vietnamese) is traditional in this omelet. It grows abundantly in garden beds, roadsides, and fields throughout North America. (See the Glossary for foraging tips.) When I don't have access to the perfumed mugwort leaves, which smell of sage and rosemary with hints of anise, I turn to a combination of Thai basil and cilantro. To these I add stronger-flavored herbs such as red perilla, tarragon, dill, or a pinch of finely chopped rosemary or sage. A scallion or a few minced garlic chives often find their way into the mix as well. Just aim for balance so no single herb overpowers.

Sometimes I make the omelet as a filling for a Bánh Mì Sandwich (page 113). My friend Suzanne, a long-term resident of Việt Nam, regularly enjoys it for breakfast or as a light lunch with slices of tomato, cucumber, and avocado on the side. **Serves 1**

FOR THE DIPPING SAUCE

Juice of ½ lime

¼ teaspoon salt

Pinch of freshly ground black pepper

¼ fresh red Thai bird chile, seeded and thinly sliced

FOR THE OMELET

¾ cup loosely packed mixed herbs—
(a balanced combination of of some of the following herbs: Thai basil, cilantro, Vietnamese cilantro, dill, tarragon, rosemary, sage—finely chopped, or mugwort leaves, picked off the stem

continues

1 large organic egg

¼ teaspoon soy sauce

Pinch of salt

Pinch of freshly ground black pepper

1 teaspoon vegetable oil

Prepare the dipping sauce: Stir together the lime juice, salt, pepper, and chile in a small bowl. Set aside.

Wash, then dry the herb leaves, thinly slicing mugwort leaves. Crack the egg into a small bowl and add the soy sauce, salt, and pepper. Use a fork to beat the egg. Add the herbs and mix thoroughly.

Drizzle the oil into an 8-inch (20 cm) skillet and tilt to evenly coat the bottom with oil. Set the pan over medium heat. When hot, tilt the egg mixture into the pan, spreading it out to cover the entire bottom with the back of a spatula. Cook for about 2 minutes, until the edges are set and the bottom is golden brown. Use a spatula to flip and cook for another minute. Remove from the heat and transfer to a cutting board. Cut the omelet into 1½-inch strips or into 6 wedges. Serve right away with the dipping sauce.

VARIATION

A chef friend in Hà Nội who runs a cooking school shared this wonderful countryside version that one of her cooks prepared for their staff meal. Simply substitute herbs or mugwort leaves with 6 pungent, slightly peppery wild betel leaves, *lá lốt*. Stem, thinly slice, then roughly chop the leaves prior to stirring them into the egg.

Fresh mugwort

FIRE-ROASTED TOMATO, CHILE, AND GARLIC SALSA

SỐT CÀ CHUA NƯỚNG

Nestled in the mountainous northwest corner of Việt Nam, the quaint hill town of Sa Pa sits fairly close to the Chinese border. I've made several trips there to observe the annual rice planting and harvest, and each time I go I stay at a small retreat several miles outside of town. There I sleep in a clay and bamboo hut perched high above the tiered rice paddies that slope down the steep hillside.

From May through the summer, rice seedlings grow and turn the valley emerald green. A few ethnic minority groups, including the Hmong, live a hard subsistence life growing rice, corn, and vegetables on these mountainous slopes. One September morning I awoke and peered out my door to see the valley glowing, yellow with ripeness, the sign that the rice harvest was about to begin. I climbed down the rice slopes to meet with a few Hmong families in the tiny village below.

The women had spent the morning hand-cutting rice stalks with scythes as the men collected the stalks and threshed them against wooden boards, releasing the grains of rice. When it came time for lunch, a few of the women, crouched under large umbrellas to shield them from the hot noon sun, offered me a taste of their meal: steamed sticky rice, some boiled greens, and this smoky, garlicky tomato salsa.

Serve this salsa as a snack with Toasted Sesame Rice Crackers (page 55) or Golden Crispy Rice Shell (page 213) or as sauce to enliven a simple rice meal. **Makes about 1 cup (250 ml)**

¾ pound (3 plum or 8 small "Campari") ripe tomatoes

1 fresh green serrano or long hot red finger chile

4 garlic cloves, unpeeled

½ teaspoon salt

2 tablespoons cilantro leaves, finely chopped

Place a fine-mesh wire rack over the top of a gas burner (or a hot charcoal or gas barbecue set to medium-high heat). Set the tomatoes on the wire rack and turn the burner to medium-high heat. Grill the tomatoes, turning occasionally with a pair of tongs, until

continues

the entire surface of the skin is blackened, blistered, and starting to peel away from the flesh (about 5 minutes for Campari tomatoes and 10 minutes for plum tomatoes). Transfer the slightly softened tomatoes to a plate to cool. Reduce the heat to medium and lay the chile and garlic cloves on the wire rack. Occasionally turn them over until the're blackened in spots and soft (8 to 10 minutes for the chile, 10 to 12 for the garlic). Transfer to the plate with the tomatoes.

Alternatively, place a rack at the top level of the oven. Set the broiler to very hot (500°F; 260°C). Lay the tomatoes, chile, and garlic separately on a baking sheet and slide into the oven. Halfway through the roasting (4 minutes for chile, 5 to 6 minutes for tomatoes and garlic), use tongs to flip them. The tomatoes, chile, and garlic cloves are ready when they are blackened and blistered and slightly soft (about 8 minutes for the chile, 10 to 12 minutes for

tomatoes and garlic). Remove from the oven and transfer to a plate to cool.

Over a bowl to catch the juices, peel the charred tomato skins away from the flesh. Chop into large chunks and scoop them, along with any juice, into the bowl of a mortar. Peel the blackened papery skin from garlic. Roughly chop and place in the bowl with the tomatoes. Pull the stems off and peel away the blackened skin from the chile. Roughly chop and place in the bowl with the tomatoes and garlic.

Sprinkle the salt over the top and use the pestle to pound gently to a rough paste. Taste and add more salt if needed. (Alternatively, transfer the ingredients to a food processor or blender and pulse 3 to 4 times so that it remains slightly chunky and is not a puree.)

Transfer to a small serving bowl and stir in the chopped cilantro just before serving. Serve warm or at room temperature.

A Hmong woman harvests rice on the terraces outside Sa Pa.

BAMBOO SHOOTS AND WILD MUSHROOMS WITH PEANUTS AND SESAME SEEDS

MĂNG NẤM XÀO

Young bamboo shoots and wild mushrooms sprout year-round in the forested hills surrounding Huế. Cooking the mushrooms separately ensures they'll brown fully and deeply, heightening both their flavor and meaty texture. The bamboo shoots offer a contrasting sweetness and refreshing crunch. Serve hot as a side dish or at room temperature as a salad.

I learned this recipe from Bội Trân, a painter who lives in Huế's southern outskirts, where serene pine forests and a number of small Buddhist monasteries dot the region. Bội Trân enjoys a peaceful existence among a number of exquisitely restored local timber houses (*nhà rường*), which form a compound. One of Huế's most skilled artisans, she regularly opens her home—which also functions as an art gallery—to visitors eager to see what she crafts from lacquer, silk, and oil.

Bội Trân is also a highly skilled cook. If you're lucky, as I was, she'll prepare you a feast of both common and historical Huế dishes.

Serves 4 as part of a multidish meal

FROM THE PANTRY/MAKE AHEAD

2 teaspoons Toasted Sesame Seeds (page 33)

½ pound (225 g) drained bamboo shoots, cut into thick matchsticks

2 tablespoons vegetable oil

½ pound (225 g) mixed mushrooms (oyster, shimeji, chanterelle, or king oyster), cleaned and cut or torn into bite-sized pieces or cut into ¼-inch-thick (6 mm) slices for king oyster

1 scallion, thinly sliced

1 fresh red Thai bird chile, seeded and finely chopped, or a pinch of dried chile flakes

¼ teaspoon salt

Freshly ground black pepper

1½ tablespoons soy sauce

½ lime

3 to 4 culantro stems, cut into 1-inch (2.5 cm) pieces or 2 Thai basil sprigs, leaves picked from stems and roughly chopped

¼ cup loosely packed Vietnamese coriander or cilantro, very roughly chopped

1 tablespoon roasted unsalted peanuts, roughly chopped

continues

Prepare the Toasted Sesame Seeds.

Bring a medium pot filled with water to a boil over high heat. Add the bamboo shoots and boil for 1 minute. Drain and set aside.

Heat the oil in a large skillet over medium-high heat. Add the mushrooms and stir or toss to coat lightly with oil. Leave undisturbed for about 2½ minutes to brown. If the mushrooms give off some liquid, cook until the moisture has completely evaporated. Shake the skillet or stir and leave undisturbed to brown for another 2 minutes. Repeat this a couple more times.

As the mushrooms cook they'll shrink a bit in volume and brown nicely all over.

If the skillet seems dry, drizzle in a teaspoon of oil and toss in the scallion and chile. Stir-fry for 10 to 20 seconds, until the chile is fragrant. Add the bamboo shoots, salt and a generous grind of black pepper and stir briefly to warm through. Drizzle in the soy sauce and a tablespoon of water. Turn off the heat, squeeze the lime over the top, and toss in the herbs. Transfer to a serving plate and garnish with peanuts and toasted sesame seeds.

OPPOSITE Bamboo Shoots and Wild Mushrooms with Peanuts and Sesame Seeds

SMOKY EGGPLANT
WITH SOY SAUCE AND CHILE

CÀ TÍM NƯỚNG

Char-grilling deep purple Japanese eggplant makes its flesh silky while imparting an intense smoky flavor. The ideal accompaniment is a drizzle of soy sauce dressing and a smattering of cilantro and toasted sesame. It's a dish whose relatively straightforward preparation and minimal ingredients list belies its considerable impact.

In some southern Vietnamese markets, vegetable vendors sell charred and peeled eggplant, making this dish even faster and simpler for home cooks to prepare. Still, it's easy to make yourself. Char the eggplant on a gas burner or over hot coals for the biggest payoff or use a broiler if you must. You can even char the eggplants a few hours before serving and rewarm them gently in a moderate oven. **Serves 4 as a side dish**

FROM THE PANTRY/MAKE AHEAD

1 tablespoon Fragrant Shallot Oil (page 38) or 2 teaspoons Annatto Seed Oil (page 35)

1 tablespoon Crispy Fried Shallots (page 37) or 1 tablespoon roasted unsalted peanuts, roughly chopped or 2 teaspoons Toasted Sesame Seeds (page 33)

1½ pounds (680 g) (about 4) firm long purple Japanese eggplants

1 tablespoon soy sauce

1 tablespoon water

½ teaspoon sugar

½ fresh red Thai bird chile, seeded and finely chopped (optional)

2 tablespoons thinly sliced scallions

2 tablespoons cilantro leaves, roughly chopped

Prepare the Fragrant Shallot Oil or Annatto Seed Oil and the Crispy Fried Shallots or Toasted Sesame Seeds, if using.

Place a small stainless-steel wire cooling rack over the top of a gas burner (or a hot charcoal or gas barbecue) on medium-high heat. Lightly prick each eggplant a few times with the tines of a fork. Lay two eggplants, each with the top 4 inches of the stem end over the flame, on the rack. Char-grill for about 10 minutes, turning frequently and gradually sliding the uncooked part of the eggplant over the flame, until the skin is mostly blistered and blackened and the flesh is just tender but not completely

continues

OPPOSITE Smoky Eggplant with Soy Sauce and Chile

soft. Transfer the char-grilled eggplants to a plate to cool and cook any remaining eggplants. (Alternatively, preheat the broiler in your oven and cook for 10 to 15 minutes or until as described, although it most likely will be less blackened and charred.)

Cool for about 5 minutes, or until you're able to handle them (they are easier to peel when still warm). Gently peel away the charred skin, using your fingers or gently scraping the side of the eggplant with a paring knife. Cut the flesh into 1½-inch (4 cm) pieces. Place on an ovenproof dish, if making them in advance and rewarming them before serving, or directly on a serving platter.

Pour the soy sauce, shallot oil, water, sugar, and chile into a small bowl and stir until the sugar is fully dissolved. Drizzle the sauce over the room-temperature or warm eggplant. Garnish with the scallions, cilantro leaves, and crispy shallots.

SOY GINGER GLAZED EGGPLANT

CÀ TÌM SỐT NƯỚC TƯƠNG GỪNG

Long slender Asian eggplants, with their thin skin and sweet flesh, shine in this easy recipe. As a cook and a busy parent, I appreciate both its speed and its depth of flavor. My wife loves the eggplant's luxurious texture and the bright spark from the ginger.

Eggplants are notorious for soaking up a good bit of oil when deep-fried, but the buttery flesh that results is hard to achieve with other methods. Shallow-frying is the next best thing. Garnish the succulent eggplant with toasted unsalted cashews. **Serves 4 as part of a multidish meal**

1 pound (454 g; about 2) long Japanese eggplants

3 tablespoons soy sauce

1 tablespoon plus 1½ teaspoons vegetarian mushroom-flavored stir-fry sauce or vegetarian hoisin sauce

¼ cup water

2 teaspoons sugar

¼ cup vegetable oil, or more as needed

1 tablespoon finely chopped ginger

½ fresh red (medium-hot) long red chile, finely chopped

¼ teaspoon freshly ground black pepper

1 scallion, thinly sliced

1 tablespoon roughly chopped cilantro

2 tablespoons cashews, toasted (optional)

Slice each eggplant in half lengthwise. Cut each half into about 3-inch (7.5 cm) pieces. Score by cutting halfway through the thickness of each piece twice at approximately 1-inch (2.5 cm) intervals.

In a small bowl, stir together the soy sauce, vegetarian mushroom-flavored stir-fry sauce, water, and sugar and set aside.

Place a paper-towel-lined plate next to the stove. Heat the oil in a large skillet over medium-high heat. Carefully place the eggplant, cut side down, into the pan (do this in two batches if necessary so as not to crowd the pan). Shallow-fry, leaving it undisturbed for about 3 minutes, or until nicely browned. Turn over to cook the skin side for another couple of minutes. Transfer to a paper-towel-lined plate. Add another tablespoon or two of oil to the skillet if the first batch of eggplant soaked up a lot of the oil. Shallow-fry the second batch.

Pour out all but 2 teaspoons of the remaining oil and discard.

continues

Reduce the heat to medium, add the ginger and chile, and briefly stir-fry until fragrant. Return the eggplant to the skillet and pour the soy sauce mixture over the top, stirring to coat the eggplant. Simmer for several minutes, stirring occasionally, until the eggplant is glazed and 1 to 2 tablespoons of liquid remains in the skillet. Transfer to a serving dish and garnish with the black pepper, scallion, cilantro, and cashews, if using.

SOY-GLAZED EGGPLANT WITH LEMONGRASS AND CHILE

Omit the ginger. Peel one or two layers from a stalk of lemongrass, and finely chop the bottom 3 inches (reserve the top of the stalk for tea or broth). Stir-fry the lemongrass and chile in the oil over medium heat for a minute or two before returning the fried eggplant to the skillet. Finish with the sauce as described.

Jackfruit hanging on a tree

STEWED JACKFRUIT
WITH VIETNAMESE CORIANDER

MÍT KHO

Ms. Vân, Việt Nam's Julia Child (see page 11 for more about Nguyễn Dzoãn Cẩm Vân), is the only vegetarian in her family, but over lunch in her home, she shared this recipe for one of her family's favorite dishes with me. As young, unripe jackfruit simmers, it becomes extra-flavorful and meaty, absorbing whatever sauce is in the pot. (Many vegans use jackfruit as a meat substitute.) If you can find Vietnamese coriander, seek it out for its distinct flavor; otherwise, use a blend of Thai basil and cilantro. Serve this dish with steamed rice, stir-fried greens, and a pomelo or green mango salad to cut its richness. Leftovers make a great filling for Bánh Mì Sandwiches (page 113).

Serves 4 as part of a multidish meal

FROM PANTRY/MAKE AHEAD

½ teaspoon Mushroom Powder (page 36)

½ cup (125 ml) fresh or canned coconut water or vegetable stock—or water enough to just cover the jackfruit

---

300 grams canned young green jackfruit (1 can; see photo on page 307), drained and cut into 1-inch thick (3 cm) and 1½-inch-wide (4 cm) pieces, if not already cut

1 tablespoon vegetable oil

¼ cup soy sauce

1 tablespoon sugar

1 tablespoon sweet soy sauce (kecap manis) or 1 tablespoon soy sauce and 1 teaspoon vegetable stir-fry sauce or molasses

1 fresh red Thai bird chile, stemmed, seeded, and finely chopped

½ cup packed (50 g) Vietnamese coriander leaves

Prepare the Mushroom Powder and the stock, if using.

Pat dry both sides of the jackfruit pieces with some paper towel or a clean dish towel.

Line a plate with paper towel and set it beside the stove. Heat the oil in a medium pot or skillet over medium-high heat. Add the jackfruit in one layer and cook for 3 minutes, or until golden brown, before carefully turning over. Cook for another 3 minutes, until the other side is golden brown. Turn off the heat and transfer the jackfruit to the paper-towel-lined plate. Pour out any oil that remains in the pot and discard.

Return the browned jackfruit to the pot. Add the soy sauce, sugar, sweet soy sauce, mushroom powder and chile. Gently mix well, not

continues

breaking the jackfruit pieces, and marinate for at least 15 minutes, and up to 8 hours or overnight.

Add all but 2 tablespoons of the Vietnamese coriander and the coconut water to the pot and mix. Bring the liquid to a simmer over medium-high heat. Cover, reduce the heat to medium, and simmer for 15 minutes. Uncover and simmer for another 10 minutes, or until the sauce is reduced to a thin, light syrup that coats the jackfruit.

Spoon the stewed jackfruit into a serving dish and garnish with the remaining Vietnamese coriander. Serve with plain steamed rice.

OPPOSITE Stewed Jackfruit with Vietnamese Coriander

CURRIED VEGETABLE STEW WITH BAGUETTE

CÀ RI CHAY

Perfumed with lemongrass and curry leaves, this aromatic coconut milk curry is a great introduction to those new to Vietnamese curries. Vietnamese curry powder has less chile heat, less cumin, and more coriander than Indian curry powders. It's also extremely versatile and shines equally bright with Vietnamese or non-Vietnamese vegetables (think celery root, Jerusalem artichokes, and parsnips, for starters). I like tearing off a piece of baguette and dunking it into the sauce as I eat. You can also spoon this curry over hot vermicelli rice noodles or steamed rice.

You can find Vietnamese curry powder (*bột cà ri* or *cà ri nị Ấn Độ*) at Asian markets, but a mild Madras curry powder makes a good substitute.

Serves 4 as a one-dish meal

FROM THE PANTRY/MAKE AHEAD

1 tablespoon Annatto Seed Oil (page 35)

A handful of Tofu Skin Chips (page 42)

———

1 tablespoon vegetable oil

2 shallots, thinly sliced

2 garlic cloves, finely chopped

1½ tablespoons Vietnamese or Madras curry powder

1 stalk curry leaves (8 to 10 leaves), leaves removed from stalk

One 14-ounce (400 ml) can unsweetened coconut milk

1¾ cups (400 ml) water

1 tablespoon soy sauce

½ teaspoon salt

1 fresh lemongrass stalk, cut into 3 pieces lengthwise and the thicker bottom part lightly bruised with the back of a knife

1 inch (2.5 cm) ginger, peeled and sliced into 3 pieces

½ pound (225 g) Asian sweet potato, peeled and cut into 1-inch (3 cm) cubes (1 cup) (see Note)

½ pound (225 g) potato or taro root, peeled and cut into 1-inch (3 cm) cubes (1 cup)

¼ pound (100 g; about 1 small) long Japanese eggplant, unpeeled, stemmed and halved lengthwise, and cut crosswise into 1½-inch (4 cm) pieces

6 pieces (80 g; 1 cup) okra, cut into 1½-inch (4 cm) lengths

¼ pound (110 g; 1 cup) oyster or button mushrooms, bottom trimmed, cut or torn into bite-sized pieces

OPPOSITE Curried Vegetable Stew with Baguette

continues

FOR GARNISH

1½ cups (5½ ounces; 150 g) bean sprouts

¼ cup Thai basil, roughly chopped

1 fresh red Thai bird chile, thinly sliced

1 lime, cut into wedges

Prepare the Annatto Seed Oil and Tofu Skin Chips.

Heat the vegetable oil and annatto seed oil in a large pot over medium-high heat. Add the shallots and garlic and stir-fry for 1 minute. Add the curry powder and curry leaves and cook for another 30 seconds. Stir in the coconut milk, water, soy sauce, salt, lemongrass, and ginger. Bring to a boil, reduce the heat to medium, and simmer for 5 minutes. Add the sweet potato and potato and simmer for 10 minutes, until half cooked. Toss in the eggplant and simmer for 5 minutes. Add the okra and mushrooms and simmer for another 5 minutes, or until all of the vegetables are tender. Check and adjust the seasoning, if necessary.

TO EAT WITH BAGUETTE

Portion into individual serving bowls and garnish with bean sprouts, chopped Thai basil and a couple of tofu skin chips. Serve with the chiles and lime segments for diners to add on their own. Serve with 6-inch baguette (or a piece of baguette) per bowl.

SERVING AS INDIVIDUAL NOODLE BOWLS

Place a portion of warm noodles in each bowl. Top with vegetables, some sauce, and garnish.

WITH STEAMED RICE

Transfer to a large serving bowl and garnish with bean sprouts, tofu skin chips and basil. Spoon over steamed rice and allow each diner to adjust the flavor with some chiles and/or lime.

Notes:

- Substitute a variety of vegetables such as celery root, kohlrabi, sunchokes/Jerusalem artichokes, parsnips, squash/pumpkin, or greens (gai lan or bok choy).
- When exposed to air, peeled raw Asian sweet potatoes brown quickly. Either peel and cut them right before adding them to the pot or immerse in a bowl of lightly acidulated (with lemon juice) water until ready to use.

OPPOSITE Freshly baked baguettes

DRINKS AND SWEETS

OPPOSITE A monk offering chilled coconut water
as a refreshment.

DRINKS

Việt Nam's vibrant café culture means the country offers an exhilarating selection of beverages. From morning to night, virtually everyone has a drink in his or her hands.

This tea-drinking nation adopted coffee as a favorite drink in the mid-nineteenth century, when the French set up coffee plantations in the central highlands. You've long been able to enjoy a plain dark rich coffee cooled over ice cubes or sweetened with condensed milk (page 270). Over time, though, local coffee houses whipped up new ways to serve coffee: over semifrozen yogurt, whisked with eggs into a thick French sabayonlike treat, or poured around a creamy coconut granita (page 273). Western coffee franchises have recently arrived in Việt Nam too, but coffee drinkers continue to flock toward an ever-growing number of independently owned cafés.

Tea (*trà*) continues to play an essential role in Vietnamese culture as well. It's customary to be offered a glass of green tea (*trà xanh*) when meeting with monks and nuns or as an accompaniment to a basic restaurant meal. Freshly picked green tea leaves infused with pandan leaves is another popular tea drink (and one of my personal favorites; see Lemongrass Pandan Mint Cooler on page 267). In Vietnamese grocers, look for a delicate tea made from lotus flowers—a sacred Buddhist symbol—or the naturally sweet and nutty artichoke tea *(trà artisô)*, which is produced from artichokes grown in Đà Lạt.

Fruit smoothies, *sinh tố,* like the Soursop Strawberry Smoothie (page 265), are also extremely popular. Almost every type of fruit is blended with ice and yogurt, coconut milk, soy milk, or even ice cream. While some fruits need to be pried open or squeezed aggressively to reach their nectar, the hard work is worth it.

The naturally sweet, lightly grassy water from young coconuts (*dừa tươi*) is another option. But nothing beats the heat like fresh sugarcane juice (*nước mía*) accented with the mandarin flavor you get from squeezing a calamansi lime.

In traditional cafés or vegetarian restaurants, you'll find some even more unusual Vietnamese drinks. On the counter or shelves, you may see large glass jars filled with fruits, like apricots or ripe mulberries, macerating in sugar or salt.

The thick syrup is mixed with still or sparkling water and ice for refreshing sipper. Or try Việt Nam's version of lemonade (*nước chanh muối*; page 262), with its salty, sour, and sweet flavors all in perfect interplay.

In the South, some cafés or drink stalls sell a cooling, healthful tonic called *nước sâm*, a tea composed of various herbs, flowers, and roots. Vegetarian restaurants serve corn water (*nước ngô*) the liquid in which corn cobs have been boiled. Not to be outdone, fresh tofu vendors sell small bags of extremely fresh soy milk.

FRUITS (QUẢ)

Việt Nam is a fruit lover's paradise. With a subtropical climate in the South and cooler weather in the central highlands and the North, a huge number of tropical and temperate fruits are available at any given moment. The fragrant aromas emitted from a market fruit stall and the sweet, floral flesh hiding behind colorful peels intoxicate the senses. Naturally tart or unripe fruits like mangoes and guavas (or even sweet pineapples) are common snacks, sprinkled with a mix of salt, chile, and sugar. When traveling in Việt Nam, be sure to try less common regional fruits. And don't assume a supermarket is too mundane a spot for exotic fruit sourcing. On the contrary, from May to August in particular, Vietnamese and Chinese supermarkets in your area offer a buffet of tropical fruits at their utmost peak.

Here's what you'll find when:

Year-round: mangoes (*quả xoài*), yellow to deep red-fleshed papayas (*quả Đu đủ*), dragon fruit with white or purple flesh (*quả thanh long*), watermelon (*quả dưa hấu*), pineapples (*quả dứa*), baby to large bananas (*quả chuối*), coconuts (*quả dừa*), star fruit (*quả khế*)

April to August: mangosteens (*quả măng cụt*), rambutans (*quả chôm chôm*), lychees (*quả vải*), longans (*quả long nhãn*), langsats (*quả bòn bon*), custard apples (*quả mãng cầu*), soursops (*quả mãng cầu xiêm*), durians (*quả sầu riêng*)

August to November: persimmons, guavas, sapodillas (*quả xa pô chê*), star apples (*quả vú sữa*)

November to April: pomelos (*quả bưởi*); mandarins (*quả quit*), sweet oranges (*quả cam* or *quả cam xành*), kumquats (*quả quất* or *quả tắc*) strawberries (*quả dâu*)

Regional-only fruits: (in the North) mulberries (*quả dâu tằm*), bayberries (*quà thanh mai*), dracontomelon (*quả sấu*); (in the South) ambarella; acerola, or West Indian cherry (*quả sơ ri*)

Fruits have special meaning in Vietnamese folklore and celebrations. Fruit vendors located outside temples sell perfect, unblemished fruits, which families use as offerings on their home's ancestral altar. During significant life events and celebrations, an artistically arranged plate or large lacquer bowl of five fruits (called *mâm ngũ quả*) sits on the altar as a symbol of honor and respect by the present generation for their ancestors. It is believed that these fruits, along with other offerings, will generate good health and harmony. The five fruits vary from region to region and change based on the season, availability, and a family's income. Some, like mango, papaya, coconut, soursop,

The unique Buddha's hand lemons for sale.

and the figlike *vả* (or *sung*) fruit are common, as these fruits' names closely resemble the words used in a prayer for abundance and wealth. Buddha's hand lemons, green bananas, pomelos, oranges, custard apples, and persimmons are other popular choices.

SWEETS

Sweets in Việt Nam are not generally served following a meal. (This holds true in many neighboring countries as well.) Instead, diners enjoy a plate of perfectly ripe seasonal fruit. Midafternoon snacks, really more like mini-meals, are a more typical time for satisfying sweet cravings. Some vendors specialize in just one or two sweet treats, while others offer a buffet of delights. These vendors are easy to spot: just look for college students or office workers congregating around the small shops or on the sidewalk in front of a home where a family has set up a table and bench for people to enjoy a quick bite.

The majority of these sweets, virtually all of them vegan, fall into a vast category called *chè*, best described as a cross between a sweet beverage and a soup. *Chè* is usually served in a tall glass or in a small bowl and eaten with a spoon (although to get to the last delicious drops a deep swig may be required). During the hot summers, *chè* is eaten with crushed ice. In cooler months, it may be served warm.

Chè might consist of pulses—such as mung beans, black beans, black-eyed peas, or kidney beans—that are soaked, simmered in water, and sweetened with sugar. Vegetables such as corn, Asian sweet potatoes, cassava, or taro may be added as well. Sometimes fruits such as mango, longan, lychee, durian, or slivers of ripe jackfruit are the *chè* stars. Cooks may add tiny pearls of tapioca, or chewy colored jellies made from agar agar, for textural contrast, as well as grain like rice, millet, black sesame seeds, or lotus seeds. A liberal splash of coconut cream adds a luxurious richness. Or you can savor *chè* in the form of dumplings, as in Gingery Sticky Rice Balls with Mung Beans (page 280).

If you prefer to serve a Western-style dessert, crème caramel or a simple bowl of ice cream—both holdovers from the French colonial era—is a typical option.

ENERGIZING LIMEADE

NƯỚC CHANH MUỐI

Made with preserved salted limes (page 264) this limeade, sweetened and served over ice, offers a refreshing respite from a humid summer day. If you've never had a drink made with a touch of salt, you may find the first sip surprising. The salt initially confuses your tongue and leads you to believe you're tasting something savory. As your palate adjusts, however, you'll discover a wonderful harmony among the salty, sour, and sweet elements of this drink. Even better, the combination of lime and salt briefly replenishes electrolytes, providing a burst of energy for the rest of the day's activities. In cooler months, mix the preserved lime with hot water, a spoonful of honey, and a thin slice of ginger to soothe a sore throat.   **Makes 1 glass**

1 preserved lime or segment of preserved lemon (recipe on page 264)

Sugar, sugar syrup, or honey

Still or sparkling water

Use a clean fork or spoon to remove a lime (or quarter of a lemon) from the jar of preserved limes and place it in a tall glass. Mash it with the back of a spoon. Add a tablespoon or two of sugar and a few ice cubes and top up with still or carbonated water. Stir, taste, and adjust the sweetness if necessary. As you drink the limeade, dilute it with more still or sparkling water if necessary.

Notes:
• If you find the drink too salty for future drinks, reduce the amount of preserved lime used and/or briefly rinse the preserved lime before making the limeade.
• If you like the salty taste and want a touch more, drizzle in a teaspoon of the salty brine.

VARIATION

ENERGIZING LEMONADE WITH PRESERVED LEMONS

Your pantry may already include preserved lemons to flavor some Moroccan dishes, which requires just the skin. Use the inner pulp, which typically ends up discarded, or sacrifice a quarter of a preserved lemon in place of the preserved lime.

OPPOSITE *Left to right*: Lychee Basil Seed Drink (page 266); Energizing Limeade with preserved lime halves; Soursop Strawberry Smoothie (page 265)

PRESERVED SALTED LIMES

CHANH MUỐI

These pickled limes are preserved over the course of one month and are an essential element in the Energizing Limeade (page 262). Select juicy, thin-skinned Key limes or Meyer lemons. Once fully preserved, they keep indefinitely as long as the brine completely covers them. I keep my jar in a prominent spot on the counter as a reminder that a glass of homemade limeade is always within easy reach.   **Makes 1 quart (1 liter)**

8 to 10 thin-skinned organic Key limes or 4 or 5 Meyer lemons, plus extra juice as needed, scrubbed clean

1 tablespoon sugar

About 1½ cups (375 ml) kosher salt

Bring a large pot of water to a boil. Sterilize a 1-quart (1-liter) canning jar in the boiling water for 10 minutes.

Place the limes in the boiling water for about 10 seconds to remove some bitterness from the skins and drain.

Spoon the sugar and a couple tablespoons of salt into the bottom of the jar. Place one layer of limes in the jar and cover with about ½ cup of the salt. Add some more limes for a second layer, pushing them down with your fingers to fit snuggly against one another. Top with another ½ cup of salt. Fit a few more limes into the jar, making sure they're below the neck of the jar. Pour on enough salt to completely cover the limes. Close tightly with a lid. (If the limes or lemons are large, cut a couple of them in half and nudge them into any open space.) Store the jar on a counter at room temperature. The salt will draw out moisture from the limes to create a brine.

After a week, open the jar and use a clean spoon to press the limes down as much as you can. Pour some freshly squeezed lime juice over the top, ensuring they're completely covered. A small amount of salt may remain undissolved on the bottom of the jar. Over time the limes discolor to a shade of military green and shrivel slightly. The limes should be fully preserved after one month. The longer the limes preserve, the browner they become.

Store the preserved limes at room temperature or in the fridge indefinitely as long as they're completely covered with salty brine.

SOURSOP STRAWBERRY SMOOTHIE

SINH TỐ MĂNG CẦU XIÊM DÂU TÂY

Fresh, ripe soursop, with its creamy flesh and pineapple-banana flavor, is dreamy in a smoothie. Fresh or frozen strawberries enhance its tropical notes. Although fresh soursop is hard to source, frozen soursop pulp is readily available in Vietnamese or Latin American grocers, where it is commonly called *guanabana*.   **Makes 1 large smoothie**

1 cup soursop pulp, partially frozen or thawed

⅓ cup (4 or 5 whole) fresh or frozen straw-berries

½ cup (2 to 3) ice cubes

Fresh milk

Sweetened condensed milk, honey, or sugar, to taste (optional)

Put the soursop, strawberries, and ice cubes into a blender. Pour just enough fresh milk to the top of the fruit and ice. Puree until smooth. Taste. If you want it a bit sweeter add some sweetened condensed milk, honey, or sugar. If you prefer a thinner smoothie add some more milk. Blend until well mixed. Serve in a large glass with a spoon or straw.

Fresh soursop (*foreground*) and lychees

LYCHEE BASIL SEED DRINK

This cooling drink combines the floral fragrance of lychee and the fun gelatinous coating of rehydrated basil seeds. Fresh lychees have a very short season—the month of June—so I use canned lychees and their syrup. Purchase basil seeds, called *hạt é* in Vietnamese, at Asian or Indian grocers under the name *falooda* or *sabja seeds*. **Makes four 7-ounce (210 ml) drinks**

2 tablespoons basil seeds

2 cups (500 ml water)

One 20-ounce (565 g) can lychees with syrup

Juice of 1 lime

Spoon the basil seeds into a medium bowl or 1-quart mason jar. Bring water to a boil, turn off heat and let sit for a minute. Pour the water over the seeds, stir, and allow the seeds to hydrate for 5 minutes. Transfer to the fridge until fully cooled. Stir in the syrup from the can and the lime juice.

Spoon 3 to 4 lychees into each glass and pour the basil seed liquid over them. Serve with a wide straw and spoon.

LEMONGRASS PANDAN MINT COOLER

A common drink offered to guests in Buddhist monasteries and vegetarian restaurants in southern Việt Nam is iced tea made from freshly picked green tea leaves and pandan leaves. The pandan leaves impart an appealing sweet herby flavor, and because of this, for my taste, the drink doesn't require any additional sweetener. Since fresh tea leaves are hard to find, I've substituted lemongrass and mint to add a bright citrusy tone. **Makes about 2 quarts (2 liters)**

6 whole lemongrass stalks, thinly sliced (1 cup)

6 frozen pandan leaves, thawed and thinly sliced (½ cup packed)

2 quarts (2 liters) water

4 to 5 mint sprigs, very roughly chopped (1 cup loosely packed)

Honey, sugar, or sugar syrup (optional)

Ice cubes

Mint sprigs for garnish (optional)

Place the lemongrass and pandan leaves in a medium pot, cover with the water, and bring to a boil. Reduce the heat and simmer gently for 4 minutes. Toss in the mint, cover, and infuse for 5 minutes. Strain through a fine-mesh strainer, taste, and sweeten with honey, sugar, or sugar syrup, if desired. Refrigerate.

Serve over ice, garnished with a mint sprig, if you like.

Lemongrass in a bundle

HIBISCUS SLUSHIE

ĐÀI QUẢ KHÔ "SLUSHIE"

For a few short weeks each September, in lanes behind Hà Nội's main Đồng Xuân market, bamboo baskets overflow with freshly picked, deep red hibiscus flowers. Steeped in water, they produce a gorgeous fuchsia-colored liquid with a lovely, tart flavor, something of a cross between black currant and cranberry. (Do add sweetener, though.) Locals use hibiscus to make jam and tea, but I like to simmer the flowers into a syrup and blend it with ice when making this lively slushie.   **Makes about 3¼ cups (800 ml) syrup, enough for about 12 slushies**

2 ounces (60 g; about 3 cups) dried hibiscus
   flowers

3 cups (750 ml) boiling water

1½ to 2 cups (300 to 400 g) sugar

1 cup ice per serving

Place the hibiscus flowers in a small pot or glass container with a wide mouth and pour the boiling water over the top. Stir, cover, and leave it to steep for at least 2 hours or overnight.

Strain through a fine-mesh strainer set over a medium pot, pushing against the flowers to get as much liquid as possible. You'll have around 2 cups. Add 1½ cups sugar, stir, and bring to a boil until the sugar is fully dissolved. Taste, and if too tart for your liking, add the remaining ½ cup of sugar and stir until fully dissolved. Remove from the heat, cool, and transfer to a jar. Refrigerate for up to a month.

To make an individual slushie, add a ¼ cup hibiscus syrup and 1 cup ice to a blender and blend until finely crushed. Garnish with a sprig of mint and serve immediately with a straw and a spoon.

OPPOSITE Lemongrass Pandan Mint Cooler
(*left*, page 267) and Hibiscus Slushie (*right*)

VIETNAMESE COFFEE

CÀ PHÊ

I love watching rich robust Vietnamese coffee drip slowly into a glass. Grown in the central highlands and made from strong dark robusta beans, Vietnamese coffee is satisfying on its own, with its hints of smoky chocolate and caramel. It's also stellar when stirred with a touch of sweetened condensed milk or, in summer, poured over ice.

Vietnamese coffee is traditionally brewed one cup at a time using a small filter (*phin*) perched atop a cup or mug. Search for a phin and Trung Nguyên brand coffee (my favorite!) in Vietnamese grocers. If you don't have a phin or want to make coffee for several people at once, opt instead for a regular drip coffeemaker or an espresso machine. Plan for ¾ cup of coffee per person. **Serves 1**

2 rounded tablespoons finely ground Vietnamese coffee or strong French roast

About ¾ cup (190 ml) just-boiled water

TO MAKE BLACK COFFEE (CÀ PHÊ ĐEN)

Place the coffee in the inner chamber of the filter and gently tap it to settle and evenly distribute the coffee. Fit the insert into the chamber, twisting it once or twice around to flatten and spread out the coffee. Screw it about three-quarters tight, leaving room for the coffee to swell. Set the filter on top of a glass or mug. Pour about ¼ cup of just-boiled water into the filter and wait about 30 seconds to a minute for the coffee grounds to moisten. Pour the remaining hot water into the filter (it should almost reach the top). Cover with the lid and let the coffee drip into the glass or mug over 3 or 4 minutes. If the coffee stops dripping before the chamber is empty, gently loosen the insert. If you're using a mug, lift the lid to check on the progress (I like using a glass cup to watch the progress of the slow dark drip.)

Drink it black or slightly sweetened with sugar.

WITH SWEETENED CONDENSED MILK (CÀ PHÊ SỮA)

Pour 1 tablespoon sweetened condensed milk into the glass or mug before brewing the coffee. Stir, taste, and adjust with more milk if desired.

WITH SWEETENED CONDENSED MILK ON ICE (CÀ PHÊ SỮA ĐÁ)

Mix sweetened condensed milk with coffee (above) and pour into a glass filled with three or four ice cubes.

OPPOSITE Vietnamese Iced Coffee with Sweetened Condensed Milk on Ice

Coconut Cream Coffee Granita at Cộng Cà Phê

COCONUT CREAM COFFEE GRANITA

SINH TỐ CỐT DỪA CÀ PHÊ

I think of this treat as a Vietnamese version of Italian *affogato*. To make it, pour strong, chilled coffee over ice-cold whipped coconut cream. On hot days I'd regularly order this popular item at my neighborhood Cộng Cà Phê, a chain of Hanoian cafés known for their kitschy retro décor and hip vibe.

Avoid the temptation to use coconut milk in place of coconut cream; only the latter has the optimal flavor and richness. Looking for a kid-friendly dessert? Simply substitute purees of tropical fruit or crushed seasonal berries for the coffee. **Serves 1**

1 Vietnamese Coffee (page 270) or a couple shots of espresso, chilled

1 cup ice

¼ cup (60 ml) sweetened condensed milk, or more to taste

3 tablespoons (45 ml) coconut cream, or more to taste

Milk (optional)

Place the ice in a blender. Pour the condensed milk and coconut cream over and blend until well crushed, about 30 seconds. If the blender needs some help processing the ice, add a touch more coconut cream or a tablespoon or two of milk. Taste and adjust the flavor with condensed milk or coconut cream if necessary.

Spoon the chilled sweetened coconut cream puree into a chilled glass with a wide mouth. Pour coffee around the side of the puree and serve immediately with a spoon.

SUMMER FRUIT WITH COCONUT MILK AND CONDENSED MILK

HOA QUẢ DẦM

My kids love this colorful, icy fruit salad that's drenched with sweetened coconut milk. It's especially good from May to September, when tropical fruits are at their peak.

Southeast Asian and Chinese markets will have a great selection of tropical fruit, so head there when planning to make this summer favorite. Aim for six to eight different types, mixing and matching tropical fruit varieties with local soft summer fruits like tender berries or plump stone fruits. If the fruit salad is well chilled, consider the crushed ice optional.   **Serves 1**

1 cup fresh ripe summer fruits, at their peak, six to eight different fruits, cut into bite-sized pieces (mango, papaya, pineapple, dragon fruit, longans, lychees, thinly sliced jackfruit, sapodilla, plums, watermelon, cantaloupe, honeydew, Asian pear, kiwi, banana, peach, nectarine, halved grapes, halved or quartered strawberries, blueberries, raspberries, blackberries, pitted cherries)

¼ cup crushed ice (optional)

2 tablespoons canned coconut milk or coconut cream

1 tablespoon sweetened condensed milk

1 tablespoon Greek yogurt

Spoon the fruit into a tall glass. Place the crushed ice over the top. In a small bowl, mix together the coconut milk, condensed milk, and yogurt. Pour over the ice and fruit. Mix with a spoon and enjoy.

OPPOSITE Summer Fruit with Coconut Milk and Condensed Milk

WARM BANANA COCONUT TAPIOCA PUDDING

CHÈ CHUỐI CHƯNG

When there's a chill in the air and I need to be carried away to someplace warm and sweet, I turn to this comforting southern Vietnamese pudding. My daughter loves the soft, chewy texture of the tiny tapioca balls, and my son always asks for extra banana slices. (He likes how they melt in his mouth.)

I'm taken with the subtle vanillalike flavor from the infusion of pandan leaves in the thick coconut milk. And my wife? She's happy to eat it any which way.

Make sure to add the tapioca pearls only when the water boils. Otherwise the liquid will become thick and gloppy.   **Serves 4**

FROM THE PANTRY/MAKE AHEAD

1½ teaspoons Toasted Sesame Seeds (page 33)

¼ cup (50 g) small tapioca pearls

One 14-ounce can (400 ml) unsweetened coconut milk

3 tablespoons sugar

¼ teaspoon salt

2 pandan leaves (optional; see Note)

3 (1 pound; 454 g) ripe medium to large bananas

FOR GARNISH

1½ tablespoons roasted unsalted peanuts, roughly chopped

2 tablespoons freshly grated coconut (optional)

Make the Toasted Sesame Seeds.

Pour 1½ cups water into a medium saucepan and bring to a boil. Sprinkle in the tapioca pearls and stir. Partially cover and reduce the heat to low. Simmer, stirring every couple of minutes so the tapioca doesn't stick to the bottom of the pan, for about 15 minutes, or until the majority of the pearls are soft and appear translucent.

Pour the coconut milk, sugar, and salt into the saucepan. Tie the pandan leaves into a knot or tear them in half and add to the pan. Increase the heat slightly to simmer, stirring occasionally, for a few minutes, until the sugar is dissolved.

As the sugar dissolves, peel the bananas and slice crosswise into 1-inch thick (2.5 cm) slices (if the bananas are not too thick, I like to slice them on a diagonal). Add the slices

OPPOSITE Warm Banana Coconut Tapioca Pudding

continues

to the saucepan and stir to completely cover them with coconut milk. Simmer gently, carefully stirring them occasionally so they don't become mushy, for 3 to 5 minutes, until they soften slightly. Turn off the heat, cover, and allow the pandan flavor to infuse into the coconut milk for about 15 minutes.

To serve, rewarm the pudding a touch, if you like, give it a good stir, as the tapioca pearls tend to settle on the bottom of the pan, and divide evenly among four bowls. Sprinkle some toasted sesame seeds, peanuts, and coconut, if using, over the top.

SUBSTITUTION

If they can't get pandan leaves, some Vietnamese cooks add a dusting of vanilla powder to the pudding. If you like, add ¼ teaspoon vanilla extract (at the time that you would add the pandan leaves). There's no need to have the coconut milk sit for 15 minutes before serving in this case.

Fruits for sale to place on religious altars outside a pagoda in Hà Nội.

SILKEN TOFU WITH GINGER SYRUP

ĐẬU HŨ NƯỚC DƯỜNG GỪNG

My family first tasted this warm dessert of custardy tofu bathed in hot, gingery syrup as we made our way to the ornate Japanese covered bridge in Hội An. We watched as a middle-aged woman pulled slices of warm, freshly made tofu from a wooden bucket. The soft tofu slid down our throats followed quickly by a hit of sweet ginger.

We've been making (and eating) this dish ever since. Try it warm or even chilled, with a spoonful or two of crushed ice. I've garnished it at times with crushed, toasted peanuts or sesame seeds. You can go in a different direction altogether and serve it with segments of oranges or tangerines. Find soft, custardy tofu at Asian markets.

FOR THE GINGER SYRUP

½ cup plus 2 tablespoons (120 g) dark palm sugar or brown sugar (see Note)

1½ inches (25 g) fresh ginger, peeled and finely grated on the smaller holes of a grater, not a zester (you should have about 1 compact tablespoon)

1½ cups (325 ml) water

———

1 pound silken tofu (sometimes labeled *tofu pudding*)

Place the palm sugar, ginger, and water in a small saucepan and bring to a boil over medium heat. The palm sugar should dissolve easily, but give it a good stir or whisk to help it along. Lower the heat to medium-low and simmer for 10 minutes, or until slightly thickened.

To serve, scoop thin slices of tofu, overlapping them, into small bowls. Heat the tofu, in the bowls, in a microwave until warm through. Drizzle 3 to 4 tablespoons of hot syrup (making sure to get some of the finely grated ginger that may have sunk to the bottom of the pan) over the tofu and garnish, if desired (see headnote). Serve with a spoon.

Transfer any leftover gingery syrup to a jar and refrigerate for up to a week. Bring to room temperature or reheat until warm to serve for future tofu treats.

Note:

If the palm sugar you purchased is in small or large rounds in a hard state, simply cut the rounds into smaller pieces or chunks to make measuring easier.

GINGERY STICKY RICE BALLS WITH MUNG BEANS

CHÈ TRÔI NƯỚC

This cold-weather dessert embodies how savory and sweet collide in the Vietnamese kitchen. (The savory mung bean filling here is the same one used in the Translucent Mung Bean Dumplings on page 123, minus the mushrooms.) Wrapping a nubbin of this filling with a dough made from glutinous rice flour creates a round mochilike dumpling that's drowned in a sweet gingery syrup. Make sure to use lukewarm water (neither hot nor cold, both of which will cause problems) when mixing the dough. **Serves 4 to 8**

FROM THE PANTRY/MAKE AHEAD

1 tablespoon plus 1 teaspoon Crispy Fried Shallots (page 37)

1 tablespoon plus 1 teaspoon Fragrant Shallot Oil (page 38)

1 tablespoon Toasted Sesame Seeds (page 33)

FOR THE FILLING

⅓ cup (2½ ounces; 70 g) dried split mung beans, covered by at least 1 inch (2.5 cm) cold water and soaked overnight or covered with hot water and soaked for 2 hours

1 teaspoon sugar

¼ teaspoon salt

FOR THE DOUGH

1½ cups (170 g) glutinous rice flour, or more as needed

½ cup plus 1 tablespoon (125 ml) lukewarm water, or more as needed

FOR THE GINGER SYRUP

½ cup plus 2 tablespoons (120 g) dark palm sugar or brown sugar (see Note on page 279)

1½ inches (25 g) fresh ginger, peeled and finely grated on the smaller holes of a grater, not a zester (you should have about 1 compact tablespoon)

1½ cups (325 ml) water

½ cup (125 ml) unsweetened coconut milk

FOR THE COCONUT SAUCE

1 tablespoon granulated sugar

2 teaspoons tapioca flour

Pinch of salt

Prepare the Crispy Fried Shallots, Fragrant Oil, and Toasted Sesame Seeds.

Drain the mung beans and spread them evenly into a bamboo or other steamer basket lined with cheesecloth or parchment. Steam for 10 to 15 minutes, until pale yellow and fully tender. Remove from the steamer and cool to room temperature.

Place the cooled mung beans, shallots, shallot oil, sugar, and salt in a food processor and pulse until well blended. Lightly oil the palms of your hands and shape the filling into tablespoon-sized balls (you'll have eight balls). Set aside.

Place the glutinous rice flour in a medium bowl. Pour in the lukewarm water and stir with a fork to mix well. Switch to using your hands and knead the dough for a couple of minutes. The dough should be soft and malleable, much like play dough. If you think the dough is a little too soft, sprinkle in a touch more glutinous rice flour; too dry, sprinkle in a teaspoon or two of water. Cover gently, pressing some plastic against the dough's surface so that it doesn't dry out, and set it aside for about 10 minutes for the flour to hydrate.

Place the palm sugar, ginger, and 1½ cups water in a small saucepan and bring to a boil over medium heat. The palm sugar should dissolve easily, but give it a good stir or whisk to help it along. Lower the heat to medium-low and simmer for 10 minutes, or until slightly thickened.

Oil your hands again and take half of the dough, keeping the other half well covered, and break it into five equal pieces about 2 tablespoons (30 g) in size. Roll them into balls. Press a ball into a flat 3½-inch (9 cm) disk. Place a mung bean ball in the center of the disk, pinch the dough together, and shape it into a ball.

Make sure you don't see any filling and there are no cracks in the dough (if so, the dough will open when boiled). Repeat until all the filling is used up and you have covered eight balls. Divide and roll the rest of the dough into 24 small balls.

Bring a large pot of water to a boil. Add the dumplings, reduce the heat, and simmer the large ones for 5 to 7 minutes; small ones for about 3 minutes. As they cook they'll swell up, become larger, and float on the surface. Once they float, cook them for at least another minute or two. Remove with a slotted spoon or spider and transfer to the warm ginger syrup.

Stir the coconut milk, granulated sugar, tapioca flour, and salt together in a small saucepan over low heat until the sugar is fully dissolved and the sauce has thickened.

To serve, equally divide the warm large and small dumplings into small bowls (1 or 2 large and several small ones per bowl). Drizzle a couple tablespoons of ginger syrup and a tablespoon of coconut sauce over the top. Garnish with some toasted sesame seeds.

Note:
You can make and cook the balls in advance and leave them to soak in the syrup. If you do and you refrigerate them, gently reheat them until warm.

FERMENTED BLACK / PURPLE STICKY RICE WITH YOGURT

SỮA CHUA NẾP CẨM

This dessert is like a toothsome, jammy rice compote. It's made by cooking black/purple sticky rice, dusting it with brewer's yeast (*men ngọt*), and leaving it to ferment for a few days. The resulting rice tastes faintly alcoholic and blends beautifully with thick, lightly-sweetened yogurt. The color contrast is stunning too.

This northern specialty is traditionally eaten on the fifth day of the fifth lunar month for the festival of Tết Đoan Ngũ. On this date, around the time of the summer solstice, the sun or male energy (*yang*) is at its highest. Northerners eat this fermented rice, and other sour or cooling (*yin*) foods, as a way to strengthen their health for the hot summer period. (The addition of yogurt can probably be traced to an innovative café owner.)

As with all fermented foods, patience is helpful as you wait for the fermentation process to complete. Plan to make this dessert at least three days before serving. And resist the urge to mix the powdered yeast entirely through the cooked rice. Layering produces optimal results. **Serves 4**

2¾ cups (500 g) black/purple sticky rice (see page 311)

About 3½ cups (875 ml) water

1 tablespoon plus 2 teaspoons (15 g; 1½) Chinese yeast balls

3 cups Greek yogurt, (sweetened with 2 to 3 tablespoons sugar—optional)

Place the rice in a large shallow bowl and cover with water. Stir with your hand several times and drain. Repeat a couple more times.

OPPOSITE Fermented Black/Purple Sticky Rice with Yogurt (*left*) and Gingery Sticky Rice Balls with Mung Beans (*right*; page 280)

Drain the rice, place in a medium pot along with 3½ cups water and set on the burner that has the most consistent lowest heat setting. Bring to a boil over medium-high heat. Cover and cook for about 8 minutes, stirring a couple of times. Reduce the heat to medium, stirring every few minutes, until the top of the rice peeks through the water, about 7 more minutes. Reduce the heat to low and cook the rice, covered and unattended, for 20 minutes longer. Uncover and stir with a fork. If some rice has stuck to the bottom of the pot, resist the urge to scrape up these crunchy bits. When the grains are separate, slightly tender, and moistly

continues

sticky, the rice is ready. If the rice is not ready, re-cover and leave on low heat for 5 more minutes. Turn off the heat and steam for another 5 minutes.

While the rice is cooking, smash the yeast balls to a fine powder with a mortar and pestle. (Alternatively, roughly chop them into marble-sized pieces and pulse to a fine powder using a mini food processor.) Sift through a fine-mesh strainer to remove any larger lumps.

Spread the rice evenly on a clean baking sheet to allow the steam to dissipate and to cool it until lightly warm to the touch, about 10 minutes.

Line a colander with plastic wrap, leaving a 4-inch (10 cm) overhang on either side of the colander. Turn the colander 90 degrees and repeat with another layer of plastic wrap. Press the plastic wrap against the contour of the colander. Cut a 1½-inch (4 cm) hole in the center of the plastic wrap.

Use the fine-mesh strainer to dust half, about 2½ teaspoons, of the yeast evenly over the entire surface of the rice.

Lift a large portion of rice with a spatula or your clean hands and flip the yeasted side down into the colander. Repeat with another portion or two of rice, placing them as close together as possible to make a single layer. Lightly dust a third of the remaining yeast over the rice in the colander. Repeat with the remaining rice and yeast, ending up with a total of three layers and with a final dusting of yeast on the top layer. Bring the edges of the plastic toward the center, folding them over each other. If the rice is not completely covered, add another piece of plastic over the top. Cover with a clean dish towel, gently folding it around the edges of the plastic. Set the colander over a smaller bowl to catch any liquid that may accumulate. Wrap the colander and bowl with another towel or two and set in a warm place.

Keep it in a warm place, checking it after a full day. A pleasant light fermented odor will develop. Ferment for another day or two. Three to four tablespoons of water should have accumulated in the bowl beneath. The rice will taste slightly sweet, faintly like red wine but without a strong alcohol flavor. Store covered and refrigerated for up to one week.

To serve, spoon ¾ cup (182 g) yogurt into a bowl or tall frosted glass and top with ¼ cup or so of fermented rice. Stir together and enjoy.

VARIATIONS

- Serve the rice over creamy frozen yogurt, stirring the two together before eating.
- Drizzle sweetened coconut milk or cream over the top before serving.

Note:
During the colder months, increase the yeast to 2½ tablespoons (20 g) or two Chinese yeast balls. Keep the layered cooked rice in a warm place such as an oven with the gas pilot or oven light on or with a warm heating pad wrapped within the towels. Increase the number of fermentation days to at least three.

ACKNOWLEDGMENTS

Throughout my life I've been very fortunate to be surrounded by many cheerleaders. While writing a book, at times there are lonely and uncertain moments, but constant guidance, love, and support from family, friends, colleagues, and strangers propelled me through this project.

First and foremost, I want to thank Ayesha Rekhi for her unconditional love and devotion. Watching her navigate family, work, and life flawlessly and seamlessly inspires me everyday to be a better person. After long days at the office she always found time to read, re-read (and re-read!) sections of the manuscript, improving it with each edit. Co-parenting with her our lovely kids, Lyla and Kiran, is an amazing experience. Lyla and Kiran learned there are many phases to writing a book and at the end of each phase would ask "Now is your book done?" I can finally say yes!

From a young age my parents, Martha and Warren, gave me many opportunities to travel, to learn new languages and about different cultures. Initially I may not have been that interested but at some point something clicked. I am deeply thankful to them for showing me that the road less traveled, although it may be longer, is always the most rewarding. I look forward to many more fabulous meals and trips with my sister and brother-in-law, Kathy and Yassine, who also share my interest of travel and languages. From the moment I met them, my in-laws, Patricia and Rajan, embraced me as a close family member. I appreciate their enthusiastic and perpetual encouragement.

This book would not exist without the initial, and continual, support of my wonderful agent, Jenni Ferrari-Adler. She saw potential in my proposal and then found a fabulous home for the book with the legendary editor Maria Guarnaschelli at W. W. Norton. Maria taught me to anticipate readers' questions and to provide answers. She forced me to be decisive and strong when backing up my arguments. Lastly, like preparing a delicious meal, she revealed that writing a book requires patience and time to get the results you desire. Nathaniel Dennett, Maria's assistant, provided helpful insights and brought levity at much needed moments. I appreciated his flexibility and communication skills as I was regularly on the move.

Writing a book is a collaborative process. I am in awe of everyone behind the scenes who shaped my messy proposal and manuscript and made them into a beautiful book. I am indebted to two fellow writers who assisted me at different stages of the book. Dianne Jacob for her engaged and thoughtful guidance in fine tuning the book's proposal. It was a pleasure to work with Cheryl Sternman Rule as she helped me trim the fat from my original manuscript.

Kim Kaechele and Kate Knapp diligently

tested many recipes and both provided helpful tips, streamlined instructions, and much enthusiam, which produced tasty results.

The week cooking and photographing the food images for the book was one of the most memorable weeks of my career. It was a fantastic experience collaborating with Evan Sung, photographer, and Erin Merhar, food stylist. I was fortunate to stay with Aunty Erica. Our early morning and late night talks brought me much laughter and energy to plough through the photo shoot. Grace Young's guidance on where to purchase Vietnamese and Asian ingredients in New York was invaluable.

Jordan MacInnis and Aristea Rizakos offered reassurances and assistance with my location photographs.

I've long admired her work, so I was thrilled when Jan Derevjanik agreed to design the book. A huge thank you to copy editor Chris Benton, who tightened, and vastly improved, this first-time author's instructions, thoughts, and words. It was fun and easy to work with the entire W. W. Norton team—especially Melanie Tortoroli, John Glusman, Susan Sanfrey, Julia Druskin, Will Scarlett, proofreader Lynne Cannon Menges, and indexer Elizabeth Parson—who were flexible, responsive, and supportive.

One of the most exciting and fun parts of writing this book was meeting home and street cooks, chefs, monks and nuns, fellow travelers, new friends, and friendly strangers who share an interest in Vietnamese food and culture. I thank them for being wonderful dinner companions, welcoming me into their homes and kitchens, and providing me with support as I traveled the country. *In Hà Nội*: Tracey Lister, Andreas Pohl, Văn Công Tú, Mark Lowerson, Rebecca Hales, Cynthia Mann, Phạm Thị Thái Hà, John Sylvan, Pete Wilkes, Suzanne Lecht, Trần Phương Dung, Linh and Quyên, Dung and Hồng. *In Huế*: To Bội Trân, Hoàng Thị Như Huy, Hương Lan, Mr. Thanh, the monks at Thiên Mụ Pagoda and nuns at Chùa Diệu Thanh, Mai Thị Trà, Thúy and her family. *In Hội An*: Cat and Mike, Loan and An, Vân from the Green Bamboo Cooking School. *In Đá Lạt*: the monks at Trúc Lam monastery and nuns at Chúa Phước Huế nunnery. *In Sài Gòn*: Ms. Nguyễn Đzoãn Cẩm Vân. *In Long Thành*: the monks at Trúc Lam Trí Đức monastery. *In Mỹ Khánh*: The abbot and monks of the Zen Buddhist monastery. *In Cần Thơ*: The nuns at Long An Tự nunnery. *In Tây Ninh*: The female Cao Đài elders at the Holy See and Huỳnh Văn Chủ.

I feel blessed by the generosity, mentorship, collective wisdom, and support from fellow cooks, food writers, colleagues, and friends. Whether it was over a lingering meal, an impromptu conversation at a conference, or via email answering a simple query, they provided me with objective, sound advice when I critically needed it. They encouraged me to work outside my comfort zone in order to see what I am capable of. Thank you to: Eleanor Kane and James Morris and all of my teachers at the Stratford Chefs School; Chef Louis Charest and the kitchen team at Rideau Hall; Naomi Duguid, Elizabeth Andoh, Susan Volland, Jody Ettenberg, Maggie Battista, Maria Speck, Jamie Schler, Fuchsia Dunlop, Deborah Madison, Andrea Nguyen, Molly Stevens, Eagranie Yuh, Nancy Singleton Hachisu, Pam Collacott, Corie Brown, and Chris Fager; all of my Zester Daily colleagues; the International Association of Culinary Professionals; Jan Campbell-Luxton; Cô Hà and Thay Mong; Natasha Pairaudeau; Erica J. Peters; Sarah Brohman; Anne Mackenzie; Deepa Mehta and David

Hamilton; Lara MacInnis and Leo Scherman; Jackie Jenkins; Malcolm Cullen; Tasha Hansen and Sean Kline; Keely Colcleugh and Graham Ferrier.

As I write this some friends and family members are unaware they'll play an important role in helping me promote this book. Thank you in advance for offering a place to stay and a kitchen to prep ingredients.

The process of writing this book would not have been as enjoyable without everyone's unconditional support. I am forever grateful.

APPENDIX: FOR THE TRAVELER

FINDING VEGETARIAN AND VEGAN RESTAURANTS IN VIỆT NAM

Unsurprisingly, vegetarian and vegan restaurants are easiest to find in larger cities and communities. The name of the restaurant will end with the word *chay* (pronounced *"chai"* and meaning vegetarian) or *cơm chay* (meaning vegetarian food) such as *Nhà Hàng Cơm Chay* (vegetarian restaurant). Vegetarian restaurants and street food options are very common in the southern cities of Sài Gòn and Tây Ninh, the center of the Cao Đài religion, and throughout the Mekong delta in Cần Thơ

and Mỹ Tho. The central cities of Huế and Đà Nẵng also have plenty of choices, while Hà Nội is slowly seeing an uptick in vegetarian restaurants. As you move north from Hà Nội into the countryside and hills near the Chinese border, options are more limited. Before your trip, search online for up-to-date information and join Facebook groups that discuss vegan or vegetarian options throughout the country or for specific cities.

HOW TO ORDER IN VIETNAMESE RESTAURANTS

Restaurants that cater to tourists are usually aware that foreign vegetarians don't eat meat and seafood and are open to eating dishes prepared with eggs and dairy. (If you're vegan, try to explain to the server what ingredients you don't eat.) Menus should have several vegetarian choices. Look for the section of vegetarian dishes called *món chay* if an English-language menu is unavailable.

The first time you leaf through a menu in a vegetarian restaurant, you may be confused. It's common for an English-language menu to be translated literally, so words like *beef*, *chicken*, and *shrimp* may appear. Don't despair! Because vegetarian dishes in Việt Nam are generally replicas of meat and seafood dishes, they are often referred to by their traditional Vietnamese name but with the word *chay*

A casual street-side vegetarian restaurant in Huế.

The chalkboard is used as a temporary sign to indicate the food stall is serving vegetarian meals on new- or full-moon days.

and seafood dishes, you may find vegetarian options like tofu in tomato sauce, stir-fried water spinach or chayote tendrils with garlic, sautéed seasonal vegetables, grilled eggplant, and a light vegetable broth with seasonal vegetables. Completely vegetarian versions of these diners, predominant in the center and south of Việt Nam, are called *cơm bình dân chay*. They offer mock meat and seafood dishes made with tofu and tofu skin, wheat gluten (*mì căn*), or textured vegetable protein (TVP). Wheat gluten and TVP are more prevalent in the northern part of the country. Inventive vegetarian cooks in the center and South also transform produce such as young jackfruit, banana flowers, and taro root into delightful meat-free dishes with a meaty quality.

A STREET FOOD PRIMER

Vietnamese street food is a wonderful fixture in the country's culinary landscape. Each vendor specializes in cooking and selling one dish. You'll often see a vendor with a bamboo pole slung over her shoulder. Bamboo baskets, each containing ingredients and cooking tools, hang on either end of the pole, called *đòn gánh tre*. Each day the vendor will set up at the same sidewalk location, or she'll roam the neighborhood, stopping to finish preparing her dish when a hungry passerby hails her.

Other street food vendors set up a basic cart with just a burner or two on the sidewalk in front of their home. They set up a few knee-high plastic tables and small stools a foot off the ground, almost like children's furniture at a pretend tea party. The seating provides just enough comfort for you to consume your meal and go on your way. Lingering isn't encouraged.

It's worth paying attention to the lunar calendar. If you're in town on the first or fifteenth

added at the end. Many vegetarian restaurants prepare a buffet to offer a wide selection of dishes to accommodate the increased demand on half- and full-moon days.

If at lunchtime, and sometimes dinner, you see people crowded around a glass display case filled with buffet-style platters of freshly prepared dishes, you've happened upon a Vietnamese-style diner. These basic restaurants, roughly translated as commoner's rice (*cơm bình dân*) or broken rice (*cơm tấm*), have no menu. I've nicknamed them "point and eat" restaurants since you point to indicate which dishes you'd like to order. Servers will scoop some rice into the center of a plate and surround it with your selections. You can then find an empty seat at a communal table to enjoy your meal. Diners like these are popular with blue-collar and office workers as they're a great value, providing a filling meal of home-style comfort foods. Alongside the meat of each lunar month, you're in luck. Apart from full-time vegetarians or vegans, most people who seriously practice Buddhism follow a periodic vegetarian diet on those days. Some believers may also eat vegetarian on the fourteenth and thirtieth. On these auspicious days, around the new and full moon, some street food vendors and some of the *cơm bình dân* restaurants serve vegetarian versions of popular dishes. At food courts of fresh food markets, scour the signs for vendors who offer vegetarian versions of dishes like *phở* or *bánh mì*. The temporary signs will end with *chay*, such as *phở chay* or *bánh mì chay*. Similarly, on these days an enterprising market vendor may offer a dish or two in the early evenings to catch people in search of a precooked vegetarian meal for dinner.

Bear in mind, several times I've returned the day after the full moon for a second tasting of a memorable vegetarian dish only to discover the street vendor is back to preparing a meat or seafood version. Similarly, some regular vegetarian restaurants close the day following a half or full moon to give their staff a break from the previous few days of hard work.

WHAT TO ORDER ON THE STREET

Although most Vietnamese street food contains meat or seafood, that shouldn't stop you from asking for vegetarian alternatives. Ask a *bánh mì* vendor, for example, to replace the meat with a fried egg (*bánh mì trứng*) or with tofu (*đậu hũ*).

Some street food cooks may not fully comprehend what a vegetarian does not eat. Even after mentioning that you don't eat meat, they may think that serving you a meat-based broth, with no pieces of meat, but with noodles, vegetables, and herbs, is acceptable. Some will consider eggs off limits, so specify whether

you eat them. If you don't feel adventurous enough to navigate some of these hurdles on your own, sign up for a street food tour with a local, knowledgeable guide.

Here are the most typical—and delicious—everyday vegetarian street foods to try:

Sticky rice dishes. On early mornings throughout the country, women crouch around large bamboo baskets selling scoops of sticky rice (*xôi*). Look for dishes such as *xôi lạc (đậu phộng)* with steamed peanuts, *xôi dừa* with shredded fresh coconut, *xôi vò* with steamed mung beans, and *xôi gấc*, an orange-hued sticky rice made with mormodica fruit (also called gac fruit). Choose from lightly salted ground peanuts and sesame seeds, fried shallots, and steamed ground mung beans as garnishes. Steer clear of the stringy light brown garnish, which is pork floss.

Tofu. For lunch in Hà Nội, try *bún đậu mắm tôm*, lightly fried pillows of custardy tofu served with bite-sized rice noodle cakes and a plate of citrusy herbs. Ask the vendor for soy sauce (*xì dầu* or *nước tương*) instead of *mắm tôm*, an odorous shrimp paste. Vegetarian rice porridge (*cháo chay*) with beans (black, kidney, or mung beans) and tofu is sometimes available too.

Vegetables. In the late afternoon throughout the country, particularly in the winter months, roadside vendors sell charcoal-roasted sweet potatoes and boiled or grilled corn. Deep-fried banana slices (*bánh chuối*), latticelike sweet potato fries (*bánh khoai lang*), and corn fritters (*bánh ngô*) prepared with a wheat-flour-based batter are cold season Hanoian favorites.

Sweets. An afternoon wouldn't be complete without sampling a Vietnamese sweet snack. The majority of these treats are vegan since they contain no dairy or eggs. Cooks prepare *chè*, a sweet gelatinous soup made with coconut milk and various cooked beans (mung, black, or kidney) or corn and tapioca pearls. Fresh fruit such as bananas or ripe jackfruit is a common garnish. Wherever you decide to eat—on the streets, in restaurants, or, most likely, in a combination of the two—I encourage you to sample your way through the country's vast and varied menus. The process of doing so is one of the best ways to engage with an unfamiliar culture. There's sure to be at least one dish, probably more, that will become a new favorite.

IF YOU HAVE GLUTEN SENSITIVITIES

If you are sensitive to gluten, watch out for several commonly used pantry products. Dishes with wheat as a main ingredient tend to have the word *bột mì* or *mỳ* in the names. Other off-limits foods are wheat gluten (*mì căn*) used in preparing mock meat dishes, wheat noodles such as Chinese egg noodles (*mì/ mỳ trứng*), macaroni noodles (*nui*), and bread (*bánh mì*). Unlike in the United States, the majority of soy sauce used on the streets, in cheaper restaurants, and in homes tends not to be made with wheat. However, it's always best to double-check, as restaurants and hotels that cater to tourists may use imported soy sauce that contains wheat. Similarly, cross-contamination may occur in oil when wheat-coated dishes are deep-fried. Again, seek confirmation from the vendor or restaurant to minimize risk.

HANDY VIETNAMESE PHRASES WHEN DINING OUT

When you don't see any vegetarian options and want to ask the kitchen to modify dishes for you, these Vietnamese phrases will come in handy:

I am/eat vegetarian.
>   *Tôi ăn chay.*

I don't eat meat, fish or seafood.
>   *Tôi không ăn thịt/cá/hải sản.*

I eat egg.
>   *Tôi ăn trưng.*

Does this dish contain _____?
>   *Món ăn này có (insert ingredient name) không?*

Can you cook this dish using (soy sauce)? [Instead of fish sauce]
>   *Bạn có thể nấu món ăn này vui (Nước tương/xì dầu) đước không?*

Can you cook this dish without . . . ?
>   *Bạn có thể nấu món ăn này không . . . ?*

Meat	*Thịt*
Chicken	*Thịt gà*
Beef	*Thịt bò*
Pork	*Thịt heo*
Seafood	*Hải sản*
Fish	*Cá*
Fish sauce	*Nước mắm*
Soy sauce	*Nước tương/ xì dầu*
Wheat flour	*Bột mì*

RESOURCES

WHERE TO BUY INGREDIENTS

Cities in North America with considerably large Vietnamese populations often have a concentration of Vietnamese grocery stores and restaurants, sometimes in an area nicknamed "Little Saigon." The size of the neighborhood will often relate directly to the size of the Vietnamese community living there. In cities with a smaller Vietnamese community, Vietnamese grocers can be found situated within areas known as "Chinatown." Vietnamese grocers should have all of the specialty items to make the recipes in this book. Other Asian grocers and large grocery stores will also carry most of the ingredients called for in this book, perhaps with the exception of the specific Vietnamese herbs. Here's a list of cities, states, and provinces and accompanying streets or neighborhoods to get you started:

Boston (Dorchester)
California (San Jose; San Diego in City Heights; Orange County)
New York City (area around Bowery and Grand)
Oklahoma City (Asia District along North Classen Blvd. from NW 22 St. to NW 32 St.)
Philadelphia (south Philadelphia)
Portland (NE Sandy Blvd. and NE and SE 82nd Ave.)

Seattle (east of the International District)
Texas (Houston in Midtown; Arlington; Garland)
Virginia (Eden Center in Falls Church)

Calgary (17th Ave)
Montreal (Jarry St. E. and intersection of St. Laurent and De La Gauchetiere St.)
Ottawa (Somerset St.)
Toronto (Spadina Ave.)
Vancouver (Powell St. and Kingsway in Burnaby)

Large grocery store chains specializing in Asian foods found largely in the suburbs of the United States and Canada include: 99 Ranch Market; H Mart; T&T Supermarket.

GROWING VIETNAMESE HERBS AND VEGETABLES

If you cannot find a regular supplier of Vietnamese herbs and vegetables you may want to try your hand at growing your own. Asian grocers sometimes have a display of packets of herbs and vegetable seeds for sale. Here are some online sources for your reference:

Baker Creek Heirloom Seeds
rareseeds.com
Evergreen Seeds
evergreenseeds.com

Flora Exotica
floraexotica.ca

The Growers Exchange
thegrowers-exchange.com

Kitazawa Seed Company
kitazawaseed.com

Richters
richters.com

Pumpkin flowers and long beans

GLOSSARY

Many ingredients for recipes in this book, such as rice paper and noodles, tofu, analog meats, and Asian vegetables, are readily available at well-stocked grocery stores. You can source some crossover pantry items like annatto seeds, banana leaves, jicama, and culantro at Latin American grocers. A well-stocked Asian grocer remains the best one-stop for affordably priced ingredients, especially Vietnamese herbs. Don't rely on what is solely written on the packages as sometimes the labeling is confusing and misleading. For example, noodles, regardless of thickness, may be called "vermicelli" and packages of specific herbs are regularly labeled "herbs." Thankfully, all types of noodles are sold in clear plastic packages that make it easy to see the shape and size of the noodles. For these reasons, include the Vietnamese (or other common) name and ingredient description to your shopping list.

DRIED GOODS

ANNATTO SEEDS / BIXA ORELLANA (*hạt điều*) Small teardrop-shaped rust-colored annatto seeds are harvested from pods grown on small shrubs in tropical areas. Annatto is most commonly used in Latin American and Caribbean cooking, where it's known as *achiote*. Heated in fat, like a neutral-flavored oil, the seeds add an orange-red color and an earthy, musky flavor to

dishes. Purchase seeds at Vietnamese or Latin American grocers.

BLACK PEPPER / PIPER NIGRUM (*tiêu đen*) Devout Mahayana Buddhists add a generous pinch of fresh, medium-coarsely ground black pepper right before serving in place of "internal heat producing" chiles. The main growing area in Việt Nam, the world's largest producer and exporter of black pepper, is the southern central highlands, but berries from the southern island of Phú Quốc, or nearby Kampot, Cambodia, are prized for their intense fruity, citrusy aroma and mild flavor.

CHILE GARLIC PASTE (*tương ớt tỏi*) Fresh chile paste, stored in a small jar with a small spoon resting on the side, is a permanent condiment on the tables of street food vendors and in most family homes. A reliable store-bought alternative is the rough chile paste (*sambal oelek*) or chile-garlic paste (*tương ớt tỏi Việt-Nam*) packaged in a plastic jar with a green screw top and recognizable Sriracha rooster logo on the side, produced by Huy Fong Foods.

CHINESE YEAST BALLS (*men ngọt*) Chinese or Shanghai yeast balls, *xiaoqu* in Mandarin, are a type of brewer's yeast the size of a Ping-Pong ball. They're used to ferment cooked glutinous rice to make rice wine (*rượu nếp*). The fermented, mildly alcoholic rice is eaten as a dessert and the alcoholic liquid drunk as wine. The rice and wine are popular in the mountainous areas where glutinous rice is grown, and locals believe it's good for gut bacteria. You'll find them at Chinese or Vietnamese grocers in clear plastic bags labeled as dried yeast. Ask if you can't find them as sometimes they're kept behind the counter.

COCONUT MILK, COCONUT CREAM, UNSWEETENED Thick coconut cream and thinner coconut milk, the former and latter extracted from the first pressing and second pressings of freshly grated coconut, are used in soups, stews, sweets, and drinks. The Thai brands Aroy-D, Chaokoh, and Mae Ploy are reliably good. If the milk has separated, a thick cream on top and thin watery milk on bottom, or solidified (when refrigerated), stir well to recombine. Transfer any leftovers from the can to a clean container and refrigerate for up to two days. For recipes in this book, don't substitute coconut milk for coconut cream. You'll often find coconut cream in the drinks aisle of well-stocked grocers.

Coconut milk (*left*); coconut cream (*right*)

CURRY POWDER (*cà ri nị Ấn Độ/bột cà ri*) Vietnamese-style curry powder, flavored with more coriander powder and less cumin, is labeled as *cà ri nị Ấn Độ* or *bột cà ri* at Asian grocers. Otherwise, use a mild or medium-hot Madras-style curry powder.

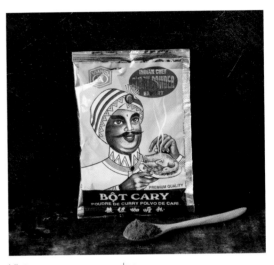

Vietnamese curry powder

FERMENTED SOYBEANS (*tương*) Fermented soybeans, a precursor to liquid soy sauce, labeled as *salted soybeans* or *soybean paste*, hail from the Chinese pantry. At markets in Việt Nam you'll find small bags or bottles of locally made bean sauces with regional variations ranging from thick to thin. Asian shops in North America sell bean sauces as whole beans or pastes; either will work in these recipes, in 8- or 16-ounce (227 g or 454 g) jars made in China, Korea, Malaysia, or Việt Nam (Yeo's brand or any Korean brand is good). Read the labels as some contain wheat. In a pinch use Lee Kum Kee brand vegetarian hoisin sauce (*tương đen chay*). The word *tương* also refers to other sauces or condiments such as small jars of smashed fresh red chiles called *tương ớt* or soy sauce (*nước tương*).

HIBISCUS / HIBISCUS SABDARIFFA (*hoa dâm bụt; hoa atiso*) Originally from West Africa, hibiscus flowers, also called *roselle*, are a recent arrival to Việt Nam and thrive in some northern provinces. The vendors confusingly call these brilliant red-purple calyxes *atiso*, the same Vietnamese name given to artichokes. They have a fabulous tart black-currant-like flavor and when steeped in water turn it a brilliant red. In Việt Nam the deep red calyxes are pro- cessed into jam, tea, syrup, and wine and the leaves used as a souring agent in soups. They're easiest to find at Latin American stores labeled as *flor de Jamaica* or *Jamaican sorrel*.

MISO See page 25.

MUNG BEANS / VIGNA RADIATA (*đậu xanh*) As a whole bean these have an olive green coat with yellow underneath. For recipes in this book use husked and split beans. Don't confuse them with larger split peas. You'll find them at Asian or Indian (*as moong dal*) and well-stocked grocery stores. The beans are made into bean sprouts, processed into noodles (bean thread or cellophane noodles), and steamed and made into paste to add to dumplings and in desserts like *chè*. Some inventive vegetarian chefs even craft them into imitation meats (see photo page 209).

SEA VEGETABLES (OR ALGAE) Soak hijiki or wakame in warm water for 20 minutes, drain, and squeeze before using. The product triples in size, so be judicious when measuring. Pound the dried seaweed in a mortar and pestle or pulse in a spice grinder to make a powder.

- **HIJIKI** / SARGASSUM FUSIFORME Sold dried in small plastic packages and looks like short black twigs or wires.

- **WAKAME** / UNDARIA PINNATIFIDA This is the seaweed you typically find in miso soup.

- **NORI** / POPHYRA TENERA Also called laver, it is sold in clear packages as thin sheets of rough black-green paper normally used to wrap sushi. Store it tightly wrapped or in a well-sealed container at room temperature to keep it crisp and fresh.

SESAME SEEDS / SESAMUM INDICUM (*mè; vừng*) The more common hulled off-white seed is delicately nutty and sweet; unhulled buff or brown seeds are slightly richer in aroma and taste; black seeds (*mè đen*) take on a complex marine flavor sprinkled over rice or simply pre- pared vegetables. Store raw seeds at room tem- perature. When toasted the seeds release their oils to the surface and can quickly turn rancid, so store them in the refrigerator or freezer.

SOY SAUCE (*nước tương; xì dầu*) Rich, salty soy sauces are used as seasoning, in dipping sauces, and in braised vegetable or tofu dishes. Vietnamese cooks predominantly use a wheat- free, tamari-like soy sauce in their cooking. Its flavor is well balanced and less aggressive than the widely available Cantonese-style soy sauce (often containing wheat). If you use tamari, seek out good quality brands like San-J wheat- free, Eden imported tamari or Clearspring. To obtain the saltiness of fish sauce without having an overwhelming soy sauce flavor, use a combination of tamari or soy sauce and salt. If you already have it in your pantry, a few squirts of rich, full-flavored mushroom soy sauce nicely completes a dipping sauce or noodle soup. The same thing can be said for Maggi seasoning sauce or Bragg Liquid Aminos, both equally effective when splashed into a bánh mì sandwhich or over a simple rice meal.

STAR ANISE / ILLICIUM VERUM (*đại hồi; hồi hương; tai hồi*) This eight-pointed star, harvested from a small evergreen grown in northern Việt Nam and China, adds a wonderful anise flavor and aroma to the broth prepared for phở. Try to purchase unbroken stars to maximize flavor. It's one of the spices in five-spice powder.

TAMARIND / TAMARINDUS INDICA (*me chua*) The ripe fruit of the tamarind tree, a reddish brown pulp encased within 3- to 4-inch, fava-bean-like pods, adds sourness to dishes. The most reliable form available, in taste and consistency, is a 14- to 16-ounce mahagony-colored block wrapped in plastic and stored at room temperature. Dilute the tamarind pulp with water before using (see page 41). Purchase at Asian or Latin American grocers, where it goes by its Spanish name, *tamarindo*. Don't buy small containers labeled *concentrated cooking tamarind*, which are weak in flavor and less sour than tamarind blocks.

TAPIOCA STARCH / TAPIOCA FLOUR (*bột năng; bột lọc*) Tapioca starch is the starch of the cassava root (also known as manioc or yuca). It's sold in 1-pound (454 g) packages at Asian shops and also available at Latin American or Caribbean shops. Sometimes tapioca starch is used as a thickener in sauces or fillings, but most often in Vietnamese cuisine it's used alone, or sometimes mixed with rice flour, to make noodles and wrappers for dumplings or rice paper, where it adds a translucent sheen and chewy, gummy texture. Tapioca starch is also used to make tapioca pearls, small round granules of varying sizes, which are key ingredients in many Vietnamese puddings, called *chè*.

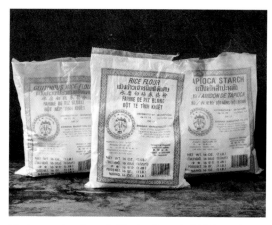

Glutinous rice flour (*left*); rice flour (*middle*); tapioca starch (*right*)

Tapioca pearls (*top right*); mung beans; star anise (*bottom left*); annatto seeds (*top left*)

VEGETARIAN FISH SAUCE (*nước mắm chay*) Although not an exact match or a perfect substitute for fish sauce, versions of vegetarian fish sauce exist. Closer in taste to tamari than soy sauce, it is made from fermented soybeans but is weaker in flavor. When sampled on its own, there's a noticeable difference in taste from soy sauce, but not as much when mixed into dressings and dips. You may find some at Vietnamese grocers. Select ones where the ingredients are soybeans, water, salt, and, sometimes, sugar. Use it instead of soy sauce, except for the braised dishes. I find brands that include peanuts, pineapple, or chiles are cloudy in flavor and unsuitable.

VEGETARIAN MUSHROOM FLAVORED STIR-FRY SAUCE As a replacement for oyster sauce, Lee Kum Kee brand vegetarian mushroom-flavored stir-fry sauce adds an extra oomph of umami to stir-fries, braises, and dips.

TOFU, SEITAN, MEAT ANALOGS
(see photo on page 56)

ANALOG MEAT, FAKE MEAT, IMITATION MEAT Made from plant proteins, these meat alternatives are similar in appearance, taste, and texture. The most common products at well-stocked grocers, in the refrigerated or freezer sections, are "meatless ground" or "chicken" strips. My preferences are Beyond Meat Beef Crumbles and Chicken Strips, although Gardein and Quorn brands are also good. Select lightly or simple seasoned meatless alternatives to use in recipes in this book. Roughly substitute 2 cups lightly packed of meatless ground for 1 pound of real ground beef. Check the labels as some products may contain textured wheat.

DRIED BEAN CURD (*Đậu hũ ky*, South; *Phù chúc*, North) Fresh, cream-colored tofu skin is highly perishable. An excellent fresh product comes from Oakland-based Hodo Soy. The dried form, the shade of a manila envelope, is sold labeled as bean curd sheets, packaged in plastic, and confusingly stocked at room temperature, in the fridge or freezer section at Asian grocers. Select packages with whole unbroken sheets. Store as bought and wrapped well. Rehydrate dried tofu skin in warm water until cream colored, soft, and pliable. A thicker version, recognizable with the imprint of cloth on either side, is not workable for recipes in this book.

DRIED BEAN CURD STICKS / TOFU SKIN STICKS is another form of tofu skin, sold in 6- or 7-ounce (170 to 200 g) packages. Before drying the sheets are rolled up into long rumpled sticks and hung. They require a long (up to 8 hours) gentle soak in water. Squeeze dry and shallow or deep-fry until crisp before adding to broths; otherwise they become mushy. Buy the tightly crumpled sticks instead of the looser, thicker-looking ones, if possible.

FERMENTED TOFU OR BEAN CURD (*chao*) At Asian grocers, look for small glass jars with white cubes of fermented tofu surrounded in its fermentation liquid, normally of rice wine, sugar, salt, and sometimes chile flakes and sesame oil. White and red fermented tofu, made in China and Taiwan, are available, but for recipes in this book use plain white fermented tofu.

SEITAN (*mì căn*) Seitan, wheat gluten, or mock meat, because of its chewy meatlike texture, is a protein-rich substitute eaten by vegetarians and many devout or lay Mahayana Buddhists in Việt Nam. It originated in Chinese Buddhist temples as a way to serve familiar dishes in a vegetarian form to nonvegetarians. It's made by washing out the starch from a wheat dough until only gluten remains or by mixing water or stock with vital wheat gluten flour, a dried form of the protein in wheat, to make a dough. Boil or steam homemade seitan before stir-frying, braising, or deep-frying it. Its bland taste easily absorbs flavors. To use in the recipes in this book, select plain or simple seasoned pre-cooked seitan, typically sold in 8-ounce (226 g) packages. Upton's Naturals and WestSoy are nationally available brands found next to tofu at well-stocked grocers or health food stores. Asian grocers also sell it canned and labeled as mock duck or mock pork. To make homemade seitan, purchase vital wheat gluten flour, such as Bob's Red Mill brand, at natural food stores or well-stocked grocers.

TOFU (*đậu hũ; đậu phụ*) Plain tofu, bean curd, is a high-protein food made from heated soybean milk to which a coagulant (gypsum or mineral salts) is added. The resulting curds are strained and pressed into a rectangle mold until the desired firmness is achieved. Vietnamese cooks prefer freshly made tofu, soft yet still firm enough to hold its shape when cut and when shallow- or deep-fried. It has an ethereal cloud-like texture. You may find such local, artisanal tofu at Vietnamese or Chinese grocers in your area. Look for Hodo Soy brand medium-firm or firm tofu blocks for a superior product. Most of the recipes in this book call for firm tofu that is sold packaged in water at major grocery stores. Once opened, store any extra tofu immersed in water, changing the water daily, and use within a couple of days.

HERBS

The lively, nuanced tastes of Vietnamese cuisine come from the abundant use of fresh herbs. Vietnamese cooks pair specific herbs to certain proteins for flavor and for their medicinal properties. These herb pairings are another way vegetarian cooks inform lay vegetarians what dish and protein the dish mimics.

ASIAN BASIL / OCIMUM SPP. (*húng quế; rau quế*) Asian basil, commonly referred to as *Thai basil*, is a tropical variety of sweet basil (*Ocimum basilicum*). The pointed medium to dark green leaves, slightly smaller than those of sweet basil, are attached to purpled-tinged stalks and often have small purple flowers sprouting at the top. Asian basil has a wonderful sharp anise flavor with a hint of spiciness or sweetness.

BETEL LEAVES, WILD / PIPER SARMENTO-SUM (*lá lốt*) The wild betel leaf is heart shaped, 3 to 4 inches (7 to 10 cm) wide, shiny green on one side, matte on the other, with fine veins running all over it. It's commonly confused with the lighter-colored, tougher betel leaf (*Piper betle*) because they're the same shape and from the same family (*Piperaceae*). That betel leaf is chewed with areca nut or tobacco as a stimulant, known as *paan*, in parts of South and Southeast Asia. Sharp, peppery wild betel leaves are mainly used in Vietnamese cuisine to wrap a piece of food or filling. The leaf releases appetizing fragrant oils and a sweet pepper aroma when heated. Eat them raw, steamed, or sautéed. Buy fresh or frozen at Vietnamese or Thai grocers. Store refrigerated, dry, and sealed in a plastic bag for up to a week.

CHINESE CELERY / APIUM GRAVEOLENS VAR. SECALINUM (*rau cần*) Stronger in flavor than common European celery, Chinese celery is sold at Asian grocers in bunches with thin foot-long stalks and leaves resembling flat Italian parsley. Use both the leaves and the less fibrous upper half of the stems, roughly chopped, in soups or stir-fries, adding it near the end of cooking. Substitute common celery leaves if necessary.

CHINESE CHIVES / ALLIUM TUBEROSUM (*hẹ*) The base of the stalk of garlic chives is tubular

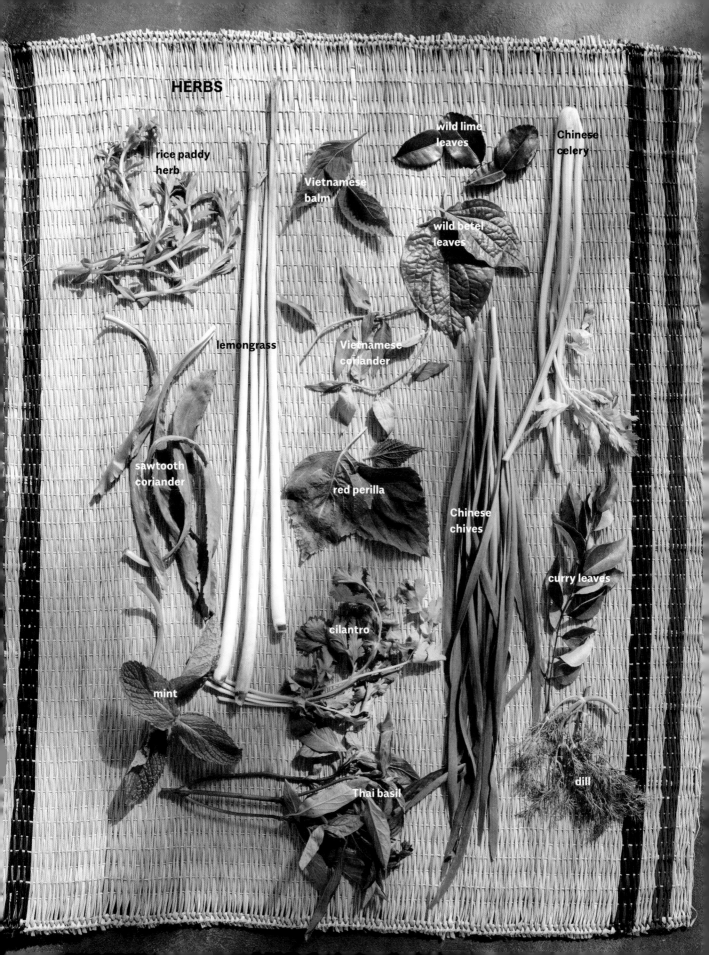

HERBS

rice paddy herb

Vietnamese balm

wild lime leaves

Chinese celery

wild betel leaves

lemongrass

Vietnamese coriander

sawtooth coriander

red perilla

Chinese chives

curry leaves

cilantro

mint

Thai basil

dill

but quickly tapers into thin, flat deep green blades. Garlic chives have a more pronounced garlicky-oniony flavor than the common European chive. The garlic taste mellows somewhat when the chives are heated, making them suitable for stir-fries or soups. Substitute regular chives or young tender garlic scapes.

CILANTRO / CORIANDRUM SATIVUM

(*ngò*) Vietnamese cooks use the leaves and tender stems of cilantro, also called *coriander* or *Chinese parsley*, as a garnish or as part of a salad plate mix. Seek out bunches with smaller, delicate-sized leaves and pick off bite-sized sprigs or very roughly chop bunches with large leaves. Cilantro is often very sandy, so wash and rinse well several times before using.

CURRY LEAF / MURRAYA KOENIGII (*lá cà ri*)

The distinct flavoring of curry leaves is used in some Vietnamese-style curries. Purchase fresh sprigs, each containing 12 to 16 small teardrop-shaped bright green leaves, from stores that cater to South Indian communities. Stir-fry briefly to bring out their flavor. Freeze them, wrapped tightly in aluminum foil, for several months. Dried curry leaves have little to no flavor.

LEMONGRASS / CYMBOPOGON CITRATUS

(*xả*) The subtle lemony flavor and fragrance from lemongrass is intrinsic to some Vietnamese dishes. Finely chopped, use it in stir-fries. Lightly bruised in large pieces, add it to broths or stews. It's sold in bundles of three or four stalks, 1½ to 2 feet long, year-round at well-stocked grocers or Asian shops. Choose firm stalks with fat faint yellow-green tight bulbs and green at the top. To use, chop off

a little of the bulb and the top, leaving about a 6-inch length. Peel away the outer two or three coarse layers (use them and the other chopped parts for infusions for tea; see page 267, Lemongrass Pandan Mint Cooler) before chopping. Store uncut stalks wrapped tightly in the fridge for up to two weeks. When frozen the flavor is diminished a bit. Precut lemongrass and dried lemongrass do not deliver the same flavor as whole fresh stalks.

LIME LEAVES / CITRUS HYSTRIX (*lá chanh*)

Lime leaves, roughly torn, tossed into a Thai-style broth or thinly sliced and sprinkled into a chicken-style phở, brighten dishes with an alluring lemon-lime aroma and flavor. Dominant in Thai cooking, the use of lime leaves in Vietnamese cuisine is fairly recent. Select packages of bright green shiny fresh leaves at grocers with a Southeast Asian clientele. For longer storage, place in a well-sealed plastic bag before freezing. Avoid purchasing brown, discolored, or dried lime leaves.

MINT / MENTHA SPICATA (*húng lũi; rau húng*)

Sprigs of spearmint add a refreshing kick to salads and salad rolls. There are a number of varieties of mint, but the one cultivated in Southeast Asia is spearmint and is a touch milder in flavor than the spearmint available at North American grocers. For that reason I suggest you thinly slice the mint leaves.

RED PERILLA / PERILLA FRUTESCENS (*tiá tô*)

The red perilla variety favored in Việt Nam has spade-shaped leaves with green on top, purple underneath, and serrated edges. It has a nuanced flavor combination of mint, basil, anise, and at times a spicy flavor reminiscent of cinnamon. At times it is called *red shiso* since it is a close relative of a Japanese type of shiso called *hojiso,* which is a good substitute.

RICE PADDY HERB (*rau ngổ ôm*) Rice paddy herb grows along the banks of flooded rice fields. It has small pale-green rounded leaves along a thick stem. Citrusy, with a touch of cumin, rice paddy herb provides an unmistakable finish to soups such as Hot and Sour Thai-Style Noodle Soup (page 184). If it's hard to find, substitute red perilla.

SAWTOOTH HERB / ERYNGIUM FOETIDUM (*ngò gai*) Sawtooth herb, native to tropical America, is grown worldwide and used in Southeast Asian, Latin American, and Caribbean cuisines. Depending on the cultural community that uses it, it is referred to as *culantro, long coriander,* or *sawtooth leaf.* Sawtooth herb is stemless and has 3- to 4-inch green leaves with finely serrated edges. It tastes like cilantro, only stronger.

VIETNAMESE BALM / ELSHOLTZIA CILIATA (*kinh giới*) With brilliant green leaves with serrated edges Vietnamese balm adds a bright lemon flavor reminiscent of lemon verbena or lemongrass to dishes. Don't confuse it with lemon balm (*Melissa officinalis*).

VIETNAMESE CORIANDER / PERSICARIA ODORATUM (*rau răm*) Vietnamese coriander is sometimes called by its botanical name, *polygonum,* Vietnamese mint, or even *laksa leaf.* Pick its long narrow pointed leaves, medium to dark green, off its pinkish stems before adding to a dish. It has a cilantrolike flavor with an additional peppery, slightly bitter distinctive lemon taste. When not available, substitute a combination of mint, coriander, and/or Asian basil.

VEGETABLES AND FRUITS

ASIAN SWEET POTATO / IPOMOEA BATATAS (*rau khoai lang*) The Japanese sweet potato (Satsuma yam) with its purple skin, white to cream color, and dry flesh is available at Asian grocers. It's simmered in soups, stews, and even desserts. Cut Asian sweet potato discolors easily when exposed to air, so add to the cooking pot right away or put directly into a bowl of water. Stir-fry the young leaves with garlic. Use orange-fleshed garnet sweet potatoes as a substitute.

BAMBOO SHOOTS / BAMBUSA VULGARIS (*rau măng*) The tender shoots of several varieties of bamboo can be eaten. To eat, all fresh bamboo should be thoroughly peeled and boiled (for some varieties to remove the toxic hydrocyanic acid before cooking and eating). It is easier to choose preboiled vacuum-packed or canned shoots. Select whole shoots over presliced ones. Boil them a minute or two to remove any strong tinny flavor.

BANANA PLANT MUSA SPP. From the bud to the stem to the leaves, the entire banana plant is used in Việt Nam.

- **BANANA BLOSSOMS** (*bắp chuối*) The violet to maroon tapered cones that grow at the end of a bunch of bananas are available year-round at grocers that stock ingredients for Southeast Asian or South Indian communities. Choose firm, unblemished blossoms with tight, overlapping leaves. Store refrigerated, tightly wrapped in plastic. Peel away the darker tough outer three to four layers of leaves, also called *bracts,* and discard or use for decoration. When sliced the pale tender inner leaves turn brown

VEGETABLES AND FRUITS

Asian sweet potato

bitter melon

water spinach

chayote

banana blossom

green papaya

Daikon radish

taro root

green mango

Japanese eggplant

kohlrabi

quickly, so immediately transfer to a bowl of acidulated water (with lime juice or rice vinegar). If brown from oxidization or heat (in a soup garnish), they are still edible. Canned banana blossoms in brine are not suitable for recipes in this book.

- **GREEN, UNRIPE BANANAS** (*chuối xanh*) are used in soups and stews. In grocery stores they are sometimes labeled as cooking bananas. Select hard, green bananas. Don't confuse them with starchy plantains, which are longer and have a thicker skin. (See photo on page 166.)

- **BANANA LEAVES** (*lá chuối*) Use as a wrapping for steamed dumplings or "cakes" (*bánh*). Blanch them in boiling water or pass them over a flame to soften and make them flexible for wrapping. You'll find packages of refrigerated fresh young, light green leaves or frozen darker green ones at Asian or Latin grocers. Wrap well, store in the freezer for up to a year, and defrost before using.

BITTER MELON / MOMORDICA CHARANTIA (*rau khổ qua*) Also called *bitter gourd*, the vegetable resembles a cucumber with a bumpy grooved skin. Green ones are slightly more bitter than ones that are light green-yellow in color. Select shiny fresh-looking ones with no blemishes or traces of brown or yellow. Scrape out the bitter seeds and pith membrane before slicing or stuffing. Eat it raw thinly sliced in salads or simmered in soups, stuffed with tofu and minced mushrooms. Purchase it at Asian or well-stocked grocers.

CHAYOTE / SECHIUM EDULE (*quả su su*) A squash native to tropical America, it grows well in the hilly areas in northern and central Việt Nam. It is pear shaped with a jade-colored skin that is somewhat prickly and wrinkly and is sometimes called *choko*. The mild-tasting white flesh is eaten raw and sweetens when cooked. The tender shoots and leaves are delicious boiled and/or sautéed as for water spinach. Look for it at well-stocked grocers or Mexican markets.

DAIKON RADISH (*rau củ cải trắng*) The flesh of this long white tapered radish is crisp and refreshing with a slight peppery bite when eaten raw. Its flavor mellows and sweetens a tad when pickled, simmered, or stir-fried. Select unblemished firm young radishes, less than a foot long, and peel before using.

JACKFRUIT / ARTOCARPUS HETEROPHYL-LUS (*quả mít*) Ripe and unripe jackfruit, the largest tree-borne fruit with a prehistoric warty skin—they can grow up to 100 pounds (45 kg)—is very popular. Young, unripe jackfruit is prepared as a vegetable used in salads, stews, and curries. The flesh has a wonderful meaty texture and mild flavor that easily absorbs seasonings. Canned young green jackfruit in brine (forgo frozen jackfruit) is

Canned jackfruit

readily available at Asian and well-stocked grocers. Don't confuse it with ripe jackfruit in sugar syrup, whose strong musky odor and firm yellow flesh is added to *chè*, Vietnamese sweet beverages, or desserts.

JICAMA / PACHYRHIZUS EROSUS (*rau củ đậu*, North; *củ sắn*, South) Jicama, also called *yam bean,* is a root vegetable widely available year-round at American supermarkets and Latin grocers, where it ranges in size from a baseball to a small bowling ball. Select a root that is firm, dry, and sand colored, with smooth skin. Before using it you need to peel it (a paring knife works well) to get to its slightly sweet, nutty, crisp white flesh. Eat it raw as crudités, in spring rolls, salads, pickled or cooked in a stew. Once cut, store in the fridge for a week.

Jicama.

MUGWORT / ARTEMISIA VULGARIS (*rau ngải cứu*) Mugwort, also referred to as St John's plant or traveler's herb (it allegedly provides strength and protection when placed in a traveler's shoes) is related to the tarragon and daisy family. The name *mugwort* is used for a lot of plants, so it's best to ensure you harvest the right species, as some are bitter or inedible.

Native to Eurasia, it's abundant in Việt Nam and grows in garden beds and along road-sides and in fields throughout much of North America. Forage and harvest it in spring, when the leaves are young, before it flowers. Look for buds and pointed-tip leaves, dark green on top, a silvery felt like underside with purplish stems. Select smaller, lighter-color leaves, as the large, darker ones are more bitter. *It's known to relax the uterus and thus should never be consumed by pregnant women or nursing mothers.* (See photo on page 238).

POMELO / CITRUS MAXIMA (*quả bưởi*) Pomelo is the largest fruit of the citrus family. Round, slightly pointed at one end, it has a thick skin and segments that are less juicy than grapefruit. Varieties vary in sweetness and juiciness and can have yellow to green skin with pale lemon to pink flesh. One variety, *bưởi Da Xanh,* green skinned with a pink flesh, from the southern province of Bến Tre in the Mekong delta, is prized for its sweetness and juiciness. Although native to southeast Asia, U.S.-grown pomelos are seasonally available from December to April. Select ones that are heavy and fragrant. An average weight is 2 to 5 pounds (1 to 2.5 kg). (See photo on page 141.)

TARO ROOT / COLOCASIA ESCULENTA (*rau khoai môn*) The natural sugars in this starchy underground stem (corm) give a slightly nutty flavor when it's cooked. The root is used in spring rolls, savory and sweet cakes, and des-serts. Larger ones are typically sold at grocers in the United States sometimes portioned and wrapped in plastic. They look like a large potato but with rings running along the length of the corm. Select ones that have no mold, soft patches, or wrinkling. The flesh is creamy white to light purple. Don't mistake the similar-looking eddoes (called *malangas* in Spanish-speaking areas) for taro. They're from the same family but not interchangeable. The corms contain calcium oxalate crystals, so cook before eating as eaten raw they may give you a sore throat. You'll most likely see two or three 8- to 10-inch lengths of taro stems (*bạc hà*) wrapped in plastic at Asian grocers. Peel and thinly slice the stalk on a bias and add to hot and sour soups. Their porous structure allows them to soak up the flavorful stock.

WATER SPINACH / IPOMOEA AQUATICA (*rau muống*) This delicious green, rich in iron and vitamin A, goes by many names; water morning glory, water convolvulus, and swamp cabbage. At Asian grocers it's most often labeled as ong choy, its Cantonese name. Select bundles with unblemished bright green narrow leaves. Stir-fry its leaves and tender hollow stems with garlic. Cooks split the less tender end of the hollow stems into long thin lengths to make a salad or to use as a garnish in noodle soups.

MUSHROOMS (*NẤM*)

Many varieties of mushrooms are well loved throughout Việt Nam. An excellent source of protein, mushrooms provide a firm to meaty texture and mild to rich umami flavor to vegetarian dishes. Interestingly, the prices for mushrooms rise around the first and fifteenth of each lunar month and special holidays, when laypeople eat more vegetarian meals.

ENOKI / FLAMMULINA VELUTIPES (*nấm kim châm*) Use these skinny stemmed white mushrooms with firm shiny caps raw in salads or rice paper rolls or add to soups a minute or two before serving. Sold in clumps in plastic bags, they keep for up to a week refrigerated. Forsake ones that are discolored and slimy.

KING OYSTER / PLEUTOTUS ERYNGII (*nấm đùi gà*) King oyster mushrooms, also called *king trumpet*, are sold at Asian and well-stocked grocers. They have thick white stems, flat tan-brown caps, and are packaged with two to six mushrooms depending on the stem's thickness. To use, trim only a little off the base. The flesh remains deliciously firm and chewy, and its woodsy, sweet flavor intensifies when cooked.

OYSTER / PLEUROTUS OSTREATUS (*nấm sò*) These white to gray, sometimes pink, fan-shaped mushrooms are said to have a very subtle sea taste but nothing like real oysters. Cultivated in Asia for ages, their mild flavor and firm texture, even after cooking, are valued in Vietnamese vegetarian dishes. Large grocery stores carry them year-round.

SHIITAKE MUSHROOMS, DRIED / LENTINULA EDODES (*nấm hương khô/nấm đông cô khô*) Dried shiitake, available in the international aisle of grocery stores, come in a variety of grades and sizes. The most prized mushrooms have thick black caps and deep white creases on top, called *flower mushrooms*. These can be found at Asian herbal shops and some Asian grocers. Buy whole, not presliced. To use, soak in hot water for 20 to 30 minutes, until soft (save hard stems and the liquid for stocks or soups). Or do a long soak of at least 8 hours for richly flavored, firm, and velvety caps. Rinse the underside to loosen any remaining grit and squeeze dry before slicing. Squeeze out excess water, cover, and refrigerate for up to 3 days. (See photo on page 36.)

MUSHROOMS

shimeji

king oyster

dried wood ear

enoki

oyster

SHIMEJI / HYPSIZYGUS TESSELLATUS (*nấm linh chi*) Also known as beech mushrooms, these small perfect light brown caps, sometimes white, are sold fresh in small clumps attached to tender stems. Slightly bitter when raw, their delicate texture and nutty flavor are great in stir-fries or added to soups at the last minute.

STRAW MUSHROOMS / VOLVARIELLA VOLVACEA (*nấm rơm*) After shiitake and wood ear mushrooms, straw mushrooms are the most popular type consumed in Việt Nam. Their name comes from the rice straw that they grow on. When fresh their mild flavor, meaty texture, and perfect bite size are prized. Fresh straw mushrooms don't travel and keep well. Use them the same day or the day after purchase. Store in a brown paper bag, refrigerated. In North America they are sold canned or dried but have an inferior texture and flavor.

WOOD EAR / AURICULARIA AURICULAJUDAE (*nấm mèo khô/mộc nhĩ khô*) Also called *cloud ear* or *black fungus mushrooms*, they're mainly sold dried, but increasingly fresh ones are available at Asian grocers. Smallish to medium sizes are preferred as they're more tender. Look for caps that are crinkled with brown-black on top and gray underneath in plastic packaging on store shelves at Asian grocers. Wood ear mushrooms, thinly sliced or finely chopped, are used for their texture, in fillings for wrapped dishes like fried spring rolls, more than for flavor. Soak them in hot water for 20 minutes and cut off the chewy center before using. Keep indefinitely in a closed container.

RICE, RICE PAPER, RICE CRACKERS, AND RICE FLOUR

LONG-GRAIN RICE (*gạo tẻ*) Fragrant jasmine rice, with long pointy white grains, is a popular variety to serve for a multidish rice meal. It cooks beautifully into slightly chewy, fluffy, individual grains. Use a ratio of 1:1.5 (rice to water) to cook white long-grain rice. Earthy and nutty brown long-grained rice (*gạo lức*) is also commonly served with vegetarian Vietnamese meals. Use a ratio of 1:2 (rice to water) to cook brown rice.

GLUTINOUS RICE (*gạo nếp*) Glutinous rice, also called *sweet* or *sticky rice*, is opaque when raw and translucent and sticky after cooking. Sticky rice requires soaking before steaming. It's available in both long-and short-grain forms at Asian grocers. Use short-grain sticky rice, such as Hakubai or Koda Farms brand, when you plan to cook the rice in advance and then reheat it. Long-grain sticky rice is best when served right away; otherwise it toughens a bit.

BLACK /PURPLE STICKY GLUTINOUS RICE (*gạo nếp cẩm/gạo nếp than*) Black glutinous rice, with its unmilled long black purplish rice grains, is not steamed like other glutinous rice but boiled. It has a slightly sweet and earthy flavor and chewy texture, reminiscent of wild rice, and is used primarily in sweets. When purchasing it, look for the following names, as they are one and the same: black glutinous rice; Thai black sticky (sweet) rice; purple sticky rice.

RICE PAPER (*bánh tráng*) Translucent rice paper is made from a thin batter of rice flour (sometimes a combination of rice flour and tapioca

toasted black
sesame rice cracker

RICE, RICE PAPER,
AND RICE CRACKERS

jasmine rice

untoasted
black sesame
rice cracker

brown
jasmine rice

8½-inch rice
paper

black/purple
sticky rice

glutinous rice

5-inch rice
paper

starch) and water that's poured and spread onto a tight muslin cloth set over simmering water, then steamed into a round sheet and left to dry on a bamboo rack. Rice paper comes in various sizes, with the 8½-inch (21.5 cm) round the most widely available. Briefly dip rice paper in a shallow bowl of lukewarm to warm water to dampen before using.

WHITE OR BLACK SESAME TAPIOCA CRAKER
(*Bánh Đa Mè Trắng or Mè Đen*) Rice crackers are thicker rice paper typically made from a batter of tapioca starch and rice flour sprinkled with white or black sesame seeds. Toast them in the oven before using. You'll find them, six to ten crackers per package, in a hard flexible clear plastic case at large Asian grocers next to the rice paper. Substitute small sesame Japanese rice crackers (*senbei*) if necessary.

GLUTINOUS RICE FLOUR (*bột nếp tinh khiêt*)
This white flour, made from ground short-grain glutinous, or sticky, rice imparts a wonderful sticky and chewy texture to dumplings and sweets. Read the label carefully to avoid confusing it with similar-looking plain rice flour, often distinguished by different-colored lettering.

RICE FLOUR (*bột té tinh khiêt*)
The creamy pale-colored flour, ground to a powder from long-grain rice, is used to make rice noodles, rice paper, and rice crackers. Most commonly sold in 1-pound (454 g) bags at Asian grocers.

NOODLES

Noodles, of varying shapes, thicknesses, and textures made from different starch bases, are added to hot soups, stir-fried, stuffed inside hot or cold rolls as a filling, or used as wrappers. Specific regional dishes call for specific noodles. Break up bundles of noodles when necessary to get the right amount required for a recipe.

RICE NOODLES/BÚN (prounouced *boon*); BÚN HUẾ; BÁNH PHỞ
Rice noodles, made from rice flour and water, are sold dried or fresh in several widths. Add thin, round vermicelli noodles (*bún*) to fresh summer rolls, to hot broths, or serve at room temperature in cold noodle dishes. A larger spaghettilike round rice noodle (*bún bò Huế*) is served in the Fragrant Lemongrass Huế-Style Noodle Soup (page 179). Flat-shaped rice noodles called *bánh phở* are available in three widths: ⅛ inch (3 mm), small; slightly less than ¼ inch (5 mm), medium; and ⅓ inch (9 mm), large; and sometimes extra-large. The thinner-width noodles are best suited when making a bowl of *phở*, while a wider noodle is good to stir-fry. Health-conscious restaurants in Việt Nam are increasingly offering brown rice vermicelli or *phở* noodles, *bún*, or *bánh phở gạo lút*. You'll find them at well-stocked grocery stores and Asian grocers.

CELLOPHANE NOODLES/BEAN THREAD/GLASS NOODLES/MIẾN (pronounced *mee-en*) or BÚN TÀU.
Thin, stringlike cellophane noodles are made primarily with mung bean starch but sometimes from tapioca starch. For ease, buy them in 2-ounce dried bundles; otherwise cut larger bundles with scissors for smaller portions. Flavorless, and nearly transparent before

and after cooking, they easily absorb other flavors and provide a chewy texture. Immerse them in just-boiled water and soak for 10 to 15 minutes, or until soft, pliable, and transparent. Cut into ½-inch (1.3 cm) pieces when using them in deep-fried spring rolls or tofu fillings. Keep in long strings if you plan on stir-frying or adding them to a soup.

EGG NOODLES/MÌ TRỨNG (pronounced *mee chung*) Thin white or pale yellow noodles made from wheat flour and eggs (*mì trứng*), also called *Chinese egg* or *chow mein noodles*, are sold in small dried bundles. You'll find fresh egg noodles in the refrigerated section of Asian grocers. Dried eggless vegan versions, found on the shelves next to the whole-egg versions, can be identified by their Vietnamese name, *mì chay*. Stir-fry them or use in wet noodle dishes like *hủ tiếu khô* (page 193) or in hot pots (see page 190).

NOODLES

fresh egg noodles

pho noodles

bún bò Huế noodles

vermicelli noodles

brown rice vermicelli noodles

cellophane noodles

SELECTED BIBLIOGRAPHY

Alford, Jeffrey, and Naomi Duguid. *Hot Sour Salty Sweet: A Culinary Journey Through Southeast Asia.* New York: Artisan, 2000.

Danell, Eric, Anna Kiss, and Martina Stohrova. *Fruits and Vegetables in Southeast Asian Markets.* Bangkok: White Lotus Press, 2011.

Kapleau, Roshi Philip. *To Cherish All Life: A Buddhist View of Animal Slaughter and Meat Eating.* Rochester: The Zen Center, 1981.

Lister, Tracey, and Andreas Pohl. *Real Vietnamese Cooking.* Melbourne: Hardie Grant Books, 2014.

Ngọc, Hữu. *Wandering Through Vietnamese Culture.* Hanoi: Thế Giới Publishers. 2008.

Ngọc, Hữu, and Lady Borton. *Huế Cuisine.* Hanoi: Thế Giới Publishers, 2006

Nguyen, Andrea. *Asian Tofu.* Berkeley, California: Ten Speed Press, 2012.

Nguyen, Andrea. *Into the Vietnamese Kitchen: Treasured Foodways, Modern Flavors.* Berkeley, California: Ten Speed Press, 2006.

Nguyễn, Thanh Xuân. *Religions in Vietnam.* Hanoi: Thế Giới Publishers, 2012.

Peters, Erica J. *Appetites and Aspirations in Vietnam.* Lanham, MD: AltaMira Press, 2012.

Pham, Mai. *Pleasures of the Vietnamese Table: Recipes and Reminiscences from Vietnam's Best Market Kitchens, Street Cafes, and Home Cooks.* New York: Harper Collins, 2001.

Shurtleff, William, and Akiko Aoyagi, *The Book of Tofu.* Berkeley: Ten Speed Press, 1998.

Solomon, Charmaine. *Encyclopedia of Asian Food.* Melbourne, Australia: William Heinemann, 1996.

VIETNAMESE COOKBOOKS

Mai Thị Trà. *Món Chay Phong Cách Huế.* Huế: Nhà Xuất Bản Thuận Hóa, 2012.

Nguyễn Dzoãn Cẩm Vân. *Món Ăn Từ Đậu Hũ.* Hà Nội: Nhà Xuất Bản Văn Hóa Thông Tin, 2013.

Nhật Thảo and Kỳ Duyên. *215 Món Ăn Chay.* Thành Phố Hồ Chí Minh: Nhà Xuất Bản Đồng Nai, 2012.

Song Phương. *208 Món Ăn Chay.* Hà Nội: Nhà Xuất Bản Lao Động, 2009.

Thục Anh. *Các Món Ăn Chay.* Hà Nội: Nhà Xuất Bản Văn Hóa Thông Tin, 2010.

Triệu Thị Chơi. *Các Món Ăn Chay Bổ Dưỡng.* Nhà Xuất Bản Tổng Hợp Thành Phố Hồ Chí Minh, 2011.

INDEX

Page references in *italics* indicate photographs.

ABOUT THE AUTHOR

Cameron Stauch is a chef, food writer, and culinary interpreter. He's spent the last two decades living and working in Asia and Canada. A former member of the cooking staff for the governor general, Queen Elizabeth's representative in Canada, he helped promote Canada's varied regional cuisines and ingredients. Currently based in Bangkok, when he's not cooking for his wife, Ayesha, and their children you'll find him cooking, traveling, and writing around Asia.